RAIDERS!

ALSO BY ALAN EISENSTOCK

In Stitches
(with Dr. Anthony Youn)

Cancer on $5 a Day
(with Robert Schimmel)

Barack Like Me
(with David Alan Grier)

Just a Guy
(with Bill Engvall)

The Kindergarten Wars

The Holy Thief
(with Rabbi Mark Borovitz)

Ten on Sunday

Sports Talk

Inside the Meat Grinder

RAIDERS!

THE STORY OF THE GREATEST
FAN FILM EVER MADE

ALAN EISENSTOCK

with

CHRIS STROMPOLOS

and

ERIC ZALA

THOMAS DUNNE BOOKS
ST. MARTIN'S PRESS
NEW YORK

THOMAS DUNNE BOOKS.
An imprint of St. Martin's Press.

www.thomasdunnebooks.com
www.stmartins.com

Design by Omar Chapa

ISBN 978-1-250-00147-4 (hardcover)
ISBN 978-1-250-01350-7 (e-book)

First Edition: November 2012

10 9 8 7 6 5 4 3 2 1

For GG

CONTENTS

ACKNOWLEDGMENTS

Chris Strompolos and Eric Zala, I am grateful for your courage, commitment, and uncanny gifts of total recall, down to conversations spoken twenty-five years ago. You opened your hearts, let me in, and trusted me. This book is the result of that trust. Thank you.

Raiders! would not exist without Thomas Dunne, Brendan Deneen, Nicole Sohl, India Cooper, Wendy Sherman, Megan Beatie, Angela Hayes, Mary Jensen, David Jensen, Elaine Stevens, Jayson Lamb, Cassie Zala, Kurt Zala, Harry Knowles, Eli Roth, Tim League, Frank Reynolds, Jenny Bent, and Jim Windolf. Thank you.

My close circle of friends and family keeps me sane: Jim Eisenstock, Jay Eisenstock, Madeline and Phil Schwarzman, Susan Pomerantz and George Weinberger, Susan Baskin and Richard Gerwitz, Linda Nussbaum, David Ritz, Katie O'Laughlin, and Michael Wilson. Thank you.

Finally, I would not be able to write anything at all if not for the loves of my life: Bobbie, Jonah, Kiva, Z., and Snickers the Wonder Dog. Thank you, thank you, thank you.

—AE

AUTHOR'S NOTE

This is a true story, though some names have been changed.

The Well of Souls

Ocean Springs, Mississippi.
Sunday, August 28, 2005.
11:46 a.m.

Stoked on his third Red Bull of the morning, Eric Zala, thirty-five, focused and wired, his natural state, adjusts his squirmy toddler, Quinn, whom he's tucked under his left arm like a football, aims the camcorder he holds with his right hand, and pans the living room of his childhood home. He trains the camera on every square inch of the hardwood floor and every piece of furniture—the couches, armchairs, coffee table, armoires— lingering on the fine china, ornate vases, and artwork, taking the care he took when he was a student at NYU film school nearly fifteen years earlier. He films the room meticulously, as if this were a postgraduate directing project that he was doing for credit. He swivels slowly, grins at Quinn's contented gurgling, and double-checks the room to be sure he hasn't missed anything. He starts to head upstairs, pivots, considers the room from this offbeat angle, decides he should shoot from here, too, get some coverage. When Eric agrees to do something—anything—he commits 100 percent. *When I say I'm in, I'm in.* Even if what he's in for is documenting the furnishings in his mother's house for insurance purposes.

Looking over the living room, he decides he actually prefers this perspective. He likes the placement of the camera, and the noon rays from the sun bounce off the water of the Gulf and bathe the normally dark interior with a soft warm light. From here, he appreciates the choices Mom and Dave made when they arranged the room, how lovingly and thoughtfully they placed each piece of furniture, not to mention how Dave, world-class carpenter and renovator, rebuilt and refinished all the walls and floors himself. The living room feels both comfortable and decorated, even staged, as if for a magazine spread. In fact, this room and many areas of the house and grounds had been photographed only a few years earlier for an article in *Vanity Fair*, although only one photo, a view of the front of the house, mostly blocked by Eric, Chris, and Jayson posing in costume, made it into the magazine.

Eric takes the stairs two at a time, jostling Quinn, who howls happily, and films the hall and all the upstairs rooms. It takes some time. The house covers a good six thousand square feet, not including the small porch outside the master bedroom where Dave keeps his bonsai tree collection and Mom her dozen or so orchids. Eric stands above the plants and tracks the camera over the cluster of leaves and flowers, then pulls away and wonders if he should move the plants inside and put them in the bathtub. No. Not practical. Later, Dave will fill the tub with water in case the storm that's predicted takes out the plumbing.

Outside, Eric jogs down the front steps and lowers Quinn onto the lawn, larger than a football field, facing the Gulf of Mexico. Behind him, David Jensen, thin, fit, seventy-plus who could pass for fifty, stands on a stepladder and hammers a sheet of plywood over a pane of a living room window.

"How's it going, Mr. Spielberg?"

"Done, I think," Eric says. "Except for the outside. I assume you want that, too."

"You might as well get everything. The oaks, the plants, the azaleas, all of it."

"Right. All the vegetation. And the cottages, of course." Screening his eyes with the flat of his palm, Eric blinks into the Gulf. The sun lasers off the placid, barely rippling water and causes a sudden shimmering glare that strikes Eric right between the eyes. The sun hits something else, a pair of glistening gunmetal hulks just to Eric's left. He blinks furiously. "What are those?"

Dave, a nail tucked into the corner of his mouth like a toothpick, scrambles down the ladder and stands next to Eric. He squints and strokes the bottom of his full white beard.

"Harvey Ellison's twin eighteen-wheelers."

"The fishmonger? He's constantly leaving rotting fish carcasses in the sun, outside his plant. The *stench*. Doesn't care what complaints are registered."

"A lovely man," Dave says. "I crossed him off my Christmas list again this year."

"He has to move those things."

"Went over to talk to him this morning, but he'd already gone."

"Son of a bitch left two semis right across from the house." Eric exhales and scoops up Quinn, who, engrossed in something crawling in the grass, starts to cry. "Come on, little man."

With Quinn now bawling, cradled into his side, Eric heads downhill to shoot up at the house so he can get it all in. He sweeps the camcorder and the word "grand" pops into his head. That's how you'd describe this house: a grand two-story colonial-style antebellum mansion perched on a hill, eight white Doric columns at intervals on the wraparound porch, a porte cochere at the side entrance, a long twisting driveway spilling out to the main road where stout twin brick pillars announce MANYOAKS. *No mystery why the house earned the name*, Eric thinks, as he walks toward the rear of the house past one of the many oak trees that dot the land. Eric steps off a fair distance and pans the five small cottages that Dave and his mom rent out, one to a close friend of Eric's, a Mississippian, who spent time in Los Angeles and returned to Ocean Springs, much more his speed. *And mine*, Eric thinks as he pans the camcorder over the last two cottages.

Finished filming, he returns to the house to say good-bye to his mom and Dave, who appear on the back porch. Mary Jensen, silver-haired, soft-spoken, her eyes clear and filled with kindness, holds a tray with three glasses.

"Eric, lemonade?"

"No, thanks, Mom. Got a lot to do."

"I know you do."

"You sure you don't want to stay with us tonight? We're a lot farther inland," Eric says.

"We'll be fine," Dave says, and arches an arm around his wife's shoulders.

"We'll call you if we need anything," Mary says.

"Okay, then. Quinn, say bye-bye to Grandma and Dave, bye-bye."

Quinn, hungry, tired, and probably wet, huffs and whams his head into Eric's chest.

Eric straps Quinn into his car seat and zips the camcorder into its faux leather case. He heads to the driver's side and waves at his mom and her third husband, a catch, a blessing.

"Third time's the charm," Eric has said more than once.

He starts to fold his six-foot frame into his tiny foreign-made hatchback, and stops. He has one more thing to do. A visitation. He steps onto the wide expanse of lawn on the side of the swamp and walks about twenty yards to a massive six-foot-high boulder at rest between cinder blocks that serve as stops. The boulder comes up to his hairline. He cranks up a smile because he knows Mom and Dave are watching and rubs the top of the boulder in a small reverent circle, for luck. Head down, he slouches back to the car, ducks inside, and backs out of the driveway.

That night, when the dark comes, Katrina hits.

*   *   *

Monday, August 29, 2005.
8:17 a.m.

Through the large bay window in his den, which for some reason he'd foolishly neglected to cover with plywood, Eric watches sheets of rain batter cars on the street and neighbors' houses and sees, with horror, the ungodly winds bend back whole trees and shear off their limbs. All night he lay awake as the rain and wind pummeled the small house, fearing that the windows he covered might shatter and that the bay window would explode. The wind now comes in surges, and at times the small house sways. Then, suddenly, a funnel of wind rises from the roof and all is calm.

He has not heard from his mother or Dave all night. He picks up the phone and hears an eerie silence. He pads through the living room and checks with the rest of the family: Cass, his wife, seven months pregnant, Quinn asleep in her arms, nods at him. He cruises by the family room where Cass's parents, both awake, have spent the night, their house dangerously close to the shore. Eric flashes what he means to be a reassuring smile and reenters the living room. He hauls on his boots and his raincoat and edges out the front door.

A tangle of tree branches lies crisscrossed on the front lawn. He steps over and between them and finds a jumble of larger branches and limbs piled up on the street, tied with a ribbon of power lines. Impossible to drive. Treacherous to walk. He flips open his cell phone and punches in his mom's number. Nothing. Dead.

He begins to walk. He negotiates the tree limbs in the center of the street, climbing over some, rolling over others, crawling by the power lines. He becomes aware of an ominous crackling sound overhead: limbs ripped away from oaks about to crash to the street. He picks up his pace. After a half mile, he veers toward the Gulf and his boots sink into a trough of mud—formerly the sidewalk. Eric swears, slogs through the muck, a thick chocolate sludge, and passes a dazed-looking man pacing on his lawn as if he's not sure where he is. Eric keeps going. People begin to come out of their houses, a few at first, then more, then a steady flow silently walking with him, all of them drawn toward the Gulf. A comic book collector from an early age, he can't help thinking of them all, himself included, as zombies from *The Walking Dead*.

Approaching the water, Eric stops, astonished. The hurricane has blown apart the bridge that yesterday spanned more than a mile and a half from Ocean Springs to Biloxi and left it in shreds. He turns toward Front Beach, in the direction of Manyoaks. He passes groups of people, hugging, crying, wandering, lost. And then he sees his mother and Dave. They see him, stare. They don't move. He reaches them and holds out his arms. His mother recoils momentarily, then allows her son to lock his arms around her.

"The house is gone," Mary says.

The words don't connect; they float right past.

"What?" Eric says.

"The house," Mary says. She pulls away and shakes her head.

"It can't be."

"It's gone," Mary says again.

"Come on," Dave says.

They walk in silence. They pass stragglers, some of whom Eric recognizes, none he can, for the moment, acknowledge. They cross the road and climb the hill toward the front of the house, which looms ahead. Eric's mouth drops open. He walks closer.

The hurricane has ripped off the front porch, smashed the eight columns into dust, pulled up the entire floor. Splintered lengths of wood lie strewn against the side of the house or in clusters on the lawn. Even from here, Eric can make out a gaping hole by the front door. Images pierce him, television footage from earthquakes in third world countries. That's what he thinks of now. His head throbbing, he adjusts his wire-rims as if that will improve his vision. Change the picture. He walks around to the back. Mary and Dave follow.

The winds have swept away the columns of the porte cochere. The overhang teeters, swinging like a hammock.

"Mom, Dave . . . how did you—?"

"We stayed upstairs," Dave says. "It was—" He swallows. "I had the camera. I took pictures."

Later, in the photos, Eric sees waves from the Gulf rising high as a cliff, roaring across the road, hurtling up the hill. With the force of monstrous rushing rapids, the waves slam into the house head-on. A wall of water blasts through the downstairs, uproots parts of the foundation, rips up the first floor, leaving the basement and garage packed in ten feet of mud.

"Come inside," Dave says, one hand linked through Mary's hand, the other one resting on Eric's forearm. As he tiptoes up the front steps, Eric feels Dave's fingers tremble.

Eric zigzags from one rickety floorboard to another until he arrives at what used to be the living room. The water has splintered the floor and collapsed the bricks of the central fireplace into rubble. More shards of wood, more mud, most of the furniture upended, most of the keepsakes smashed. A foul stench hits Eric, a nostril-slicing mix of rot and filth as if from a long-unattended toilet. He braces himself, forces himself not to gag. He raises his arm and buries his nose in his jacket sleeve.

He trails Mary and Dave into the kitchen. The floor tilts dramatically to the right, a section torn away, revealing the basement below.

"My God," Eric says. "My God."

"We were lucky," Mary says.

"I can't even begin . . . ," Dave says. He lowers his head, rests his hands on his knees.

Through a slant of the kitchen window, Eric sees that three of the five cottages have been leveled, reduced to woodpiles. Resting against one is an unfamiliar oblong metal box.

"What the hell?"

"Ellison's eighteen-wheelers," Dave says, his voice flat. "The water lifted them both, catapulted them toward us. They flew right past, missed the house and hit the cottages. Unbelievable. I watched it all. I thought we were dead."

"I couldn't look," Mary says.

"A miracle you're alive," Eric says.

"This house . . . ," Dave says.

He sighs, a deep exhausted exhale. David Jensen, career air force, with Mary at his side, had taken this old worn-down dowager of a house and remodeled, repainted, and upgraded each room, every wall, every floor, every inch himself until Manyoaks had become a showplace, a Sunday morning gathering spot where their church often held mass and they hosted lunch afterward, the *grand* dame it was meant to be. And now—

"This house has a soul," Dave says. "It really does. I feel . . . lucky. And I feel kicked in the gut."

Mary rubs his arm. Her eyes fill up. "We had many wonderful years here. We've been very happy. We'll be okay somewhere else. We'll be fine. We'll live in a smaller house—"

"Wait," Eric says. "You can't—"

He doesn't finish. Dave's eyes cloud up in defeat. *It's over. We lost.*

Eric feels his legs buckle. He leans against the kitchen counter, caked in brown dust and globs of mud, and holds on as if he is trapped in a flimsy boat about to tip. He has heard every word, especially his mother saying that they will move, and yet he cannot absorb it, cannot allow these words to penetrate, cannot allow this life change. He cannot allow—

This house. The house of his childhood.

No.

This house *was* his childhood.

His comfort. His constant. The house withstood divorce and bankruptcy, survived fire and ice.

His home. And Chris's.

"No," he says.

He bursts out of the kitchen and stumbles onto the lawn.

*   *   *

For the next three days, Eric lives in what feels like both a dream and a disaster movie. He returns to Manyoaks the morning of August 30 with a digital camera and the camcorder and he documents the aftermath—the devastation, the muck, the three slabs where the cottages stood, the blown-apart porch, the tenuously hanging roof over the nonexistent porte cochere, the rubble inside and out—all while holding his breath against the rancid odor that nearly swallows him. As he aims his camera, he imagines himself a crime scene photographer taking autopsy photos of a corpse. Finished, he kneels on the grass on the side of the house near the swamp and surveys the landscape and the damage.

Only then does he realize that the boulder is gone.

He shudders, stands, begins to scan the lawn trying to find his bearings, and then Dave appears, coming toward Eric.

"Eric, listen," Dave says. "I can't imagine how you feel. I only know how I feel. I feel so . . . tired. I'm not a young man. I celebrated seventy years on this earth a while ago."

"I know," Eric says.

"I can't do it," Dave says. "The cleanup alone—"

"You won't have to do it yourself. We'll help. We'll get help."

"There's no point."

"Dave, please."

"I'm sorry," Dave says. A whisper. His legs unsteady, he heads back toward the demolished front porch.

*   *   *

For three days, they are cut off from the outside world: no phones, no television, no electricity. The nearest airport, in Gulfport, has been wrecked, runways torn up, buildings smashed. Late the second day, in Ocean Springs, a few scattered stores open. Lines at gas stations snake for miles from the small business district all the way to the highway. Broome's Grocery, the local market, opens on the third day, cash only, and crowds line up for hours. Stories, some tragic, some triumphant, begin circulating from nearby Biloxi and Gulfport, and from New Orleans, only ninety miles away. Eric hears of a neighbor, a man in a house a few streets away, who fought to hold on to his wife's hand as water raged through their living room and then swept her away into higher water where she drowned. Other neighbors tell of looters cleaning out stores, even in Mayberry-like Ocean Springs where no one ever locks a door. Signs begin appearing in store windows: YOU LOOT, WE SHOOT. Eric borrows a loaded handgun and keeps it with him at home. He has never fired a gun in his life. He—and everyone he knows—stumbles through the day on edge, jittery, on the verge of some kind of communal breakdown.

Day four, cell phone service returns.

Eric calls his brothers Kurt, Michael, and Jeff, and his sister, Cynthia. They have all been panicked, sick with worry. He tells them about the house. Kurt, closest in age to Eric, and the sibling who grew up in the house with him, promises to leave his home in Boston the next morning, pick up Cynthia, who has also settled in Boston, and head down to Mississippi to help. Michael and Jeff, construction guys, say they will load up their truck and trailer with all the supplies Dave needs to start the cleanup. They'll leave in the morning from Denver.

"It's no use," Dave says. "It's impossible."

"Tell you what," Jeff says on the phone to Eric. "Have Dave make a list of everything he needs and fax it to us. We'll take care of it."

Eric cups the phone, relays Jeff's message.

"I don't know." Dave swallows, then allows himself a small, appreciative grin. "Okay, I guess. Fine."

As Eric answers Jeff's questions and fills in details, Dave begins writing a list. In characteristic David Jensen style—careful, thoughtful, complete—as Eric talks on the phone, Dave scribbles a list that goes on for three pages. When he sees it, Eric smiles. This is the first sign of life he's seen in Dave in almost a week.

A few days later, Michael and Jeff, from Denver, hauling a trailer (they've spray-painted TEAM AMERICA—KATRINA CLEANUP on a crate of supplies), and Kurt and Cynthia, from Boston, arrive at Manyoaks just before dusk, within one hour of each other.

*   *   *

Finally, Eric calls his other brother in Los Angeles, his non-blood brother. "Chris."

"Eric! Holy *shit*. I am so glad you called, man. So fucking relieved to hear your voice. *Man*. I've been worried sick. I've been calling like every fucking hour. There's no service. I finally got through to my mom in Gulf-port. She's okay. Shaky, but okay. What is going on down there? What is happening?"

"We're okay. But Mom's house . . ."

"What?"

"It's gone, man. It's gone. The house is gone."

And then Eric starts to sob. Safe on the phone with Chris, he allows the loss he's been keeping squashed inside him to gush out and ravage him. On the line in Los Angeles, Chris loses it. He cries along with Eric.

"I feel like it was my house, too, man," Chris says, pulling himself together.

"It was your house," Eric says. "It is your house."

"I'm coming down to help."

"Good, great, come over and help."

Come over and help.

Come over. As if it's a summer day twenty years ago and Chris still lives at the Riverhouse five minutes away.

*   *   *

Maybe it's the makeup of this family or maybe it's the natural energy that courses through them as they pull together for this unique purpose, but their collective spirit never sags, never darkens, never dissolves into self-pity. Typical of most family reunions, everyone congregates in the kitchen. Except this kitchen tilts sharply to one side like the floor of a funhouse and sunlight streams through a widening gap at everyone's feet. They convene in the kitchen to share drinks from a cooler, to escape from the mosquitoes, to catch their breath, to check in with each other, and, remarkably, to laugh despite the brutal early September heat that bakes the inside of the house and carries with it the nauseating stench of hardening marsh mud. Between the smell and the lack of electricity—meaning no air-conditioning—the family bonds in the kitchen but sleeps on the lawn.

"I don't remember when I've had so much fun," Dave says, sawing through a length of wood that he'll use as a support beam.

Yes, Dave is back. It took him a few days, but gradually he located his infectious enthusiasm and uncompromising resolve.

Day one. The family votes him foreman. He refuses. He says he just doesn't feel up to it; Katrina has broken his heart. Refusing to accept Dave's decision, the family waits an hour and votes again—this election is also rigged—and again, Dave wins.

"David, don't make us vote again," Mary says.

"Yes. I'm pretty sure I can predict the outcome of that one as well."

So, a reluctant foreman, Dave hands out the assignments: construction for Michael, Jeff, and him, outside cleanup for Eric and Kurt, kitchen cleanup for Mary and Cynthia. Eric can't pinpoint the moment that Dave comes all the way back, but one morning, standing in the kitchen with him, Dave sipping a cup of coffee, Eric swigging a Red Bull, Dave swipes his lip with the back of his hand and says, "You know, maybe, just maybe, we can pull this off."

The next day, Cass picks Chris up at the closest working airport, in Mobile, Alabama, fifty miles away. Cass parks in the driveway several yards from the house. Chris steps out of Eric's car and collapses into a crouch.

"Fuck." He stares ahead at the front of Manyoaks, the demolished porch covered with sheets of blue tarp. "I'm in shock. I'm in fucking shock."

Chris bows his head, removes his glasses, rubs the bridge of his nose, forces himself to stand up. When he does, he sees Eric striding toward him.

"Hey," Eric says.

They throw their arms around each other and hold tight.

"This is fucked," Chris mutters into Eric's shoulder.

"Indeed," Eric says.

They pull apart and look each other over: Eric, thicker around the waist, hair grown out, full beard the color of chocolate, wire-rims askew and streaked with Katrina dirt; Chris, looking just a little bit L.A., broad-chested, as if he's been working out, his potential shock of wavy black hair buzzed Melrose Avenue short.

"I like the beard," Chris says.

"Yeah? I don't know. I've been so distracted I honestly wasn't aware I had grown it, and then one day, there it was."

"Keep it."

"I'll take your recommendation under advisement."

"Nice. Okay." He rubs his hands together as if he's about to crack a safe. "Put me to work."

*　　*　　*

When Mary sees Chris, they both cry. She clasps him tight, as if he is her own son. He breaks from her and hugs all the others, except for a silly im-provised soul handshake with Kurt, followed by a huge laugh and a hug. Then Dave banishes Chris and Eric to the basement.

"Where we belong, man," Chris says. "At the bottom."

"Where we can do the least harm," Eric says.

Chris, balancing two shovels over his shoulder, walks behind Eric, who struggles to maneuver a temperamental wheelbarrow loaded with wooden planks. They wind around to the back of the house and face the yawning crater where the garage and porte cochere used to be. A few more steps and they sink up to their ankles in muck, which they wade through until they confront a six-foot wall of hard-packed mud, blocking what was the door to the basement.

"I left L.A. for this?" They lay the planks down; Chris hands Eric a shovel and slams his into the mud. "We have broken ground."

They begin to dig.

They lose track of time. They fill the wheelbarrow with mud, push it across the planks, dump the load into the bed of an old pickup. When the pickup is full, they drive to a divot the pounding rains dug out of the side of the hill and dump the mud, creating a landfill. Straining, groaning, progressing literally an inch at a time, they finally reach the basement itself. Their faces blotched and dirty as coal miners', their heads swimming from exhaustion and the sweltering sun, every part of them soaked and sticky with sweat—their feet, their thighs, their eyebrows—their lips hard, dry, and split, they stop digging and stare inside at what's left of the back wall of the basement. Water has blasted through and toppled most of it, but a small portion of the wall still stands. Chris and Eric gape at what they painted on it twenty years ago.

Hieroglyphics.

"The Well of Souls," Eric says.

"Remember how long it took to paint those walls?"

"I do. Forever."

"And as soon as we finished, my mom knocked it over," Chris says, and laughs.

"You were not laughing then," Eric says.

"Hell, no."

"This house is like the ancient temple. It survived Katrina and your mom," Eric says.

Chris grunts. "Unreal. Here we are again, slaving away in the basement. We've come full circle."

Leaning on their shovels, blinking into the dark of the basement, a maze of hidden rooms where they spent so much of their childhood, so much of their *lives*, Eric Zala and Chris Strompolos stand shoulder to shoulder and peer into their past.

Babe I'm Gonna Leave You

Chicago, Illinois.
1974.

Chris Strompolos, three, lies in bed and waits for the green clown.

This is when he comes. Nights like this. When his parents host a party and he is left alone, confined to his room, when the crazy high-pitched laughter, screeching rock music, and awful smell of something rotten burning seep through the flimsy walls and drown out his thoughts, the green clown appears in a mist at the foot of his bed. The clown pulses and glows like a neon light. He rockets off the floor, his giant clown shoes flapping in the air, and floats above Chris. Chris tries to scream, tries to call to his parents for help, but no sound comes out. The green clown has savaged his breath, stolen his voice. Chris lies in his bed, petrified, immobile, having no choice but to wait for the clown to take him. As the green clown hovers, his wild eyes wide, his horrible green mouth opening, the green fangs flashing, Chris fights twin feelings of terror and relief and this secret truth: He wants the clown to take him.

And then he wakes up.

Drenched in sweat, shaking, unsure he is really awake, missing his mom, needing his dad, he's out of bed, his legs carrying him down the short hallway, through a doorway strung with beads that jingle as he pushes through them and into a large living room filled with smoke, frantic dancing adults, and "Stairway to Heaven" blasting through speakers taller than he is. Through a haze of semisleep and confusion, he searches for his parents. He can't find them. Everyone in this room looks alike, men and women. Long scraggly hair, loud-colored shirts, sandals. He thinks he sees a woman in the corner kissing a man who might be his dad. Chris moves closer and identifies the man as someone he's seen around a few times. The woman turns away. He panics. Is he alone? Have they left him here in an apartment full of strangers? His world a blur, he stumbles, crashes into two people entwined on the floor. They pass a pipe and blow out a funnel of foul-smelling smoke. The smoke rises from the floor and swirls into his nostrils. Chris coughs but doesn't move. He wants to stay right where he is because he doesn't think the green clown will find him in here. He loses track of time and space, his head throbs and spins, and when he wakes up the next day, somehow back in his bed, bright sunlight knifes through the smudged bare window, stabbing him in his eyes and in his heart.

*   *   *

A year later.

His parents have divorced.

He splits his time with them, living sometimes with his mom and grandparents in Gulfport, Mississippi, and sometimes with his dad in Malibu, California. His grandparents are cool and strange, in a good way. His grandmother, Irene, whom he calls YiaYia, stays at home, cooks, runs the house, hangs out with her black housekeeper. His grandfather, Gus—Chris calls him Papou—owns a nightclub he calls Gus Stevens' Hot Groceries, the first nightclub ever to open on the Gulf Coast, where Jayne Mansfield once pranced and Elvis Presley once played. Papou, a barrel-chested man with thick wavy hair and an olive complexion, speaks in a mishmash of Cajun, English, and Greek. Chris often has no idea what he's saying. Papou practically lives at the nightclub. If not, "They'll steal me blind." Chris isn't sure how he'll know he's been stolen blind since Papou never throws anything away, which is why the backyard, the size of a base-ball field, is filled with everything from old clothes to rusted stoves to stacks of lumber to stuffed fish that used to hang on the wall of the night-club. Chris loves this backyard. He builds forts and hideouts and creates imaginary worlds where he, as Superman or other superheroes, stars in his rich fantasy life.

His dad, meanwhile, leaves Chicago and moves to Los Angeles, where he becomes a talent manager in the music business. He books one good client, the singer Mimi Hines. Mimi demands his dad's constant presence, so when Chris visits, they are always on the go. They accompany Mimi as if they are members of her band, schlepping from his dad's bachelor pad in Malibu to spectacular homes on stilts in the Hollywood Hills or traveling on Mimi's tour bus, to clubs in different cities where she performs. Shuttling between Gulfport and Malibu, Chris never feels settled; he feels like a tennis ball batted back and forth from the Deep South to the West Coast. If someone asks where he lives, he shrugs.

Chris turns five and starts school in Mississippi. After kindergarten, he moves with his mom, Elaine, to Queens, New York. She's landed a job on *The Dick Cavett Show*, where she's in charge of lining up audiences. They live in a cramped one-bedroom apartment in a sketchy neighborhood. Her new job keeps her away for long hours. Divorced from his dad, she seems to have married the show. Chris, stuck for hours alone in their creepy apartment, craves her attention. Elaine enrolls Chris in a Montessori school for first grade. It's a bad fit. Chris complains that he hates his new school, hates New York, and misses his dad. Elaine tries to reason with him. Embracing her well-meaning hippie values, she suggests they talk openly and explore his feelings. Chris, six, mainly feels abandoned, lonely, and angry. One day, Chris goes into the bathroom at school and kicks his foot through the wall. Shortly after, fighting to stay financially solvent and trying to establish herself in her career, Elaine ships Chris back to Mississippi to live with her parents.

Back in Gulfport, Chris's grandmother helps him carry his suitcase to the room she's made up for him—a weird room with scratchy puke brown shag carpeting and blackout curtains over every window blocking out any light. Chris can already imagine the green clown salivating in the closet, preparing to pounce that night. But the green clown never shows. An omen. A sign that Chris is growing up and that despite sleeping in a room dark and cold as a cell, living with his grandparents might not be so bad. In fact, Chris spends more time outside, in the wide cluttered backyard, climbing in, around, and over empty refrigerator crates and bulging boxes that held restaurant equipment, making up games and creating action heroes, using the piles of old clothes as costumes. His grandparents, distracted with keeping the nightclub going and having already raised a family of their own, give Chris the run of the big house and rarely impose discipline. YiaYia and Papou trust him, allow him to make his own rules. He can take care of himself. He's old enough. He's eight.

For the next year and a half, Chris spends the school year in Mississippi and summers, long weekends, and alternate holidays in Hollywood. He travels back and forth between two magic kingdoms—Gus's backyard paradise full of junk and Mimi Hines's tour bus. What he doesn't feel, most of the time, is included, or, frankly, wanted. His mom calls him often and sees him when she can, but these calls and quick visits just make him miss her more. Over Christmas break, his dad tries to include him by taking him along on Mimi's gigs, including bringing him on the tour bus to Vegas where Mimi tapes *The Hollywood Squares*, with, among other stars, Paul Lynde, Vincent Price, and Dick Van Dyke. By the time they get to Vegas, a five-hour drive from L.A., Chris has fallen asleep. He wakes up in the bus, alone, his nose burning from the smell of exhaust fumes mixed with pot. He looks out the window of the bus and sees that they have parked in the lot of a famous Vegas hotel. He tries the door. It's locked. He's trapped, caged inside the eerie empty bus. He bangs on the door and screams for help. His words bounce back at him. He runs down the aisle, sees an open window, yanks it open all the way, pushes out the screen, and climbs out. He hangs out the window by his fingers and looks down. He hasn't realized that the tour bus is a double-decker and he's twenty feet off the ground. He shouts for help again, dangles for a moment, and then, summoning the courage of Superman, drops to the pavement. He feels a sharp pain in his knee and sees blood leaking through his pants, his knee cut in a jagged line. Limping, he wanders through the parking lot and finds the backstage door of the hotel. A security guard blocks his way. Chris announces himself, and the security guard lets him pass. At the end of a long hallway, he spots Mimi and his dad. Paul Lynde paces near them, muttering, "Why do they need so many fucking lights? Are they doing this show for the blind? My makeup is gonna melt. This show is such a piece of crap."

"Chris?" His father. Seeing him stagger toward him. Eyes landing on his bloody knee. "What happened?"

"Nothing. I jumped off the top of the tour bus."

"Kid's gonna be a stuntman," somebody says.

A few days later, Chris's knee stitched, Chris's dad brings him to a New Year's Eve pool party in West Hollywood hosted by a drag queen couple, Ronald and Donald. Perhaps not the best choice for an eight-year-old, but Mimi, beloved in the gay community and the guest of honor, insists that her manager accompany her. At the party, Chris's dad Velcros himself to Mimi and leaves his son alone in the living room by a coffee table adorned with a mound of black gunk, caviar, and a pair of size fourteen strapless high-heel sandals. Surrounding him and ignoring him, drunk and stoned drag queens squeal, bump, and grind to "Stayin' Alive" and "Hot Stuff" blaring through ceiling speakers. Ronald and Donald and dozens of their close friends usher out 1979 and the end of a supremely troubled decade by obliterating themselves on drugs and disco. The only person under thirty in sight, Chris, a chubby kid, feeling underdressed and embarrassed in the swimsuit he was told to wear, his field of vision obliterated by wall-to-wall drag queens, weaves out of the living room and wanders toward the pool. He passes drag queens in costume, Aretha Franklin making out with Cher. He wonders if these guys, who he assumes are gay, prefer men or—what's the deal? He shrugs, hugs his knees, and cannonballs into the pool. He dog-paddles to the side, flips over, shoves off with his feet, and floats on his back, asking himself this one confounding question: *Where am I?* Getting no answer, having no clue, he heaves himself out of the pool and, dripping, climbs the spiral staircase to an upstairs bedroom, where he left his clothes in a paper bag when he and his dad arrived. He strips off his swimsuit, towels off, drops his towel, and is reaching for his clothes when Ronald, wearing a slinky dinner dress accentuating his runner's calves and hairy legs, walks in. Chris scrambles to cover himself.

"Oh, honey, please," Ronald says. "I've seen a million of 'em."

Later, scrunched on a loveseat between his dad and Mimi, Chris joins the applause as Ronald, now dressed in a sequined gown, feather boa, platinum blond Carol Channing wig, and size eleven strapless fuck-me shoes, a cigarette holder pinched between thumb and pointer, descends the spiral staircase. His dad and Mimi stand, applaud and whistle, then lurch off toward the bar. A few minutes later, Ronald or Donald or Aretha or Cher, he's not sure who, the faces have all melded into something scarier than any green clown, hands him his first-ever joint. He smokes the thing to a roach, choking it down without a single cough, eventually passes out, and wakes up stuffed in the back of a limousine, clear-eyed and starving, longing for Mississippi.

*   *   *

Chicago.
June 12, 1981. Midnight.

Chris, ten, every nerve ending crackling, stands with his dad in a massive line that loops around the block for the premiere of *Raiders of the Lost Ark*, Steven Spielberg's highly anticipated action-adventure film. Chris, a devout fan of *Star Wars* and Harrison Ford, has been collecting *Star Wars* figures and subscribing to *Star Wars* newsletters for at least two years. As the date for the *Raiders* premiere approaches, he has gotten swept up in the hype for the new movie. The newsletter promises that *Raiders* will blow your mind with nonstop action and predicts that Harrison, superb as Han Solo, will bust out as Indiana Jones. For months, Chris has begged his dad to score tickets for the film's opening. His dad, no fan of *Star Wars* or waiting in long lines, buys the tickets at the last minute. To make sure they get good seats, Chris drags him to the theater two hours early. To their shock, people have been waiting in line all day and they have to settle for the back of the pack.

The movie thrills Chris. It turns out to be what the newsletter promised and more—exciting, scary, romantic, funny, and filled with magic. But the film affects him on an even deeper level. Watching Harrison Ford as Indiana Jones escape one impossible cliff-hanger after another, Chris thinks, *I can do that. I can do all that: get into trouble, get out of trouble, leap into cars, defeat the bad guys, get the girl. Man, what would that be like? I don't know. I just know I can do it. I know I can create that world. I can be that guy.*

*   *   *

As Chris's dad commutes between Chicago and California, Elaine leaves her job in New York and returns to Mississippi, where she gets hired as a radio DJ doing the midnight to 3:00 A.M. shift. She and Chris move into a small apartment, and she enrolls him in Christ Episcopal Day School, a private school in Bay Saint Louis, a manageable bus ride away. So far, as schools go, Chris has not found the right match. He seems determined to approach every new school as a gig and each classroom as a comedy club. Elaine hopes that CEDS, with its reputation for rigorous academics and stern discipline, will straighten Chris out. The principal warns her that the school favors paddling. Elaine, fed up with being called into principals' offices to discuss Chris's questionable attitude and shenanigans at Montessori and other touchy-feely progressive schools, is ready for a change. If it will make a difference, she's not opposed to an occasional whap on her son's ass.

As Chris starts fifth grade at CEDS, Elaine rises rapidly at WLOX, from radio DJ to on-camera reporter to anchoring the evening news; meanwhile, Chris claims the title as class clown and raconteur. One day, for an oral assignment in which each student is to tell a short autobiographical story in front of the class, Chris recounts a story not from his current life but from a previous one. The class and teacher listen, captivated.

"In my past life, I was a dog," Chris says. "I had a job guarding a warehouse. One night, some thieves broke in and shot me in the neck." The class gasps. "If you touch the right spot, you can still feel the lump where the bullet got lodged when I was a dog. Go ahead. Feel it."

He cranes his neck toward his teacher. She reaches out her hand. Chris barks. The teacher screams. Livid, she sends Chris to the principal's office. He spends the rest of the day copying passages out of the Bible. Then the principal strolls in, shuts the door, lowers the shade, and paddles his butt like a drum. Chris doesn't flinch. He's recently been cast as the Artful Dodger in the school play, *Oliver!*, and nothing can hurt him now.

He doesn't know why, but for some strange reason, he believes that attending this school is going to change his life.

Survivors Have It Tough

Ocean Springs, Mississippi.
1981.
7:07 a.m.

Eric Zala, eleven, in uniform—white button-down shirt, red tie, dark blue pants, shined brown tie shoes—waits for the morning bus at the Whistle Stop, a former train station. In his own world, not thinking about when the bus will arrive, he sits on the cold metal bench outside the old train tracks, opens the composition notebook he's tucked under his arm, and sketches a cartoon character he's made up, a superhero he calls Shape Shifter. In a few minutes, he feels the ground rumble and hears the crunch of the school bus grinding over the gravel of the parking lot. The doors hiss open, and Kool and the Gang singing "Celebration" pours out of the large radio that the driver, Frank, keeps lashed onto the dashboard with one of his old belts.

"Well, good morning, Eric," Frank says.

"Good morning, Frank."

"You look spiffy this morning," Frank says as Eric closes the notebook, grabs his backpack by one strap, and climbs into the bus.

"That's because it's Wednesday," Eric says, and reflexively tightens his tie.

Frank closes the doors and cranks the radio up as Eric chooses his seat. A creature of habit, Eric goes right side, middle back, window. He can pick any seat he wants because today, as every day, Eric is the first passenger on the bus. No reason to shake up the routine. Eric always chooses the same seat. Eric drops his backpack onto the seat next to him, leans his head against the window, and continues drawing. He's volunteered to create a comic strip featuring Shape Shifter for the school newspaper, and he has been arduously working out the storyline, in his spare time, of course.

Homework comes first. Not a problem. Eric pulls A's in everything but
choral music, the result of a tin ear and a voice that sends dogs fleeing, and
almost always finishes his homework on the long bus ride home. This
morning, even though Eric draws slowly, with great attention to detail,
color, and shading, he will have plenty of time to complete this sketch,
start another, and possibly finish that, too. The drive from the Whistle
Stop to Christ Episcopal Day School goes from Ocean Springs over the
bridge to Biloxi, then to Gulfport, Long Beach, Pass Christian, and then
over a long bridge to Bay Saint Louis, covering a distance of thirty-two
miles. The ride, including stops, takes over an hour. Twice a day. Five days
a week. Mary Zala, Eric's mother, has made it clear that education, no matter what the cost, always comes first for Eric and his brother, Kurt, and so
has enrolled them in CEDS, the best private elementary school in the area.

Aside from school, at this point in his life, the beginning of sixth
grade, Eric puts most of his energy, time, and focus into collecting and
drawing comics. By his count, he has amassed a collection of over six hundred, mostly DC, some Marvel, all of which he's purchased by carefully
parceling out his allowance. Although he's drawing "Shape Shifter" for an
elementary school newspaper, he considers this a career opportunity. He's
already committed to becoming a comic book artist, a future Jack Kirby,
and this could be his big break.

As he draws and writes the thought balloons and sidebar text, he becomes vaguely aware of the first group of kids rushing onto the bus. He
knows some of the kids, but not as well as his close friends, Robert Parker
and Callie Gottsche, who come on later. They'll want to see a preview of
the first installment of "Shape Shifter," and he'll happily show them.

This morning, though, a roar of laughter interrupts him as three kids
climb aboard. The first two shriek hysterically, annoyingly, like hyenas,
as the third one, a chubby dark-haired kid with a black Members Only
jacket slung over his white shirt, his red tie wrapped around his head like
a headband, follows them. Eric doesn't recognize this kid. He must be
new to the bus, or new to school, or a fifth grader. The chubby kid flashes
a wide halogen smile and hits the other two kids with the punch line:
"When you can't stand your own farts? Man. That's when you know they're
really bad."

Big laugh. Nothing more surefire to a fifth-grade audience than a fart joke. Eric grins a little—the chubby kid's joke is actually funny and true—and keeps drawing. He raises his head and sees that the three kids claim seats two rows in front of him. The chubby kid, keeping his voice low, but not so low that Eric can't hear, launches into a story about the school play, *Oliver!*. He's playing the Artful Dodger and tantalizes his friends with juicy backstage gossip about one of the teachers being a closet lesbian.

Eric leans forward to get a better view. The new kid doesn't look familiar. Definitely a fifth grader, though, he's sure of that. He can't put his finger on it, but there's something about him. The kid laughs, throws an arm across the back of the seat, pulls his tie off his head and circles it around his neck like a noose. He sticks his tongue out and makes a grotesque face like a man dying. Even bigger laugh.

Yes. Definitely. Something about him.

*   *   *

The first thing Eric does at school is avoid Page Murphy. Although a few weeks have passed since the Disaster, he still can't help feeling the heat rise to his head and cheeks, can't help feeling that his legs will turn to jelly and he will crumple to the floor whenever he thinks of her. He assumes everyone can see him turn the shade of a lobster. No good reason he should subject himself to more pain or further dejection.

Once he's off the bus, instead of heading straight to class, he circles around to the back of the building, comes in by the far hallway, ducks into his seat in Mr. Bienvenu's sixth-grade class, and buries his head in a book so he won't have to see her come in.

A few years earlier—

Valentine's Day.

Third grade.

Eric, nine, has fallen hard. Page Murphy, petite, brown hair in a flip down to her shoulders, coy smile, brown eyes that flutter with both passion and intelligence, sits one row away. Eric dreams of her; Eric draws her. He's too shy, too clumsy to speak to her. How can he ever reveal his true feelings to her?

He doesn't have to. She reveals her feelings to him. She presents him with a small red wooden heart on which she's painted in bold black letters: I LOVE YOU, ERIC Z.

He'd sing if he could. He'd shout if he dared. He'd dance, but his legs feel rubbery, incapable of holding up his lanky frame. He whispers the inscription, "I love you," and then says, low, "I love you, too, Page."

Ten minutes later, he sees that she's given identical hearts to each of the Bandini brothers, twin idiots, who wouldn't recognize true love if it bit them on both their substantial asses.

Shake it off, Eric! Shake it off!

So what if Page gave them hearts, too? At least she didn't give a heart to everyone in the class. This just means he has a couple of rivals. Rivals! Ha! Together their IQs wouldn't add up to his average in math. He will dispose of these two morons like a wad of toilet paper stuck to his shoe.

A year later.

Valentine's Day.

Fourth grade.

No sign of the Bandini twins backing off. If anything, they step up their pursuit of Page. They hover around her at lunch like a couple of fat flies. Meanwhile, Eric's love for her has multiplied by a factor of ten million. He can't sleep, he misses meals, he draws her face over and over, he fills entire composition books with *Mrs. Page Zala* until his fingers ache.

He has to take bold action. He scrapes together every penny he has to his name and asks his mom to drive him to a candy store, where he spends twelve dollars, his entire savings, on a heart-shaped box of chocolates. Concealing Page's box of candy in his backpack, he rides the bus, rehearsing what he will say to her, how he will finally proclaim his love.

He'll do it at recess. He'll make his move while most of the class rushes outside.

The recess bell rings. Page sits at her desk gathering her books, talking to a couple of friends. He approaches, head down, eyes locked on the floor, and places the heart-shaped box on her desk. She mutters a muted thank-you while her friends gasp. Or giggle. He's not sure. He begins mumbling his rehearsed speech, "Page, the first time I laid eyes on you—"

Maybe he hits the word "laid" too hard, because her friends burst out laughing and Page blushes. The rest is hazy. He runs out of the classroom, down the hall, out of the building.

At lunch, he sees Page with his candy, sharing the chocolates with a group of kids. He doesn't know half of them. *The love of my life is sharing my candy, the chocolates I paid for with my life savings, with a bunch of strangers?* Then she notices Eric and offers him the box. His heart flips. He takes one, unsure whether his chest is pounding from love or heart failure.

A year later.

Fifth grade.

A rumor circulates that Robert Parker, Eric's closest friend, and Page kissed behind the school bus. Impossible! Robert has told him repeatedly that he doesn't like her. Why would he kiss her? And knowing that he doesn't like her, why would she kiss him? Doesn't make sense. Eric dismisses this whole Robert-Page kissing rumor as ugly gossip.

Finally—a year later.

Sixth grade.

The Disaster.

Second week of school. Mr. Bienvenu—bald, bearded, funny, kind—assigns an essay that each student must read in front of the class. The subject: "What would your life look like as adults?" Eric envisions himself moving to a large city, New York perhaps, and creating his own comic book with a superhero not unlike Shape Shifter. The comic book becomes popular, and Eric enjoys some fame. Not too much. Just enough to bring him financial security and the freedom to spend the rest of his life doing what he loves—writing and drawing comic books. He finishes reading his essay, lowers his head, and goes back to his seat to polite applause.

Up next, Page reads her essay. She imagines that she and Robert Parker are married and living in an amazing house of the future featuring an automatic toilet that flushes by itself when you drop toilet paper into it.

Eric feels tears burning down his cheeks. The lunch bell rings. He bolts out of the classroom, sprints across the school's adjacent field, and hides out behind his favorite oak tree. Realizing that he's wasted five years and his life savings loving a girl who all this time has loved his best friend, he weeps.

Now, a month after the Disaster, Milton Bienvenu comes to Eric's emotional rescue.

He announces a new project—a class film that Mr. Bienvenu plans to direct. The class, as a group, will choose the story, write the script, and act in the movie. Mr. Bienvenu stands at the chalkboard, writing key words as everyone starts spitballing ideas. Somehow, he filters every idea until everyone agrees to this basic storyline: a cruise ship goes down in a storm, and the survivors wash up on a desert island where they discover . . . *they are not alone!* Inspired, Mr. Bienvenu writes his idea for a title on the board— "Survivors Have It Tough." The class stares, clueless, then Mr. Bienvenu circles the first letter of each word: *S, H, I* . . . and the class erupts. "Survivors Have It Tough" will be their title, and "SHIT" will be their hilarious little secret.

Mr. Bienvenu invites the class to invent their own characters. Eric remembers the villain Toht from *Raiders of the Lost Ark*, the extremely cool movie he saw in Gulfport a few months ago. He decides to model his character after the black-trench-coat-wearing Gestapo henchman. He will call his creation Himmler and he will speak with a sinister German accent. Yes. Eric Zala, model citizen, CEDS's poster boy, whose worst offense in seven years was once pocketing a Communion wafer, will play a terrifying Nazi bad guy. No more Mr. Nice Guy. Where does being nice get you, anyway? Nowhere. Certainly not living in some super house of the future with the girl of your dreams and self-flushing toilets.

On the bus ride home, Eric finishes all his homework—it takes less than a half hour—and thinks about the class movie. He starts a new page in his composition book, draws a rough sketch of his character, and jots down a few notes for possible scenes that he'll suggest to Mr. Bienvenu tomorrow. He's only peripherally aware of kids getting off the bus. He finally closes his composition notebook, puts away his pen and pencils, and stretches. He then notices the chubby kid sitting across from him in the seat next to the window, reading a comic book. He's reading what appears to be a deluxe edition of *Raiders of the Lost Ark*. The kid turns the last page and puts the comic on the seat next to him where Eric can get a closer look. Way cool cover. Indiana Jones. Marion. The Ark of the Covenant. Squares filled with action scenes from the movie.

"Hey." Eric blurts the word.

The kid turns, faces Eric. "Yeah?"

"Could I borrow your comic book? I'll give it right back."

"Sure."

He hands it to Eric. No hesitation. Eric likes that. It makes him feel as if the kid trusts him.

Eric opens the comic book. He pores over every page, and as he does, he remembers how thrilled he felt watching *Raiders*, how amazed he was at the special effects and nonstop action. He gets to the last page just as Frank grinds the bus to a stop. The chubby kid starts gathering up his stuff. Eric hands him back the comic book.

"Thanks."

"You can borrow it again sometime," the kid says.

"Cool," Eric says.

He seems like a pretty good kid, Eric thinks. *He seemed like such a wiseass this morning.*

What a nerd, thinks Chris.

*   *   *

Several weeks later, *Oliver!* plays to a packed house in the school's assembly hall, and the cast, among them Chris Strompolos as the Artful Dodger, receives a standing ovation. Unfortunately, Eric's comic "Shape Shifter" falls flat in the school paper. Not his fault. Reproduced on the school's moody mimeograph machine, the comic comes out blotchy, runny, and smeared. You can barely read Eric's thought balloons and sidebars. After two frustrating issues, Eric abandons the strip and puts his energy into "Survivors Have It Tough," creating funny dialogue and melodramatic scenes and working out the story from the villains' point of view. Mr. Bienvenu accepts each of Eric's suggestions eagerly, laughing out loud at some of them. Finally, the script completed, filled with many of Eric's contributions, Mr. Bienvenu shoots "Survivors Have It Tough" over the course of three days using his clunky Super 8 camera. They shoot at the Pass Christian Yacht Club for the ship's interiors, the adjoining beach for the island, the woods near the school for the jungle. Mr. Bienvenu zooms in to a close-up of a plastic model of a ship and "sinks" it for the big special effect. He edits the twenty-minute film, shows it to the class—they go crazy—and announces that the school will host the world premiere one evening for the entire student body and parents.

"SHIT" does not stink; it triumphs. The audience laughs in all the right places and in a couple of wrong places, including during the supposedly horrific moment when the ship sinks, but that makes even Eric laugh. When the lights come up, the audience stands and applauds, and Eric feels a new sensation, a rush. He loved working on the movie. The whole process was more than fun; it lit a kind of spark within him. Even as he accepts congratulations from his mom and Kurt and his close friends Callie and that traitor Robert Parker, he starts thinking about doing a sequel.

*   *   *

Eric's final day at CEDS hits him hard. During the send-off ceremony at the church, a montage of moments, like a slide show, clicks through his mind: his hour bus ride each way, Frank cranking up Kool and the Gang as Eric completes his homework or draws "Shape Shifter"; his passionate and futile pursuit of Page Murphy; the close friends he made, people he spent virtually every moment with and who he realizes he may never see again; and, of course, "Survivors Have It Tough," the excitement he felt as he helped create the film and as he watched the finished movie with an audience.

After the send-off ceremony, he drifts from friends to teachers, saving his most heartfelt handshake for Mr. Bienvenu.

"Good luck at Ocean Springs," the teacher says, pumping Eric's hand. "We'll miss you."

"Thank you," Eric says, trying to smile, noticing for the first time that he has shot up in the past year and has grown almost as tall as Mr. Bienvenu. "I'll come back and visit," Eric says, his smile fading, knowing that he never will.

Finally, alone, Eric stands beneath the white bell tower and wonders how he will manage in the fall at Ocean Springs Junior High, a public school closer to home yet somehow farther away. He wishes he had told Mr. Bienvenu that he will miss him, too, that he will miss this place, the place that has become his second home.

"I just wanted to say congratulations."

A woman's voice. Deep. Musical.

Standing before him, exuding the same charisma that she does on television, dressed sharply as if for broadcast, more petite than she appears on TV, Elaine Stevens, anchorwoman on WLOX, the ABC affiliate, extends her hand for Eric to shake. "You were brilliant."

Eric takes her hand even though he has no idea what she means. He wonders what she's doing here.

"In 'Survivors Have It Tough.' That wonderful little movie. You were great as a Nazi. Scary."

"Oh. Thank you."

"I've got my eye on you. I'm expecting big things."

Beaming—how often does an eleven-year-old kid receive a compliment from an actual television celebrity?—Eric shrugs and drops his eyes, not sure where to look. Elaine Stevens powers up that smile, the same welcoming grin she offers to all of southern Mississippi Monday through Friday nights at six and ten. She turns from him in a little pirouette. He watches her walk away until she reaches the chubby kid whose comic book he read on the bus. She drapes an arm around his hefty shoulders as they walk into the parking lot and dissolve in the sunlight.

Perhaps he's high from Elaine Stevens's compliment or perhaps his creative juices have simply been flowing hot since working on the movie, but Eric spends a solid few weeks of the summer working on his own private sequel to "Survivors Have It Tough." In "SHIT 2," the good guys return to civilization and their former lives. They don't know that the bad guys have left the island and are going after them with designs to inflict further damage and heartbreak. He scribbles down ideas, plot points, funny lines of dialogue, slapstick bits. He even clips photos of possible locations from magazines such as *National Geographic*. He expands his scribbles into full-fledged scenes. He sketches a few characters just for fun. And that's what this is really, fun, a way to spend the summer before he starts seventh grade. Yes. Just fun. Nothing serious.

Then he gets the call that changes his life.

Fire

YEAR ONE

"I don't know. I'm making this up as I go."   —Indiana Jones

Summer 1982.

A stifling early July afternoon. Heat that punishes you. Humidity so thick you have to push through it. Perfect day to find a cool spot inside and do nothing, and so Eric holes up in his dad's law office and plays computer games. He sits at the front desk, lost in *Star Trek* on his dad's Apple IIe, manipulating murky green characters against a night-black screen. The game mesmerizes him, the soundtrack's *beep-beep-beep* practically singing him to sleep. As the afternoon slogs along and the heat seeps into the tiny office through hairline cracks in the window screens and under the front door, Eric, in T-shirt and shorts, cranes his neck up to the slowly whirring ceiling fan to try to find some relief. At least this room is cooler than the back room, where, door closed, his dad and his part-time secretary work over some legal briefs. Eric's dad rarely receives walk-in customers—he practices bankruptcy law, and most of his clients prefer to call him dis-creetly on his private number—so Eric can sit at the front desk and play computer games all day if he wants, as long as he answers the office's main line, his only responsibility. That and not to disturb his dad.

When the phone does ring, Eric stares at it in surprise for a full two seconds before he slides over and picks it up, answering in his practiced professional voice, "James Zala's law office."

"Oh, yeah, hi. Is Eric there?"

Someone is calling for *him*? At his dad's office?

"Yes. This is Eric."

"Cool. I wasn't sure I got the right number. Anyway, Eric, this is Chris

Strompolos." Chris allows a pause for his name to register and for Eric to place it. "Remember me? We rode the bus to school together? You borrowed my *Raiders of the Lost Ark* comic book?"

The chubby kid. Fart jokes. Famous mom.

"Yeah, sure, I remember," Eric says. "So. What's going on?"

"Not much. Hey, I'm doing a remake of *Raiders of the Lost Ark*. I'm playing Indiana Jones. It's gonna be really cool. You were great in that 'Survivors Have It Tough' thing, which was also very cool, and I was wondering if you wanted to help. You know, with *Raiders*."

In the next three seconds—Chris holding on the line—Eric goes silent as a barrage of thoughts and questions rushes through his mind:

Wow. Raiders of the Lost Ark. *Cool movie. Amazing movie, actually. I can see him as Indiana Jones. He did well as the Artful Dodger. Makes sense that he should choose the leading role. I wonder who else he's cast. Who's playing Marion? Sounds like he's pretty far along. I wonder how he built all those sets. Has he scouted locations? Does he have a submarine? How is he going to do the snakes? I am* curious.

"Sure," Eric says. "I'll help."

"Great! Terrific! When do you want to get together?"

"I don't know. You want to come over tomorrow?"

"Perfect."

Eric gives Chris his address and directions; they set a time and hang up. Eric keeps his hand on the receiver for another few seconds and confirms *Yeah, this is cool,* then slides back to the computer and resumes playing *Star Trek*.

*   *   *

Two weeks earlier.

Chris, back in Chicago, staying with his dad at his grandmother's house in the suburbs, begs his dad to take him to the re-release of *Raiders of the Lost Ark*.

"You want to see that movie *again?*" his dad asks. "Harrison Ford is a horrible actor. I don't know why you like him so much."

Chris prevails, and one afternoon he and his dad see *Raiders* a second time, only this time his dad sleeps through most of it. Afterward, blinking into the late afternoon sun, his dad's opinion about Harrison Ford has been confirmed. "That guy is the worst."

Probably not the best time for Chris to tell his dad that he's begun writing a revised version of the film based on the comic book, in which he plans to star as Indiana Jones. And one morning, when his dad knocks on the bathroom door after Chris has locked himself in there for thirty minutes, shouting, "What are you doing in there?" he doesn't dare tell him that he's been practicing Indy's signature smirk in the mirror.

Later, while his dad phones the Coast, attempting to calm Mimi Hines down over one crisis or another, Chris sneaks out to the driveway, cupping the remote to his grandmother's automatic garage door. He clicks the remote—the garage door lifts—paces off ten feet, faces the garage, hits the remote, and as the garage door lowers, runs to the garage and dives inside, easily making it before the garage door clanks down. He tries the same move from fifteen paces, then twenty, then finally begins at the end of the driveway, all the way down to the sidewalk. He lowers himself into a sprinter's crouch, presses the remote, bolts for the garage as the door shimmies and lowers, and rolls beneath the door a breath before the door slams onto the driveway.

Time to up the stakes.

Time to add the whip.

Looking around the garage, he spies an old broomstick. He saws it in half with a hacksaw and attaches a length of clothesline to the end with duct tape. He tries it out in the garage. Slings it. *Plop!* Good enough. Now for the real test. He lays the bullwhip on the driveway a foot away from the landing point of the garage door. Blowing into his hands, he saunters back to the end of the driveway. He faces the garage. Aims the remote. Clicks. He sprints toward the garage. He lowers his body, dives, rolls into the garage, reaches back, and yanks the bullwhip into the garage with him— a hair before the door crashes down. On the dark, cool, greasy floor of the garage, he lies on his stomach and raises both arms. Yes!

He practices this—sprint, dive, slide, reach back for the bullwhip—a hundred times until the move becomes second nature, until he's ready, until he's sent back to Mississippi for the rest of the summer.

That's when he calls Eric.

*   *   *

Eric waits on the porch for Chris to arrive. At exactly two, the appointed time, an unfamiliar car pulls off the road, past the twin pillars announcing MANYOAKS, eases up the long gentle hill, and coasts to a stop by the porte cochere. Eric bounds down the stairs as Elaine Stevens pops her head out of the driver's side window and, with a flick of a finger, lowers her oversized sunglasses. Chris swings out of the other side of the car.

"I *love* this house," Elaine says. "Wow."

"Yes, well, thank you," Eric says. "Of course, we could do with a fresh coat of paint—"

"Stop," Elaine says, drawling the word out to two syllables. "It's perfect."

"Bye, Mom," Chris says as he materializes next to Eric. Elaine notices how tall Eric has become since the end of school. Chris, a year younger, comes up to Eric's chin.

"Bye, honey, pick you up at six. You boys have fun."

Sunglasses back in position, she completes a U-turn in the driveway and barrels down the hill toward the highway. The boys never look back.

Eric opens the screen door leading into the kitchen. "You want the grand tour?"

"Sure, cool."

"Okay, well, this is the kitchen."

"Really?"

"I know, obvious, right? Well, this, of course, is the dining room. And, obviously, here we are in the living room. Oh. I was wondering. Who have you cast as Marion?"

"Nobody yet. Where do those stairs go?"

"Upstairs. My room and my brother's. Kurt. I doubt you've met. He's three years younger."

"Nah."

"Oh, and I don't know if you have a location for the tent scene yet, but if not, I was thinking we could shoot it here. In the living room."

"Wow." Chris steps farther into the living room and scans the space, hands on hips like a buyer about to make an offer. "Definitely. This'll work."

Why do I think he's not very far along? Eric thinks. *What am I getting myself into?*

"Oh, I wanted to show you this." Chris roots in the side pocket of his cargo shorts and pulls out a paperback. "Check this out."

Eric, taking the paperback, reads aloud, "*Raiders of the Lost Ark: The Published Screenplay.*"

"Got that at the mall," Chris says.

Eric nods, flips through the screenplay. *Okay, good, I'm wrong, he's on top of this.*

"So, what kind of camera do you have?" Eric asks. "Super 8?"

"Don't have a camera," Chris says.

Eric nods again, eyes locked on the pages of the screenplay, doubt starting to flutter in his belly. "So, have you cast any of the other parts?"

"Nope," Chris says. "Not yet. I was thinking you might play Toht."

"Toht?"

"Yeah. The face-melting Nazi? You'd be great."

Eric purses his lips, eyes still on the pages of the paperback. He actually could see himself as Toht. He pulled off the Nazi role in "Survivors Have It Tough" very convincingly and to great acclaim. Well, great acclaim meaning Mr. Bienvenu, his mother, and Chris's mom, who called him brilliant. And she's a professional.

"What do you think? About Toht?"

"Yeah, okay, sure."

"Cool." Chris wanders to the French doors that open out to the wide front lawn. He peers at the calm shimmering Gulf. "This is a great house. We could shoot some of the movie here, you know?"

The doubt in his gut rising steadily, settling into a simple phrase—*this kid has nothing*—Eric closes the paperback and hands it to Chris. "You haven't seen the best part," he says.

*   *   *

In the dark, Eric fumbles with the ends of two yellow extension cords bright as bananas, connects them, and finds the wall socket. The lights twitch on and, in a flicker, it's a twelve-year-old boy's version of heaven: a

brown, damp, marsh-smelling fifteen-foot-high basement room illumi-
nated by a series of cheap aluminum-domed clip-on lights from Kmart.

"Awesome!" Chris says.

"I was thinking that maybe we could shoot the bar scene in here."

"Incredible. Perfect."

"Then I thought that room back there would be a good place for the
snake scene, you know, where Indy finds the Ark? We could paint hieroglyphics on the walls." Eric gestures toward another room, straight ahead,
past the main room. "Check this out."

He points to an elevated ledge in the center of the room and climbs up
on it. Chris scrambles after him. Eric whips around and nearly clunks
heads with Chris.

"Oof! My head. Oh, man, I'm seeing stars, planets," Chris says, mas-
saging his forehead violently. "Ohhhh."

"I'm sorry, did I—?"

"Nah. Just messing with you."

Chris laughs, and Eric, unsure, gives in and joins him.

"Be careful. You can't stand up here," Eric says.

"Gotcha."

The boys, squeezed knee to knee, crouch in the hazy light, the tops of
their heads brushing the low ceiling.

"I have something here," Eric says. "There might be stuff on this we
can use."

He leans forward and drags over a small dusty record player. Next to
it, a few LPs rest against a beam. He removes a record from its sleeve, places
it on the turntable. "I had been toying with the idea of putting on stage
productions down here for little kids. I figured I would set up folding
chairs over there for the parents. My brother and I would perform, and I
would provide the music, the ambience. I know, stupid, right? It was just
an idea. Never came to pass. Anyway, maybe we'll find this record useful."

"What is it?"

Eric holds up a finger and smiles. He doesn't want to ruin the moment.
"Listen."

The record spins, crackles, and then the sound of a grotesque *WHACK*
followed by a *CRUNCH*.

Eric, reading the record jacket, says in a mock DJ's voice, "That was 'Arm Chopped Off.'"

Now he and Chris both laugh. Eric hands him the record jacket.

"*Sound Effects: Death & Horror,*" Chris reads.

"Listen to this next one. You know when Toht threatens Marion with the red-hot poker?"

From the record a *SIZZLE* and a *SQUISH*. Then a louder *SIZZLE* and a *SQUISH* followed by a B-movie scream.

"'Red-Hot Poker into Eye,'" the boys read together and then dissolve in laughter, Chris going breathless, resting a beefy arm on Eric's shoulder.

They listen to the whole record, both sides, losing it time after time to the crazy sounds of horror, effects such as "Sawing Head Off," "Neck Twisted and Broken," "Execution and Torture," "Head Chopped Off," and the cheesiest and most bizarre sound of all, "Souls Leaving Body."

"Man, that was so cool," Chris says.

"I know, right? 'Red-Hot Poker into Eye.'"

"*So* cool."

A final laugh, Chris losing it again briefly, wiping a tear with his palm. "*Man.*"

"So, Chris, seriously, how are we going to do this?"

Eric doesn't mean this as a challenge. He's already bought his ticket. He's in. Committed. He likes Chris, likes his energy, his passion, his silly sense of humor. Chris, sober now, blinks, watches as Eric, in his crouch, spreads both arms wide as he can, as if he were some weird oversized bird attempting to lift off from this impossible trapped perch.

"I mean, *Raiders* is a big movie. Think about it. An exploding airplane, live snakes, a burning bar, faces melting, heads blowing up, a submarine, Indy being dragged on his stomach behind a *truck*—how are we gonna do all this?"

Eric somehow stretches his arms wider, then pulls them in and locks his fingers in his lap as if in prayer.

"Oh," he says quieter. "We also have to find a girl who wants to play Marion."

Then arms wide again, voice rising, "And how are we gonna do the *boulder?*"

Eric sighs. He drops his head, pretending to study the label on the record on the turntable even though the letters are upside down. "We don't even have a camera," he says.

"Yeah," Chris says. "You almost forgot to mention that."

This actually makes Eric laugh. Chris rises out of his crouch slightly, so that he almost assumes a sitting position. He reaches a hand toward Eric's slumped head and neck and rests his palm on his new friend's sunken shoulder.

"Well," Chris says. "We could pool our allowance money and buy fake snakes from Toys 'R' Us. My grandfather has all this crap in his backyard, tons of junk. We can find a lot of props and stuff there. My mom works at the TV station. We could totally get help from her and all the people she works with. Cameras, cables, whatever we need, and advice and stuff. And, Eric, what about all *this*?" He spreads his arms wide. "Look at all these cool rooms we could make into *sets*. Just like you said. It'll be unbelievable."

Eric's mouth crinkles into something close to a smile. "Costumes. We need costumes."

"My grandfather has tons of old clothes. They smell like my grandfather but—"

He laughs, more breath than sound. It seems to be all that Eric needs. Eric's doubt about the making of this movie gets swallowed up in the dank of the basement. And by expressing it now, he forever lets it go.

"It'll be an adventure," he says.

"Big-time," Chris says.

"I'll enlist my brother," Eric says, tapping his finger on the side of the record player. "He'll do anything I say. He may even be helpful with the effects. He's not as dumb as he appears. And for some reason, he has a lot of friends, why is anybody's guess. But I'll get him to recruit his friends for the crowd scenes and to play the Nazis and Arabs and natives and whatnot."

"Now you're talking. We're rolling, man."

They clasp hands, sealing their commitment with a handshake.

"So, how long you think it'll take us to make the movie?"

Eric rolls his head from side to side, thinking, considering, figuring this complication and that, trying to be conservative, adding additional time to account for overage, setbacks, uncooperative actors, bad weather, family vacations. "I'd say at least until the end of the summer."

*   *   *

Just before Elaine returns at six, the boys, officially partners, coproducers, and costars, agree to meet in three days at Chris's grandparents' house. In the meantime, they assign each other homework. Chris will find or create Indy's signature fedora and leather jacket. Eric will retype the entire published screenplay into the word processing program on his dad's computer.

"Tell me again why we have to retype the whole thing?" Chris asks, his mom's car rolling to a stop near the back porch.

"For the cast," Eric says. "Everybody will need a copy of the script to learn their lines."

"Right," Chris says, smacking his forehead with the palm of his hand. "Duh."

Elaine, sunglasses sitting on top of her head, folds her arms out the car window. "So, how did it go? Did you have fun?"

"Yeah," Eric says. "We did."

"We're getting together again in three days, at Papou's," Chris says, sliding into the passenger seat. "I invited Eric to sleep over."

"Well, all right," Elaine says.

"We're working on something," Chris says.

"What?" Elaine says, lifting her arms back into the car, her eyes traveling from Eric to Chris.

Chris, cool, elbow out his window, smiles narrowly toward the porch where Eric stands and waves. "A movie."

*   *   *

Scavengers on a mission, they prowl among Gus's endless junk heap in search of props. In truth, they aren't sure where to look or even what to look for, but excavating through this crap, all fair game, seems as good a place as any. Swimming through tires, cracked plastic tubing, empty cardboard crates, rows of dented restaurant equipment, strange curvy Styrofoam packing, and space-age-looking fiberglass walls, they excavate, digging for anything resembling a bullwhip, golden idol, scimitar, bows, arrows, breakaway liquor bottles, or exotic knickknacks that could work as the property of Arabian street vendors. Rummaging through a stack of bent and rusted silverware, Eric hollers at Chris, a pile away, "Wow, look at this!" He holds up a pink smoking pipe. "Maybe we can use this for Captain Katanga's pipe. In the submarine scene."

Chris scratches his head. "It's *pink*. And Captain Katanga smokes a cigar."

"Well, I was thinking, as a backup—"

"We're not doing *Raiders of La Cage aux Folles*."

"You're right," Eric says, but pockets the pipe, just in case.

An hour later, frustrated, sweaty, empty-handed, Eric stands up, places his fists on his hips, and squints at Chris, who's sorting through a bag of broken picture frames. "I'm not sure we're getting anywhere."

Chris swabs his perspiring forehead with the bottom of his shirt. "I know. This is kind of a waste." He winks at Eric. "But I finished my homework assignment."

*   *   *

Eric sits on one of the twin beds upstairs in Chris's room and accepts the worn herringbone hat Chris places in his hands. Eric runs his fingers over the brim.

"Stole that from my grandfather's closet," Chris says. "He won't miss it."

Eric nods, rotates the hat like a nervous job applicant.

"Indy's fedora," Chris says.

"I know, yeah, I guess this could work. Except it's the wrong color. It's gray."

"Not a problem." Chris opens the rickety scuffed drawer of his night-stand and pulls out a can of brown spray paint. "Voilà."

Chris snatches the hat and bolts from the room, shaking the paint can all the way downstairs and out to the driveway, Eric a step behind. Chris places the hat on the cement, pops off the top of the can, and starts to spray. They circle the hat, shielding their eyes from the spray, crinkling their noses, their slim defense against the rising fumes, and, taking turns, douse the old herringbone until it's dripping the color of chocolate pudding.

"Fast drying," Chris says. "We'll have it in fifteen minutes."

"Good job, Indy," Eric says, watching a small wave of brown paint spill off the hat's brim and plop onto the driveway.

"Thanks, man. But I'm not done. I got more surprises."

He tosses the spray can to Eric, who snatches it, caps it, then speed-walks to catch up to Chris, who heads back up to his room.

Chris greets him holding his black Members Only jacket, which he has also spray-painted brown. "Neat, huh?"

"Oh, wow, looks just like Indy's leather jacket."

Eric's voice cracks. His long fingers curl around the cool metal of the spray can, which feels strangely comforting. The jacket looks nothing like Indy's leather jacket. It looks exactly like a black Members Only jacket spray-painted brown. You can still see the MEMBERS ONLY logo.

"Fits, too." Chris slips into the jacket, not noticing that a road of brown paint has come off the jacket and streaked his fingers. Chris steps up to the mirror over his dresser and fires up his practiced Indy smirk. He turns sideways, checks his profile. What he doesn't see is that every time he moves, brown paint flakes fly off the jacket in a mini dust storm.

"I'm just making this up as I go," Chris says to the mirror, channeling Harrison Ford, then swipes his mouth with the back of his hand. He backs away, and more brown flakes erupt and explode off the shoulder of the jacket. Pained, Chris brushes his shoulder and knocks off the entire layer of brown paint.

"This sucks," Chris says.

"Well, I wouldn't say it sucks—"

"I would. It *sucks*."

They laugh, hard, taking turns slapping the jacket and watching sections of brown paint fall off in clumps. The jacket really does suck.

But it sucks less than the fedora, which refuses to absorb any of the spray paint and instead leaves a blotch of brown on the driveway in the shape of Nevada, and when Chris tries the hat on, it balances atop his big wavy hair like a yarmulke.

After dinner, sitting in the living room, Chris presents his final and, hopefully, most successful surprise. First, though, he plays Eric his favorite song. He spreads the twin doors of a large walnut cabinet built into the wall, revealing his grandparents' entertainment center—record player, tape deck, RCA television, and stereo speakers, all in one convenient location. Chris lays a 45 on the record player and turns the volume up.

"Dig this," Chris says. He snaps his fingers and "Valley Girl" by Frank Zappa, his daughter Moon Unit singing lead, blasts through the built-in bass-heavy speakers. Chris sings along and, moved by the music, adds a few nifty dance moves.

"*Encino is like so bitchin' (Valley Girl)*," Chris sings. "*Like fer sure.*"

He knows every word. The song ends and Chris bows. Eric claps.

"Thank you," Chris says. "Thank you. No, please. Okay, one more time."

He plays the song again and sings along, louder.

Eric watches, slightly stunned, struck mute, amazed not only that Chris knows the lyrics and all the "Valley Girl" inflections to this crazy song but that he has an excellent voice.

*   *   *

Back in his room, Chris unveils the third surprise.

"I started writing down the shots," Chris says. "The ones I could remember, anyway."

Seated on Chris's bed, Eric opens the notebook Chris has handed to him and reads the first entry aloud: "*Medium shot. Jungle. Indy walks. Natives walk behind.* "Wow," he says, eyes riveted on the page. "This is great."

"It's just a start. We'll have to go through the whole script."

"I know, yes, of course. This is so good, though."

Eric nods solemnly at the few shots Chris has written down. This *is* great. It's early—they've only been moviemakers for three days—but so far, they've experienced only setbacks: looking for props and coming up empty, the Members Only jacket fiasco, and the too-small and too-gray hat that could never pass as a fedora. This feels like a beginning.

"Since I haven't finished retyping the screenplay, I'd be happy to continue writing down the shots," Eric says.

"You got it," Chris says, and drops back onto his elbows. Suddenly, Eric hops off the bed, nearly capsizing Chris. He paces, his bare feet crunching through the blades of the industrial shag carpet, rough as sandpaper. He plops down on the other bed, opposite Chris, the one he'll be sleeping in. He nods slowly to himself and then goes eerily silent.

"What?" Chris says.

Eric doesn't seem to hear him. He's off somewhere, adrift in space.

"Eric, yoo-hoo, what?"

Eric blinks himself back to earth and focuses on Chris, an idea clearly spinning in his head. "I was just thinking. We have the published screenplay, I'm retyping it, all good. But maybe what we also need is an actual *recording* of the movie, to hear exactly what's being said, with the proper inflection. How else to direct the actors?"

"Oh, totally, man, absolutely," Chris says. "What the hell are you talking about?"

Eric leans into Chris. "We need to sneak into the movie and tape it. The whole thing."

"We can use my grandfather's tape recorder," Chris says. "He won't care. He doesn't remember he has one." Chris scoots up, presses his back into the headboard. The mattress wheezes and the headboard creaks. Sounds like a piece of timber ready to go. "So, okay, who should do it?"

"Well," Eric says. "We want to be fair. We could choose up, draw lots, draw straws, cut cards, one of us could think of a number—"

"Never mind. I'll do it."

*   *   *

The next afternoon, his grandfather's audiocassette recorder the size of a cigar box strapped to his chest with duct tape, the microphone taped to the side of the recorder so it will face the screen, Chris stands in suffocating two o'clock heat outside the Gulfport Twin Cinemas, in line to see *Raiders of the Lost Ark*. He wears pleated cargo shorts and a billowing shirt to hide the recorder. He shifts his weight and tries to soak up the pool of sweat on his forehead with the palm of his hand.

I gotta get inside. If I don't, I'm gonna pass out right here. I'm gonna fall

*face-first and crush Papou's tape recorder. Or it will drive right through my chest
and kill me.*

He shuffles his feet, drops into a deep knee bend. Why? He has no
idea. He's just trying to find a comfortable position with this metal death
box strapped to his chest.

My underwear feels like an oven. Man, am I sweating. I'm sopping wet.

And then it occurs to him.

*Once I'm inside and I turn on this tape recorder, all this moisture will
electrocute me. I'm gonna light up like a Christmas tree. I'll be buzzing so loud,
I'll drown out the movie. Shit! Open the door!*

That's when he notices the usher walking toward him.

Kid about eighteen. Dressed like a dweeb in that uniform. Acne
spread over his face like a map of Mars.

The line starts moving.

Chris whispers "Thank you" to the sky, and begins the slow shuffle
into the air-conditioned lobby. He reaches the acne-faced usher dweeb and
smiles right at him.

"How ya doin'? Man. Am I glad to be getting out of that heat."

The kid's nose twitches as if he's gotten a whiff of sour milk. He lasers
two beady eyes at Chris, looks from the lake on his forehead down. He
stops at Chris's stomach. "You're not that fat."

"What?"

"Step out of the line."

"Come on. I'm dying out here. I'm sweating like a pig."

"Raise your arms."

He's so light-headed from the heat that he doesn't resist. He lazily
lifts his arms. The usher goes right for his midsection and taps the cassette
recorder full on. He grins, showing a mouthful of braces.

"Busted," the dweeb says.

*   *   *

Two nights later, Chris brings Eric the cassette recorder. Together they strap
it in place to Eric's thinner frame, lash it to his T-shirt. Eric slips a short-
sleeved shirt over that. Chris, hands on hips, circles him. "Looks good."

"Well concealed?"

"Walk."

Eric takes a few stiff steps.

"Walk normal. You look like you got a pole up your ass."

Eric fastens his arms to his side, walks casually across the room.

"Better," Chris says.

"All right then." Eric blows out a funnel of air that brushes Chris from across the room.

"You don't have to do this."

"No, no. We need it for the movie."

"Okay, but—"

Eric shoots Chris a hot stare. "When I say I'm in, I'm in."

*　　*　　*

Different day. Different show time. Same usher.

Standing in the line for *Raiders*, which twists another block behind him, Eric taps his foot and whistles to calm his nerves. For some reason, he looks skyward. A shadow, real or imagined, a patch of darkness, hovers over him.

The shadow is a sign. A symbol of the dark side. Makes sense since he feels like a criminal. In his entire twelve-plus years of life, Eric has never done anything remotely close to this. Break the law? Sneak into a movie with a tape recorder and *record* the film? That's a crime. That's copyright infringement. He's heard that phrase bandied about somewhere. Probably picked it up from some lawyer show on TV. Or maybe from his dad. Eric presumes that what he's doing, should he get caught, carries a stiff penalty, a huge fine, possibly jail time. Wow. Would they really put him in jail? They'd have to consider his impeccable past, his unblemished permanent record, his academic accomplishments, his devotion to extra credit, his good nature, his cooperativeness with students and teachers, his volunteer work in the community. He's never committed any sort of crime, ever. Well, except for pilfering that Communion wafer, but that was in the third grade, and that was—he's not sure what that was, but it wasn't this. Today, Eric Zala, model citizen, rising seventh grader, aspiring cartoonist, fledgling filmmaker, winner of a one-hundred-dollar savings bond for Best Traffic Safety Poster, is about to commit a felony.

He feels kind of good about it.

Then the fleeting feeling of wanting to get caught, of deserving to get nabbed, leaves. Maybe that's what the shadow symbolizes: Deep down, beneath his straight-arrow exterior, beats the heart of evil. But there's nothing wrong with pushing the goody-two-shoes stuff aside now and then for the sake of your *art*. That's what this is really about. The movie. Doing what you have to do to make this movie. No matter what. Of course, he won't cross a line. He won't hold up liquor stores to finance this film. He won't knock down old ladies and run off with their purses. Nothing like that. Nothing heinous. But he *will* do pretty much anything else. He will sneak into a movie theater and record *Raiders*. Yes, he'll do almost anything for their movie. And he realizes—although they have been friends for only a week—that he would do anything for Chris.

The line moves. He inches forward, stretches to see how far he is from getting inside. Then the dweeb usher Chris described appears, hands clasped behind his back like a storm trooper, scoping out every person in line, flashing his metallic smile. He stops at Eric.

"Hey," Eric says.

The usher looks Eric up and down. The kid not only has cheeks overrun with zits but he smells of witch hazel. "Have you seen this movie?"

"Yeah," Eric says, and then his throat dries up and he nearly gags before he speaks. "This is my second time. No. My third time. Is it my third time? Or my second? I can't remember if I've seen it two or three times."

"I see it five times a *day*. I'm so sick of it."

"Ha! Wow. Yeah, I can imagine that would make anyone—"

But the dweeb has gone. Moved past. Pulled up to a shady-looking character several people away. Old guy with a bulging man purse. The line surges, and in a matter of seconds Eric steps into the lobby, the temperature inside a blissful sixty degrees, then he's moving down the aisle, his legs carrying him along mechanically, and he's sidestepping into a middle row and taking a seat, just as he planned, his hand slipping inside his shirt for the ON switch like an outlaw reaching for his gun.

*   *   *

"I got it!" Eric shouts into the phone.

"Unbelievable! How does it sound?"

"Well, muffled, in parts. You can hear most of it. But when Indy shoots the Arab swordsman?"

"Yeah?"

"Drowned out by applause."

"Okay. But still."

"Yeah. Worth it. Totally worth it."

"You rock, Eric! You did it, man!"

Eric beams into the phone. "No, *we* did it."

*   *   *

They establish a routine. Mornings, they work on the shot list or retype the screenplay, and when they get bored figuring out shots or typing, they listen to the crude cassette recording and memorize whole sections of the movie, acting out scenes and dialogue—Indy's, Toht's, Marion's, and all the other characters'. Afternoons, Elaine and Mary take turns driving them to one of two nearby malls, where they scour stores for props and costumes. Their moms see the two boys hanging out, sleeping over, forming an inseparable friendship. Eric and Chris call this pre-production.

Most southern Mississippians spend their afternoons cruising the mall, plodding from store to store, shopping leisurely, escaping the crushing heat, killing time. Eric and Chris bolt from their moms' respective minivans with no time to waste, explorers on a mission. No telling which store may contain bounty, treasure, possible props. Of course, this treasure costs money.

They pool their allowances and rarely come up with more than five dollars. Less than that, actually, since Chris usually begins each mall adventure by popping into the arcade inside the front entrance and dropping a quarter or two in a quick game of *Dragon Slayer*, *Galaga*, or *Pac-Man*.

"Okay, got that out of my system. Let's go." Chris, patting his palms dry on his cargo shorts, bursts out of the flashing, beeping arcade din.

For the most part, their four bucks and change won't buy them any-thing. Instead, they consider these mall stops fact-finding excursions where they'll identify what they need to save for or ask for for birthdays or Christmas. They do manage a few purchases: at the Sound Shop, two LPs, the *Raiders* soundtrack, which contains John Williams's soaring score, and *Raiders of the Lost Ark: The Movie on Record*, loaded with valuable sound effects from the film—Indy throwing a punch, his whip lashing out, Nazis screaming, natives shouting, as well as an inside sleeve full of photos; at Waldenbooks, a *Raiders* calendar and a coffee table book on "Movie-Making Magic," which gives a glimpse inside Lucasfilm's Industrial Light & Magic division; at the hobby store, starter pistols, with blanks; at Toys "R" Us, realistic-looking rubber snakes; and, at World Bazaar, cheap replicas of metal-tipped spears and scimitars.

Soon Eric finishes typing the screenplay and they complete the shot list. Possessors now of a handful of props, a list of shots, and a retyped screenplay, they convene in Eric's living room and consider what they have accomplished so far.

"It's good," Eric says. "All this. The list. The shots. Glad we got it done."

"Definitely." Chris blows his breath onto a pane of glass in one of the French doors and with his index finger draws a stick figure of Indiana Jones. He laughs at his own terrible sketch. "Wish I could draw."

"Well," Eric says, his mind elsewhere. He pushes himself off the couch and picks up the published screenplay on the coffee table. He leafs through the pages, slams through the illustrations, stops at a drawing. "Hey, Chris, look at this."

Chris rubs out his drawing with his thumb and walks over to Eric. He stares over his shoulder. "Yeah?"

"See this? It's a storyboard."

"Like a sketch of—"

"Each shot," Eric says.

"So, I guess that's how it's done—"

"Yes. How Spielberg planned each shot," Eric says. "I've been trying to figure this out. I keep thinking, we've made the list, great, now what are we gonna do with it? The list doesn't tell us that much."

"I know. *Medium shot. Indy.* So what?"

"Exactly. So, this is what we need to do. We need to make storyboards."

"For every shot?"

Eric slaps the page. "Exactly. Draw one for every shot."

"What's this?" Chris points to a sidebar next to the storyboard filled with nearly illegible handwriting.

"Spielberg's scribbling," Eric says. "Notes for the cameraman." Like a kid in math class finally catching on to the secret of word problems, he grins at Chris. "I got it now."

He rushes out of the living room to Mary's office, which she works out of part-time selling insurance policies, an adjacent open area with desk, typewriter, and copy machine. He moves so fast that Chris stays pinned to his spot, not sure where to go, watching Eric, a blur, place the page of the book with the storyboard face down on the copy machine, power up, and press COPY.

"Okay, cool. What are you doing?"

Eric's smile widens. "Turning our shots into storyboards."

The machine whirs, spits out a copy. Eric snatches the copy of the storyboard page from the machine, stands at Mary's desk, twists open the stubborn bottle of Liquid Paper he finds, and paints over anything that's written inside the storyboard form. By now, Chris has moved to Eric's elbow. Together, they blow on the copy to dry the Liquid Paper; then Eric puts this copy into the copy machine.

"I get it," Chris says. "You're making a blank storyboard."

"Yep."

After a moment, the copy machine flashes green, whirs, and kicks out a fresh storyboard, warm to the touch. Eric pulls this one out carefully and scans it like a proofreader, looking it over for any random line, scratch, word, or blemish.

"Perfect," he says, a word that rarely crosses his lips.

"Looks great. How many storyboards do you think we need to make?"

Eric considers this as he blows the blank storyboard dry. "Maybe a hundred."

*   *   *

On a table in the corner of the living room, they spread out everything *Raiders* that they have collected: the *Raiders of the Lost Ark* storybook; the *Raiders of the Lost Ark* children's record; the John Williams soundtrack album; the inside sleeve and photos from the *Movie on Record* LP; a coffee table book from Industrial Light & Magic; *The Making of Raiders of the Lost Ark*, a paperback by Derek Taylor, a key reference; *Starlog* magazine, the *Raiders* issue; the published screenplay; and their bootlegged audiocassette recording. Eric puts the soundtrack on the record player, turns it up, and begins to draw. Across from him, watching, then getting up, pacing, nodding—frenetic movement in contrast to Eric's focused stillness— Chris observes Eric at work. After thirty minutes, Eric mumbles, "Okay," and hands the storyboard he's drawn to Chris. For a solid ten seconds, Chris does nothing but stare.

"Amazing," Chris says, his voice flat-lined in awe. "Professional."

"Thanks. I just tried to reproduce what Spielberg did."

"Unbelievable."

Eric has, in fact, sketched something that looks like a cross between a storyboard and a comic strip. Relying mostly on his memory and the drone of the cassette recording, Eric has drawn Indiana Jones in close-up walking into the jungle looking remarkably like *Indiana Jones*—leather jacket, fedora, hand on whip. Eric has even somehow captured a sense of the Indiana Jones spirit, his cockiness.

"I'm sorry it took so long," he says quietly. "I wanted to do this right."

"Wow. I mean *wow*."

"Well, so, that's the idea. Got a lot more of them to do." He nods at the pile of blank storyboard forms, shakes out his fingers as if they've cramped up, and, consulting the shot list, begins to tackle storyboard number two. Chris slides an empty storyboard form in front of himself, rolls a pencil into his fingers, and, tongue out, begins to draw. Fifteen minutes later, Chris completes his first storyboard. Eric, pausing and restarting the cassette recorder, has not even begun shading his second one.

"I don't like mine," Chris says.

Eric, dialed in, doesn't answer.

"Mine's a piece of shit," Chris says.

Eric doesn't hear him or doesn't care.

"I'll do one more," Chris says.

"Umm," Eric says.

Within ten minutes, Chris finishes his second storyboard. He lowers his chin onto the table and blows the sheet across the table. The storyboard flutters up against Eric's cheek. Eric peels it off. "You finished?"

"I've done two."

"Really? Great."

"No, Eric, not great. Horrible. Gross. I hate my drawing. My drawing sucks. You do it. I can't." He presses his palms flat onto the table, pushes off, heads for his spot facing the Gulf.

"I don't mind doing them," Eric says. "Truth be told, I enjoy it."

"Good. Because truth be told, I hate doing it. Hate it like a rash. I can't fucking *draw*. We won't be able to use mine at all. I'm just wasting our time."

"Umm," Eric says, back to the drawing board, literally. "Less than a hundred to go. It shouldn't take too long."

It takes all summer. Eric runs out of blank storyboard forms and copies more. Stealing thirty minutes here and there, late at night, before anyone wakes in the morning, on a family road trip, in sketchy motel rooms, alone by a drained motel swimming pool at dawn, Eric draws, and draws, and draws, storyboard after storyboard, each one a complete and worthy cartoon panel.

He guesses low. By summer's end, the number of storyboards he completes, including Chris's two, tallies 602.

*   *   *

Not to be outdone by Eric's obsession with storyboarding, Chris plunges into conceiving, planning, and gathering materials for the biggest, most daunting prop in the movie.

The boulder. The huge terrifying rolling rock that explodes out of the Peruvian cave, crashes toward Indy, and nearly crushes him. The movie's signature effect.

Around the time Eric puts pencil to paper for storyboard number 300, Chris invites Eric for what he calls a major *Raiders* sleepover. He refuses to reveal details. When Eric walks into Chris's room, he passes a stack of cardboard boxes in the hall, only to find a second stack in Chris's room along with two rolls of silver duct tape, two pairs of scissors, and a pile of bamboo stalks, precisely cut, on the floor.

"What's all this?" Eric asks, stowing his overnight bag on the bed across from Chris's bed.

"Are you ready for the big one? We're gonna build the boulder, man."

"Indy, I was born ready."

"I'm very excited. *Very* excited." To prove it, Chris does a little dance shuffle on the carpet.

"Where did you get the bamboo stalks?"

"Next door. The neighbors' yard." Chris dances to his dresser and fiddles with a new addition to his room, a twelve-inch black-and-white television he confiscated from his cousin's abandoned room downstairs. He tunes in a snowy channel showing reruns of *Sanford and Son*.

"Do the neighbors know?"

"I doubt it. They weren't home. Well, they might know by now."

"Excellent. And if anyone asks, I don't know you."

"Okayyy." Chris runs a hand through his thick hair, musses the middle, then picks up a sheet of notebook paper from his bed and studies a ragged-looking sketch he's made. "I wrote out a plan. The boulder has to look great. I mean, you think *Raiders*, you think boulder."

"Agreed," Eric says.

"I figure it has to be at least six feet around. No less. What do you think?"

Chris hands Eric the rough sketch of the boulder. Eric clicks his tongue, considers the math. "Seems about right."

"All right then." Chris plops a hand on Eric's shoulder. "Let's do this."

Working silently, intently, Chris's sheet of instructions in front of them on the floor, fumbling with the light but awkward bamboo, they swathe duct tape around the stalks and crisscross them in the center to form a frame. As the evening light fades, they cut and tape lengths of cardboard to the flimsy frame, painstakingly filling in the surface. Canned sitcom laughter the only sound in the room, they work on their knees, cutting, ducttaping—foot by foot—creating a massive misshapen cardboard orb in the center of Chris's bedroom. At two in the morning, the sitcoms replaced by a test pattern, the boys stitch the last square of cardboard onto the enormous boulder. The boulder completed, they sit on the floor and stare at it without expression. They lean back against their beds, too exhausted to move, too dazed to absorb their accomplishment.

"I'm totaled," Chris says. "Hey, Eric?"

"Yes, Chris?" Eric says.

"Did we just make the fucking boulder?"

"I believe so. It's kind of a blur."

Chris falls onto the floor sideways and pretends to snore. Then, laughing, without changing their clothes, the boys climb onto their beds and collapse.

The sun wakes them.

Eric stirs. Chris sits up. The huge cardboard boulder towers in the corner, its shadow filling up the room.

"It wasn't a dream," Chris says.

Eric sits up. Yawns. Stretches. "Nope. There it is."

"We did it, Eric," Chris says.

"I know—"

"WE DID IT!"

Chris rolls out of his bed, reaches his arms around the boulder, hugs the cardboard body, kisses the top, slow dances with it.

"I love you, boulder," he says.

Eric kicks off his covers, shouts, "I love you, too."

"We are trying this out *now*," Chris says.

"Get in front of it!" Eric runs behind the boulder, ready to push.

"Dude, let's try this out downstairs," Chris says. "My mom is gonna be thrilled."

Together, the boys shove the boulder toward the door.

Thwack.

The boulder spans the entire doorway, dwarfs it. It quivers and rolls back to them.

"No," Chris says.

"I can't believe that we didn't calculate—"

"NO!"

"—that the boulder might be too wide for the doorway. In retrospect, that was pretty dumb—"

"Shit! God damn it, sonofabitch, FUUUCCCCCKKKKK!"

"Christopher Andrew Strompolos!" Elaine. Downstairs. Her voice morphing from patient mom to broadcaster with breaking news. "You do *not* use that language in this house!"

"Shit," Chris says, a stage whisper. He sinks to the floor. "What are we gonna do?"

Eric scans the room. "The window's not an option. Even smaller than the door. There's no way to disassemble the boulder, not the way we taped the whole thing—"

"No way," Chris says. "Out of the question."

"I see no choice other than to force it through the doorway. Then cross our fingers."

"That's your plan?"

Eric bobs his head. "I admit it. It's not a great plan."

"It's lame."

"It's all I got. You have to admit, though, the boulder is pretty sturdy. My guess is that it'll fold up momentarily, then pop right back to its original shape."

Chris pinches the bridge of his nose. He looks up at Eric from the floor. "I got nothing better."

He reaches his hand up to Eric. Eric grabs his wrist and hauls him to his feet. The boys station themselves behind the boulder, nod in unison, and jam the boulder into the doorway.

The boulder grunts and freezes, stuck.

"Push!" Eric shouts.

The boys shove the boulder with all they have. The boulder gasps, belches a stream of air, and then something inside it snaps. Chris flinches, paralyzed in midpush.

"Don't stop!" Eric says.

"You stupid *boulder*—" Chris lowers his head and charges into the cardboard like a linebacker.

The boulder whimpers. Then its bamboo guts splinter and *crack*. Its midsection groans and sags.

The boys give one more push, and the boulder, formerly a cardboard planet, now a pathetic half-moon, slides easily through the doorway, and—*fawoosh*—deflates like a punctured beach ball. For one last nostalgic second, the boys cling to the remains of the boulder's emaciated, ragged carcass. Without looking at each other, they release the useless mound of smashed cardboard and allow it to bang down the stairs. It flops to rest in the entryway against the front door.

Elaine, hands on hips, appears in the hallway. She follows their gaze. "What are you doing? Why are you throwing that hunk of junk down the stairs?"

Chris, miserable, his eyes on the wreck below, says, "That's no hunk of junk. That was our boulder."

*   *   *

With only a few props gathered, no costumes—thanks to Chris's fedora and leather jacket spray-paint disaster—the boulder demolished, and hundreds of storyboards to go, the boys decide to concentrate on the one area they know they can handle: stunts. Chris, showing off his practiced Indiana Jones swagger, approaches each day as if it's the day that they might somehow get hold of a camera and actually *film* this thing. He vows to be ready. He sets his sights on the pit scene, where Indy leaps over an open pit to escape the collapsing temple cave by swinging from tree branch to tree branch. The boys find the perfect tree right outside Gus and Irene's house—a sturdy white pine in a neighbor's front yard—climb it, and prepare to "rehearse." That's the word they use. Because every thought, every action, every play date, every trip to the mall, every conversation, every nickel they save or spend goes into what will be their *Raiders*.

Standing on a tree limb ten feet above the ground, the boys prepare to jump to a branch hanging close by in the next tree almost within their grasp, certainly within Eric's reach. Why is Eric practicing stunts? He's not Indiana Jones. He's playing Toht, the bespectacled, trench-coat-wearing Nazi who never goes flying in the air. No reason. Except that Chris and Eric are twelve, and climbing trees and swinging from branches is what twelve-year-old boys do.

Chris goes first. Indy smirk stitched in place, he shoots out of his crouch, leaps, and easily grabs the branch in front of him. He flashes Eric a wide grin, pounds his chest, and howls like Tarzan. Eric, much less athletic and much more nervous, measures his leap. He hesitates. Swings his arms back and forth like a monkey. Wipes his suddenly slippery palms on his thighs.

"Don't think about it. Just do it," Chris calls from the tree across.

Eric nods, crouches the way Chris did, jumps, and latches onto the branch in front of him. He did it! Eric resists the temptation to yelp in victory. He hangs in midair for a full second, his legs scissoring, and then his grip slips, and he falls. He hits the ground hard. Pain blazes across his shoulder, but he holds back his tears. He bites his lip.

"Shit." Chris shimmies down the tree trunk, jumps to the ground.

"It's broken," Eric says, tears welling. "I know it."

"I got you, man," Chris says, circling an arm around Eric's waist. "Lean on me."

Eric rests his right arm on Chris's shoulder. Chris helps him up as gently as he can. Eric cries out, a muffled roar of agony, and Chris walks him across the neighbor's lawn and into his grandparents's house, chanting, "It's gonna be all right," the whole way.

He half-carries him into the living room and eases him onto the couch. He stuffs a pillow under Eric's head.

"I'll be right back. Don't move."

Chris races into the kitchen, calls his mom at work and Mary at Manyoaks, and jogs back into the living room. "My mom will be here in five minutes. What the hell were you doing swinging in a tree anyway? Who do you think you are, Indiana Jones?"

Eric sniffles, then laughs. He can't help it.

"Here, man. A little something to cheer you up. A candy cane. You love candy."

"Chocolate," Eric says.

"Well, fuck you."

Eric winces. "Don't make me laugh."

"Sorry." Chris yanks the cellophane off the candy cane with his teeth and hands it to Eric. "Merry Christmas."

"Happy New Year." Eric sniffs, pops the candy cane in his mouth, and closes his eyes so Chris won't see him cry.

Later, in the hospital, both moms hovering, Chris pacing, a candy cane of his own plugged into the corner of his mouth like a new father's cigar, a doctor finishes setting Eric's broken shoulder, then doses him with morphine to help him float above the pain.

"Who gave him the candy cane?" the doctor says.

"I did." Chris looks from his mom to Mary, expecting a reprimand from the doctor and a punishment from Elaine later.

"Very smart," the doctor says. "The body experiences shock when breaking a bone. The candy kept his blood sugar up, helped ward off some of the shock's intensity. Good job."

"Thanks, Chris," Eric says, his face folding into a goofy, wacked-out morphine-laced grin. "I feel *great*."

Just before Eric drifts off into sleepy, druggy heaven, it occurs to him that they may not finish *Raiders* that summer.

YEAR TWO

"I have the perfect man for this kind of work."   —*Colonel Dietrich*

1982–1983.

Eric, on bed rest while his shoulder heals, looks forward to his daily visits from Chris. They listen to the *Raiders* soundtrack and the crude cassette recording until they memorize every line of dialogue of every character in the movie. When Chris leaves, Eric throws himself into completing the last of the storyboards before school starts. He finishes with several days to spare. Rather than exhausting him, drawing the equivalent of six hundred detailed cartoon strips ignites Eric's imagination, leaves him feeling high. He craves more creativity, more *Raiders*, and so he starts to sketch costumes: Indy's, Toht's; the white-suited Belloq, Indy's rival and the movie's main villain; Marion, Indy's love interest, fetching in both a flowing white dress and a bar owner's outfit; Indy's friend Sallah's traditional Arab garb— all drawn with typical Eric detail. The day before school starts, he buys school supplies for the coming year and adds in an extra spiral-bound notebook. He fills this with the 602 storyboards, the shot list, and the costume sketches. In black marker, he labels the cover of the notebook *Raiders of the Lost Ark Book of Ideas and Memos. Indy and Toht's Notes: Don't Touch!!* and hides it in a drawer. Despite breaking his shoulder, busting the boulder, and the other *Raiders* setbacks, he doesn't want the summer to end.

In September, Chris returns to CEDS for sixth grade, and Eric enters seventh grade at Ocean Springs Junior High. The one-year grade difference and attending separate schools naturally distances them, but only a little. They talk regularly and hang out on weekends, planning for next summer, when they are determined to shoot their film. They talk casting

(Who can they recruit to play natives, Nazis, Marion? What part will Eric rope his little brother, Kurt, into playing?); stunt casting (Chris has begun training his dog, Snickers, to take on the part of the Nazi monkey); costumes (Eric's mom has a bunch of stuff tucked away in a hall closet and a sewing machine, and Eric can sew, so that's a start); props (more outings to Irene and Gus's backyard, the Salvation Army store, but where are they going to get a whip?); stunts ("Chris, I'll take a pass on that one"); effects (blood spurting, exploding heads, melting faces, corpses pincushioned with arrows—*help!*); shooting schedule (Eric's on it); camera, or lack of one ("Elaine? Can you rent one for us? Or 'borrow' one from the TV station?"); and, finally, the dark cloud that hangs over them: the boulder (no idea). The months drag by. They long for summer, talking about jumping back into *Raiders* the same way other kids talk about returning to their favorite sleep-away camp.

One fall day, the boys bike to the Salvation Army store on Government Street in search of a real leather jacket and a fedora that fits. They again pool their allowances and enter the store flush with cash, their stash close to twenty dollars. The store, a sad dark musty place crammed with racks of donated clothes sprayed with disinfectant, creeps them out. They split up and methodically comb through the clothing, arranged in no particular order. After a few minutes, Chris cries out, "Eric! Over here!"

Eric finds Chris standing by a clothing rack, holding a fake—possibly vinyl—brown leather jacket. The collar ends stick up, pointy and too wide, and the color is off, but otherwise it's perfect, certainly a big improvement over Chris's Members Only jacket. A few minutes later, they rummage through a bin of hats and come up with a fine-looking fedora, close enough to pass for the one Indy wears. Leaving the store with the leather jacket, the fedora, and *change*, the boys hop on their bikes, dizzy with success. A couple of months later, they fill in the rest of Indy's costume. For Christmas, Chris's dad gives him a single present, the only thing he's asked for: a replica of the Indiana Jones bullwhip, purchased at a Hollywood prop house.

As New Year's approaches, Chris, now twelve, faces abrupt and severe changes at home as a result of Elaine's romantic life. Elaine, charismatic and popular and never lacking for dates since her divorce, seems on edge, more prone to secrecy. She begins keeping odd hours, skulking around like a spy. She finally admits to Chris that she's seeing someone new, a guy she's crazy about—handsome, smart, rich, powerful, and her boss. Jimmy Love III. Gulf Coast royalty. Southern aristocracy. Moneyed beyond belief— owner of a string of funeral homes across the state, bed-and-breakfasts, yachts, apartment in New York, pillared mansion on the river called, fittingly, the Riverhouse, and owner, with his sister, of WLOX-TV. She asks for Chris's cooperation as her clandestine relationship with Jimmy heats up, and when he comes over during the day—lunchtime, late afternoons, before and after work—she asks Chris for privacy.

One Friday night, Elaine, flushed and in a hurry, charges into Chris's room. "Pack some things. Jimmy's taking us to New York City. We leave in an hour."

The weekend feels like a dream. Chris, once shuttled from Gulfport to Malibu and back again, an underage outsider on Mimi Hines's tour bus, a child visitor at a Hollywood party, now rides shotgun to the pilot on Jimmy Love III's private plane, then sits in the back of a stretch limo, sipping a soda while his mom and Jimmy fill flutes with Dom Pérignon on the way to Jimmy's penthouse on the Upper West Side across from Lincoln Center. After dressing for dinner and a Broadway play, Chris finds his mom alone in the living room, taking in the view of the city.

"What are we doing here, Ma?" he says.

"Starting over," Elaine says.

At dinner at Le Cirque, after a performance of *Cats*, watching his mom and Jimmy giddily clink glasses, she, luminous, a star, all eyes on her as she accepts her seat at the best table in the place, as if a spotlight has fallen on her, he, happily at her side but unquestionably in charge, maroon-cheeked from this moment of bliss and from imbibing half a bottle of an expensive Burgundy, the picture of a Southern gentleman in his signature white linen suit, Chris thinks, *This lifestyle—private plane, Broadway shows, five-star restaurants, the penthouse, the privilege, the money—I could get used to this.*

*   *   *

Meanwhile, at Manyoaks, Eric experiences violent sea change.

Most days, he finishes his schoolwork as soon as he gets home and then draws costume sketches or fiddles with a shooting schedule in anticipation of summer. His dad, James, always a heavy drinker but one who could hold it, seems more ornery, more adrift in his own house. It's common now that James will leave his office by midday and plunk himself down in the living room, silent, a glass of wine in his hand and a scowl on his face.

Manyoaks itself has hit an all-time low. The seaside elements have battered the house inside and out. The roof leaks whenever it rains and creaks and sags in the wind. Most of the floorboards buckle. Paint peels off the walls. Cracked plaster falls like snow from every ceiling. Mary, soft-spoken but insistent when she wants to be, hates living like this and asks James to repaint a few of the rooms—the kitchen, the boys' rooms, their room. James laughs her off. He's too busy. One day, refilling his wineglass in the living room, he tells Mary that many of his clients have left him and he's had to declare bankruptcy. He doesn't realize that Eric is sitting in the kitchen within earshot, taking this in.

Mary decides that she will fight for the house. She increases her hours with Mutual of Omaha, ratchets up her efforts to sell more policies, cleans out the five abandoned cottages behind the house, and rents them out to a collection of characters who preferably can pay in cash. Among her tenants is Peter Keefer, an actor who played a zombie in *Dawn of the Dead*.

"So cool," Eric tells Chris on the phone. "We've got a celebrity living out back."

When bills need to be paid and Mary comes up short, she dips into their rapidly dwindling savings. James responds by spending even less time at the office, by disappearing for hours during the day, and by starting to drink even earlier.

One evening after several glasses of wine, his dad sits in the living room, a blank, dead look on his face. Eric sits at the table, hunched over his *Raiders* notebook, lost in concentration as he sketches a costume for one of the Arab street vendors.

"What are you doing?" James says.

"Working on the costumes for *Raiders*."

His dad fills his empty glass from a jug of wine at his elbow. "You're not working," he says. "You're playing."

*   *   *

Summer 1983.

The week school ends, Elaine and Jimmy Love III marry. Sometime after
the wedding, Chris invites Eric for a sleepover at his new home, the Riverhouse. Inside the vast boxy white mansion that smells of wealth, Eric follows Chris up a metal spiral staircase painted ghost white to a small room
on the third floor, the converted attic. Chris's bunk bed rests in the middle
of a shaggy blue throw rug. The room, angled oddly this way and that, has
windows on all four sides and a view of the Tchoutacabouffa River. A ceiling fan whirs lazily, a portable stereo and a black-and-white TV with a
VCR hug the corner, and Chris's prize, a motorized disco ball he un-
earthed from a pile in his grandfather's backyard, swings below the fan.
Shortly, Chris adds a strobe light, splashes splotches of bright colors on
the walls, and hangs his *Star Wars* posters, survival knife, camouflage
pants, and other oddities. He blasts the Stones or Hall & Oates and powers up the pulsating strobe, which burns so hot it licks the paint off the
back wall. To Eric, the room feels completely Chris—loud, funny, wild,
and warm.

Eric gets the opposite feeling when Chris gives him a tour through the
rest of Riverhouse.

Carpeting so thick it covers your ankles. A cook's kitchen with gleam-
ing stainless steel appliances. L-shaped leather couches in a media room
facing a huge TV and LaserDisc player. A wet bar. A wet bar in every room,
actually. Eric loses count of the number of bathrooms. Hallways polished
slick and long as bowling alleys. Chris allows Eric a peek into Jimmy's
study—dark mahogany shelves crammed with leather-bound books, a mahogany desk the size of a conference table, bloodred armchairs, brandy
snifters, a humidor, wineglasses that sparkle, and a wet bar stocked with
single malt Scotches, whiskeys aged forever, and highly touted wines from
Sonoma. Jimmy's study feels dark, cool, and formidable, not unlike Jimmy
himself.

Elaine and Jimmy live in their own separate wing on the second floor
in a master bedroom suite that makes Eric imagine a Manhattan

penthouse—master bath with two sinks, a bidet, a circular bathtub with Jacuzzi jets, and a walk-in closet for Elaine that's bigger than the apartment she and Chris just vacated. Their wing connects to another wing where Jimmy's son, Chris's age, and his two younger daughters live. Overall, the Riverhouse envelops Eric in a kind of solemnity, heaviness. He feels, except in Chris's room, an absence of light. And despite the June Mississippi heat starting to press in, the inside of the Riverhouse feels freezing. Jimmy has the air conditioner turned way up blowing arctic air.

Ever since the weekend months ago that they spent in New York, Chris hasn't quite been able to get a handle on his new stepfather. Everything about Jimmy Love III seems different, foreign. Chris is used to a world of Greek men—cooks and club owners—who speak in loud booming voices, who laugh and cry without hesitation, who eat, drink, sing, and dance on tables, and who'll hug the hell out of you because Greek men *hug*, and hug hard.

Jimmy keeps his distance. He stands back. He observes. He judges. He criticizes. He has the right to, Chris believes, because he has made a fortune and earned entry into a world his dad and grandfathers never knew, a world of culture and education and breeding. A world to which Jimmy has offered him entry.

"He may not be the warmest man in the world," Elaine says, "but he sees something in you. He believes you have promise."

Chris, draped over the leather couch in the media room, says nothing. He's riveted for the millionth time on his favorite movie of the moment, *Red Dawn*.

"I'm not asking you to like him," Elaine says. "Just respect him."

Chris turns the volume up, returns to his movie. He admits that he's intrigued by Jimmy Love III's world, a world that he will soon experience firsthand. In September, he will enter seventh grade in a posh boarding school on Long Island.

"You will learn a lot there," Jimmy says, pouring brandy into a snifter and taking a deep whiff before he downs it in one swallow.

Respect him, his mother says to Chris.

Chris respects his *world*. He wants to be part of it. But he wants no part of Jimmy Love III himself.

Especially since he made his mom quit her job as WLOX-TV's first and only female news anchorwoman.

"No wife of mine is going to work," he said.

Elaine accepted Jimmy's decision, unhappily. She did what he said and walked away from her career. To keep harmony in the Riverhouse. To keep Jimmy Love III happy and feeling in charge. She did it for Chris. For Chris's future.

She did it for her son.

*　　*　　*

The boys have a problem. With the first planned day of shooting only a week away, they have nobody to play Dr. René Belloq, Indy's natty white-suit-wearing villainous rival portrayed in *Raiders of the Lost Ark* by Paul Freeman with a sketchy French accent and effective horror-film cackle.

"What about Ted Ross?" Chris says. Chris knows Ted and his brother Jason from Gulfport, where they were neighbors.

"He's too short," Eric says, "and much too young. He's a kid. He's my brother's age. Belloq is a major role. We can't trust it to a kid."

"True. It's the third lead," Chris says. "A kid could flake on us. We have to guard against premature flake-age."

"Well," Eric says. He lies on his bed, his arms locked behind his head. Chris sits on a chair next to an open window absently knotting and unknotting the Venetian blind cord, one leg dangling over an arm of the chair.

"I suppose—"

"What?"

"I mean, if we had no other choice."

"You?" Chris looks at Eric. The cord drops out of his hand and swings against the arm of the chair.

Eric pushes himself off the bed and walks toward Chris. He bends at the waist, deepens his voice, and speaks in his own sketchy French accent: "*Dr. Chones, again we see there is nozzing you can possess vich I cannot take avay.*"

"That is scary," Chris says. "Close my eyes and you are Belloq."

"Seriously? Do I really sound like Paul Freeman?"

"You're his fucking clone."

"All right, I'll do it. Problem solved. Now, what about Toht?"

Chris snatches the cord in midswing and starts tying it into a tiny noose. "We'll hold auditions."

"Like a screen test? We don't have a camera."

"Screw a camera. Whoever fits into the costume gets the part."

It's summer. Pickings are slim. They contact the only two possibilities they can think of—Ted Ross and Kurt, Eric's little brother. Eric walks downstairs to the backyard and corners Kurt, who's pumping up a bicycle tire. Kurt shrugs, says sure, he'll try out, why not, holding back a smile that suggests he's glad to be asked. Chris calls Ted on the phone, waking him up. It's noon. They set the audition for Eric's room, two o'clock sharp.

Ted goes first. Eric and Chris hand him Toht's costume on a wire hanger, labeled and ironed, and shoo him into a spare bedroom to change. A few minutes later, Ted slouches into the bedroom, the black overcoat, black hat, white button-down shirt, red tie, and black pants hanging off him at least two sizes too big. He looks like a derelict who mugged a much taller businessman and stole his clothes.

"You want me to say anything?" Ted asks.

"No. You're great. We'll call you," Chris says.

"Hand the costume to Kurt on your way out," Eric says.

"What did you think?" Chris says after Ted closes the door behind him.

"He lacks Toht's creepy energy," Eric says. "I felt no menace. No sense of danger when he walked into the room. Then again, he's ten."

"I thought he looked like a slob," Chris says.

"He is appropriately round, though. Add the proper glasses and he might be able to pull it off."

"I'm ready to give the part to Kurt, sight unseen."

On cue, the door opens and Kurt, the Toht costume falling off his scrawny frame—*five* sizes too big—penguins into the room doing a bad Charlie Chaplin impression. He doffs the hat, wobbles it down his arm before it skids off.

"Kurt!" Eric says. "You're supposed to be a sinister Nazi henchman. Quit screwing around!"

Kurt whips off his hat and curtsies.

"Go! Leave! You're not playing Toht!" Eric whirls on Chris. "He's not playing Toht. We're casting Ross."

"Hey," Kurt says, crushed. "I'm your *brother.*"

"Don't remind me," Eric says. Eric stands, towering over his brother. "This is serious stuff, Kurt. We're making a movie. If you want to help, fine, but we're not fooling around."

"I want to help," Kurt says quietly.

"Okay, but you're not playing Toht. You blew that."

"Fine," Kurt says, and slowly leaves the room. He crouches in the hallway outside the room he shares with Eric and sulks before he returns to his deflated bike tire. Chris calls Ted Ross with the good news: He got the part.

"Oh, okay," Ted says. "It's so boring in the summer. At least now I have something to do."

"Was he excited?" Eric asks when Chris hangs up the phone.

"Jacked," Chris says.

*   *   *

With the first day of filming approaching, Eric spreads the storyboards on the table in the living room. He glances at them, lifts his head, and stares into the Gulf.

"Uh-oh," Chris says, sitting across from him, working on his second Popsicle in less than a minute. "You got that *look.* What's the problem?"

"This." Eric reaches over to the chair next to him and cradles a small plastic skull that the boys purchased for five dollars at the mall. "Makeup. Special effects. We need Forrestal's corpse to burst into view impaled on a row of spikes, and we need Barranca's bloody corpse to fall at your feet, his back riddled with poison darts. Derek Taylor's book explains the big effects, the exploding head and so forth, but not this stuff. Not the normal run-of-the-mill blood and gore. How are we going to do this? We don't want it to look amateurish. It has to look convincing."

Chris removes the Popsicle, which he's slurped down to the nub, his face smeared red with raspberry. "That's your problem? The blood, guts, and gore?"

"Yes. *And* the spikes and poison darts."

Chris taps the Popsicle stick, sucked dry, on the table like a drumstick. He leans his chair back into the wall and flashes a grin at Eric.

"I know a guy," Chris says.

*   *   *

Jayson Lamb sits in front of the television, mesmerized. While channel surfing, he's come upon a documentary on PBS about the makeup artist Rick Baker, who won the first Academy Award ever given out for makeup for his work in *An American Werewolf in London*. Jayson feels a profound connection to Rick Baker, to his process, and to his world, a world Baker has realized out of the mythic creatures in *Grimm's Fairy Tales*, Jean Cocteau's *Beauty and the Beast*, his imagination, and his dreams. Baker's creatures project heart and humanity and they scare the shit out of you. Jayson feels drawn in, and then he feels as if a fire has been lit inside him. He knows what he wants to do for the rest of his life. He has found his calling.

"I'm going to be a special-effects artist," he says to Rick Baker's American werewolf.

When he thinks about it, becoming a special effects artist is totally logical. Since the first grade, Jayson has been building his own puppets. He's given them names, personalities, and voices and created stories for them in which they sometimes end in a gruesome death. Not to worry. In these fantasies, he brings the dead back to life. Usually. If it suits the story. Lately, though, he's shelved the puppets and devoted his alone time—he has plenty of that—to magic tricks. He prefers tricks that unnerve you, creepy tricks, special effects, ones that involve severed hands and fingers and a lot of gushing fake blood. Pick a card, any card? Not his style. He likes to treat his audiences, usually his brother and sister, to a little gore.

Jayson's big break, his Rick Baker moment—now that he knows who Rick Baker is—happens at school, CEDS, at Halloween. With his teacher's encouragement, Jayson turns his fifth-grade classroom into a gory, scary haunted house. His teacher invites everyone in the school to enter Jayson's House of Horrors. Most kids, especially the older boys, strut into the darkened classroom, strobe lights pulsing, creepy music playing, sound effects blasting, peeled grapes as eyeballs popping out of bloody skulls, trying to put on a cool, even blasé, attitude. After Jayson's fright fest, many of the kids come out screaming. One of the fifth graders, Chris Strompolos, the heavy kid, the new kid, comes out beaming, shaking his head with respect.

"Did you do all that yourself?" Chris asks Jayson, who stands shyly in the hallway. Chris towers over Jayson. Well, everybody does. A series of allergies when he was a baby that kept him bedridden, and then contracting Legg-Calve-Perthes disease stunted Jayson's growth. As a fifth grader, Jayson has barely broken four feet in height. Eventually, he will experience a mild growth spurt and stop growing when he hits five feet two inches.

"Yeah," Jayson says, smiling at the floor. "I did it."

"Totally gross, man," Chris says. "Awesome."

Later, riding on the bus, Chris notices Jayson sitting alone, munching on carrot sticks. Chris bounces down the aisle and slides in next to him. Jayson raises his free hand in greeting and offers Chris a carrot.

"No, thanks. Beef jerky?"

"Ah. No. I'm a vegetarian."

"Seriously?" Chris has never known a ten-year-old vegetarian. He's met a few older vegetarians, mostly emaciated drag queens who tagged along with Mimi Hines, popping vitamins by the fistful and pounding wheatgrass like shots of whiskey. Chris comes from a Greek family of enthusiastic cooks and passionate eaters, worshipers of lamb and beef and grilled whole fish in succulent sauces.

"I'm also a Buddhist," Jayson says.

Chris cocks his head and passes his eyes over this weird little kid, who neatly folds up his empty carrot bag and stuffs it into his shirt pocket. Chris notices then that Jayson wears a leather medicine bag fringed like a moccasin slung around his neck with twine.

"You want to hang out?" Chris says.

They do, on the weekend, at Chris's grandparents' place. Unlike most fifth graders, who might show up for a play date with a ball or a glove or a board game, Jayson arrives with a makeup kit. Chris finds this odd, a little endearing, and very cool. The boys watch a movie, then fool around with Jayson's makeup, creating fake bloody injuries, and then Jayson decides to treat Chris and his grandmother to a little gore, too. He rigs a harness around Chris's waist and chest inside his shirt, fashions a noose out of a length of clothesline he's brought along, and drapes the noose around Chris's neck. He tightens the noose enough to make it look like an authentic suicide attempt, swings the end of the rope onto a hook he finds in the closet, fills an empty plastic pill capsule with red food coloring, and stuffs it into the corner of Chris's mouth. Then they wait. Chris knows that soon his grandmother will climb the stairs with a tray of freshly baked cookies. As soon as they hear her heavy footsteps coming up the stairs, Jayson turns on the closet light and ducks behind the bed, and Chris bites down on the capsule. Blood spurts into his cheek and spills onto his white shirt.

"Chris, I brought you some cookies I made . . . *AHHHH!*" Chris's grandmother screams and flings the tray of cookies over her shoulder. She slams both hands over her mouth in horror.

"Hi, Grandma," Chris says.

"Christopher Strompolos! You give me heart attack!"

"Sorry. What kind of cookies?

*   *   *

That Jayson has discovered his calling, his career, at such an early age surprises Jayson's recently divorced parents—his dad, a doctor and former air force colonel turned pacifist and practicing Buddhist who's moved to California, and his mom, a photographer—because Jayson began so many other things so late.

Talking, for instance.

Jayson didn't speak until he was five years old.

Legg-Calve-Perthes disease, an uncommon ailment that shuts down the blood flow to the hips, forced Jayson to remain in bed for the first three years of his life. He learned to walk slowly, painfully, wearing clunky, unwieldy leg braces. Gradually his condition improved and he was able to walk without the braces. But being confined to his room for practically his entire life, Jayson felt scarred socially. He had learned words, could form sentences, but he didn't know what to say. So he simply didn't speak. Doctors could find nothing physically wrong with him. A succession of speech therapists failed to get him to talk. Jayson lived in silence and for the most part alone. In fact, he tried to disappear, or at least to escape. He would spend much of the day in his closet, dragging his puppets and pop-up books with him into his dark imaginary world.

By law, when he turned five, he had to start school. For kindergarten, his parents enrolled him in a Montessori school. His mom would wait for him to get settled before she would leave, but as soon as she drove away, Jayson headed right into the classroom's closet. The teacher would gently pull him out, but the moment she turned her attention to another child, he rushed back in. One day, a girl known by her classmates as June Bug, whose freckled face mirrored Jayson's, watched him with something more than curiosity as his mom left him for the day. He waited for a moment, gathered his puppets and pop-up books, and shut himself in the closet. With no hesitation, June Bug walked to the closet door, pulled it open, stepped inside, and closed the door behind her. Jayson and June Bug stayed in the closet until the teacher called them out for snack.

That evening at dinner, Jayson pushed the food around on his plate, his head cupped in his other hand. He looked lost in thought.

"Seems like you got something on your mind," his mom said.

"Oh, I'm just thinking about me and my girlfriend, June Bug."

His parents froze. Other than a random word or two, Jayson had never spoken an entire sentence. Not once in five years.

"Well," his mom said, summoning every ounce of her resolve to keep herself from crying. "That's nice. You have a girlfriend."

"Yeah. We're gonna get married and live in a big white house with a big white car. Have a couple kids. Maybe three. You never know."

And now, beginning seventh grade, Jayson Lamb, not quite five feet tall, confirmed vegetarian, Buddhist magician, special effects expert, and supreme conversationalist, answers the phone on the first ring.

"Jayson? Chris."

Jayson talks softly and carefully, as if he's speaking from a long distance and late at night, as if he's far away. "How goes it?"

"Got a situation. We need your help."

"Yeah?"

"Remember in show-and-tell or whatever it was back in like fifth grade I showed the class pictures of me dressed as Indiana Jones? I said I was remaking *Raiders of the Lost Ark?*"

"I remember. That was cool."

"Well, I'm doing it for real. We're shooting in two days."

"Nice."

"Totally. Except we got jammed up in pre-production. We're trying to make that corpse in the beginning of the movie, the one with the spikes through it? And also that corpse that falls over with the poison darts in its back? We need that, too."

"Yeah. You gotta have them."

"I know. But, okay, here's the thing. Me and Eric? We have no clue. If we do the corpse and the skull ourselves, it will *suck*."

Jayson laughs a little, from that distance. "It might."

"We'd really like you to come aboard."

"Okay."

"Great. Excellent. Come over to Eric's house as soon as you can. Bring your makeup kit."

Jayson huffs into the phone. "I always bring my makeup kit."

*   *   *

Standing in the service porch attached to the kitchen, Eric, at least a head taller than Jayson, presses the plastic skull into Jayson's hands. "Jayson, please make this skull work."

"I will. Can I use this table?"

"Yes, sure. Let me just spread some newspaper under it so my mom doesn't have a conniption."

As Eric and Chris lay out the morning's paper on the table, Jayson digs around in his makeup kit. He takes his time, breathing a slow cleansing breath to relax because he feels a little nervous. Eric and Jayson are the same age—Jayson may actually be a month or two older—but as a result of Jayson's illness and his dyslexia, diagnosed in the first grade, the school and his parents held him back a year. Now here he is making a movie with Eric Zala, a grade above him, someone he always admired because of his appearance in "SHIT" and his ill-fated "Shape Shifter" comic strip, but someone he has never spoken to.

"I liked your comic strip," Jayson mutters, rummaging through his makeup bag.

"Oh, thank you. It became too difficult to pull off on a weekly basis because of the school's ancient mimeograph machine. Horrible reproduction quality. Characters all smudged. Ink smearing the captions. Very frustrating. That's why I gave it up."

"Too bad," Jayson says. "I know I have some clay in here. I just hope I have enough."

He pulls out makeup brushes, fake blood, a couple of false ears, some bloodshot glass eyeballs, and a half-empty jar of clay.

"Not enough," he says. "This won't cover the skull."

"Now what?" Chris says.

"We need to go to the store and buy some more."

Jayson might as well have suggested that they pull stockings over their faces and hold up the store.

"We don't have any money," Eric says.

"Well." Jayson shoots them a helpless, slightly embarrassed smile. "I have to find something I can substitute for clay."

"You can use anything in the house," Eric says. "Everything is fair game."

"Let's take a look." Jayson heads straight for the kitchen sink. He pulls open the cabinet doors below. "People usually keep their good stuff in here." He sits on the floor, pokes his head inside, and hunts through an assortment of cleaning supplies. He pulls out caulking putty, a box of Brillo pads, and a small can of brown paint.

"Bingo," he says.

*   *   *

While Jayson works on the skull and the corpse in the service porch, Eric and Chris walk along the perimeter of the Zalas' backyard. Near the property line, they stop at a small swamp, the water green and hazy, red flowers blooming, butterflies flapping above so loudly they buzz. They move on, enter a lush section of woods, passing trees they've heard described as cot-tonwood and indigo bush.

"This could be Peru right here," Chris says.

"That's what I was thinking, too," Eric says. "Then if we push through here—"

Eric circles back and Chris follows to an opening that leads them back to the backyard. Facing the woods, Eric holds his hands in front of his face and makes a frame with his fingers. "I thought this is where we could shoot you—Indy—rushing out of the jungle, the Hovitos in hot pursuit. The backyard here will easily serve as the clearing that Indy runs into, don't you think?"

"Definitely."

Eric moves a few feet to his right. "As the storyboard indicates, if we place the camera right here, we'll re-create the shot almost exactly."

Chris rubs his chin, a gesture he's copied from Harrison Ford. "Eric?"

"Yeah?"

"You want to direct? You have the storyboards down cold, and you seem to know where the camera should go. What do you think?"

"Okay. Sure."

"Great."

And that's how Eric becomes the director.

                    *   *   *

Later, in the service porch, the afternoon turning hot, Jayson takes his shirt off as he works on the skull. Chris yanks open the freezer compartment of the Zalas' fridge, hacks at a chunk of ice with a screwdriver, and scoops ice chips into three plastic cups. He hands cups of ice to Eric and Jayson and keeps one for himself. They chew the ice, allowing the shock of the cold to spread into the backs of their mouths.

"Chris tells me you're into photography," Eric says, a wad of ice packed into his cheek like a chaw of tobacco. The cold stings. He winces and spits the ice into his cup.

"Yeah. My mom's a photographer. I picked up a couple things from her."

"So you know cameras?"

Jayson bites into an ice chip, swirls it around. "Little bit."

"What about movie cameras?"

Jayson scratches his bare stomach. "Guess I could learn."

"We might have to expand your job description," Eric says.

Chris hauls open the freezer again, chops another wedge of ice with the screwdriver. "Eric's the director."

"Cool," Jayson says, keeping his voice calm and distant, even though he wants to scream. A few hours ago, he was sitting at home bored as hell, wondering what he would do all summer. Now he has a *job* and he feels needed. Better, he feels wanted. He even feels, for the moment, important.

"Die, ice, die," Chris says, brutally stabbing the ice in the freezer. Pieces of shaved ice fly everywhere. "Man, it is fucking *hot*."

He knees the freezer closed, takes a small slice of shaved ice, and drops it down the front of his pants.

"Ahhh," he says, then shudders.

Eric, recently named director of the movie, and Jayson, head of makeup and master of special effects, crack up as the leading man wiggles his crotch and moans in fake ecstasy.

*   *   *

Two hours earlier than expected, Elaine's minivan turns up the drive at Manyoaks and pulls up outside the back porch. Elaine lowers her window and waves at the boys. "You guys ready to go?"

Chris, confused, squints into the sun. "You're early, Ma."

"I called her." Mary appears behind the three boys. She lightly places her hand on Eric's shoulder. "I'm sorry, boys. We're going to have to call it a day."

"I'll take you home, too, Jayson," Elaine says.

Eric looks up at his mom, trying to determine what has happened. He sees only a stony stare. It's a look he hasn't seen before. At first he thinks he's done something wrong, but his mind whips through the events of the morning, then scrolls through the days before, and he can think of nothing. Mary lowers her head, and Eric sees that her eyes look red and puffy and realizes that she has been crying.

"Well, okay, guys," Eric says. "Um, Mom, tomorrow we're scheduled to start shooting—"

Mary nods, tries a smile.

"Oh, that's *on*," Elaine says. "We're gonna pick up the camera right now. I called ahead and reserved it at that video store, Captain Phil or whatever that pervert's name is."

"Good. Thank you. Mom, I told everybody ten o'clock," Eric says. "Eight for the three of us. Is that still—?"

"That's fine," Mary says, but she's no longer looking at him. She's trained her eyes on something in the distance. She gazes over Elaine's car, past the front lawn, her eyes resting on the Gulf.

"Okay, well, see you guys tomorrow, eight sharp," Eric says.

Jayson balls up his shirt, nods at the plastic skull and the spike he's started to stick into it. "What should I do with this stuff?"

"Leave it," Mary says. "It'll be fine. I'm sorry—"

"No big thing," Elaine says. "You'll pick up where you left off tomorrow."

"Yes," Mary says.

Before Eric can find his bearings, Chris and Jayson bound down the back stairs and pile into Elaine's minivan. Jayson laughs at something Chris says or does, and Elaine says, "Christopher, that's terrible!" but she laughs, too, and then they're gone.

"Get Kurt," Mary says. "Meet us in the living room."

"Should I put this stuff away first or—"

"No, Eric. Now."

She disappears into the house.

In a few minutes, not yet four o'clock on a hot June afternoon, Eric and Kurt sit on the couch across from their father, who stands propped against the wall, rubbing the top of his head. Mary sits at the table in the corner, her back erect, her hands folded in front of her. Her mouth looks caked, dry. Eric and Kurt sit at the edge of the couch.

"Tell them, Jim," Mary says, her voice cracking.

In that moment, Eric knows what his father is about to say. He pictures the words hanging above his dad as if captured in a bubble in a cartoon just as his dad pushes himself away from the wall and steps toward the couch, his hands dangling at his sides—

We've run out of money and we have to move.

Where will we go? Eric thinks. *Will we leave this summer? And* Raiders? *We'll have to figure out another location—*

"Your mother and I have decided to get a divorce."

His father projects his voice louder than he needs to. It sounds as if he's standing on a stage playing a part, speaking to the back row so that he's sure to be heard. "I'll be moving out tonight."

Eric lowers his head, looks at the floor to steady himself, but the floor is swimming, making him dizzy. A wave of nausea ripples through him, curdling into the back of his throat. Then he hears a howl, a cry of pain. He thinks their dog outside may be hurt. He whips his head toward the sound and sees Kurt doubled over, his hands gripping his midsection. He sobs, his body shaking. Eric starts to reach an arm to his brother, but before he can move, Kurt shoots off the couch, stumbles, and runs upstairs. Eric fastens his eyes back onto the floor. He wants to look at his mother, but he's afraid he'll raise his head and catch his father's eyes, and he doesn't want to look at him at all. He wishes that his father would somehow disappear. But then he feels his father's presence. He's moving toward him, coming closer. Eric smells liquor on his breath mixed with mint. He wants to go to his mother and he wants to tell his father to just go, to leave, to get the hell away. And he wants to tell him to stay. Eric wishes he could dissolve into the couch.

He forces himself to look up. He turns toward his mom. She sits at the table, a hand covering her face, her eyes closed. He can't see if she's crying, but her shoulders are heaving. His father has retreated to his spot against the wall and he's looking at his hands now, rubbing them in front of him as if he's trying to keep warm. He nods at them, at his hands, and says, simply, "I guess I'll go pack," but he doesn't move.

Eric looks straight ahead, at nothing. He sees his father out of the corner of his eye and his body is shimmering, and Eric thinks, *He's going, but he was never here.*

Eric gets up from the couch, moves to his mother, and throws his arms around her. She grips his forearm and buries her head in his chest. She doesn't seem to be crying. She seems as if she's gathered herself, collected her strength, and she raises her head and catches Eric's eyes. Something he sees in her tells him that she feels robbed, that's all, that her husband has stolen something from her.

"We're going to be all right," she whispers. "We'll figure it out."

"Are we going to stay here?"

"I'm not giving this place up, Eric," Mary says. "He might be changing his life, but we're not changing ours."

Eric nods, not sure what she means. In a matter of a few weeks, he'll find out. He learns that his father decided to leave his mother for his secretary.

Now his mom brushes Eric's hair off his forehead. "You okay?"

Eric sniffs, nods. "You?"

"I will be."

Eric nods again. He turns then to his father, still in retreat against the wall, his eyes clouded, his mouth lined into a frown. He seems stuck in that spot, not sure where he should be.

"Excuse me," Eric says, drilling his father with his eyes. "I have work to do."

*   *   *

He begins by planning what scenes they'll shoot and in what order. The first scene, he decides, will be a simple shot of Indiana Jones on the ground, surrounded by hostile natives, their bows and arrows and spears aimed at him. He has recruited Kurt and four of his friends to play the spear-throwing, arrow-shooting Hovitos who in subsequent shots will chase Indy out of the jungle (the woods next to the house), across a clearing (the backyard), and into the river (the Tchoutacabouffa River next to the River-house). They will have to pick up and move the production to that location. His mom and Elaine, the transportation captains, have agreed to drive the entire production staff and cast members.

Eric moves downstairs to his mom's office. He spreads out the story-boards and lists the shots in order on a sheet of paper that he attaches to a spare clipboard he finds. He powers up his mom's Xerox machine and copies the scenes he needs on the back of a stack of used Mutual of Omaha stationery.

Then he goes upstairs and checks the costumes. He makes sure he has enough beads for the kids to wear and enough spears, bows, and arrows to go around. He double-checks the idol, a small statue he made out of a cork shrimp-net bobber, duct-taping half a Christmas ornament to the top, carving a face with a knife, and spray-painting it gold. He turns it over in his hands the way Indy does and decides that it doesn't look half bad. He's sure it will look even better on film. He opens a drawer and takes out a purple Crown Royal bag he confiscated a week ago from one of his father's empties. His father's sole contribution to the film and he doesn't even know it.

At eleven, getting ready for bed, he grips the bathroom sink with both hands. He slowly blows out some air to steady himself. This day feels shattered into a thousand pieces like a jigsaw puzzle that's been thrown onto the floor. His father, a man who has always seemed so far away, so disconnected from him, now feels almost unreal, a shadow. Kurt feels upended, he knows. But Eric feels oddly calm. Resigned. He will lose himself in his work. No. He will *find* himself in his work, in this movie, in his friends, in his best friend.

He lies down on his bed, his matching twin bed, next to Kurt. Kurt breathes heavily. Eric can't tell if he's asleep. He wants to say something to his little brother, some words to try to soothe him, make him feel better, but he doesn't know what those words would be. He considers calling Chris and telling him about his father. They have something else in common now besides their love of *Raiders of the Lost Ark*. They have parents who have split, dads at a distance. He wonders suddenly, *Am I the man of the house now? I'm thirteen years old. Am I supposed to take care of things now? Am I supposed to take care of my mother? How? What does all this mean?*

He focuses on being the director. He's not sure what that means either, but he imagines that he is supposed to know what to do. He's the one who has the answers. The one who makes the decisions. The one with the final say. The one in charge. The dad.

Wide awake now, the ceiling fan humming, Eric realizes that he never heard his father leave, that he never said good-bye.

*   *   *

They meet on the service porch, wearing their costumes, Chris in his fake leather jacket and fedora they found at the Salvation Army store, Eric in khaki pants and shirt he discovered hanging upstairs in a closet and a pith helmet Kurt came across somewhere. Inspired by his costume, he tries out Belloq's accent, and Jayson laughs. "You sound just like him."

"He does, right?" Chris says. He rubs his chin. "Guys, I need stubble. Indy has beard stubble."

"I thought about that," Jayson says. He unscrews a jar of Vaseline he takes from his makeup kit and smears it over Chris's cheeks.

"You think that's *enough?* This is my face, not a baby's ass."

"That should do it." Jayson steps back. "Okay, now." He reaches into a brown paper bag, sweeps up a handful of ashes, and pats Chris's cheeks.

"What is that shit?" Chris says.

"Ashes. From Eric's fireplace. You said everything was fair game."

"Indeed," Eric says.

Jayson steps back again, studies Chris, and grins.

"Wow," Eric says. "Check this out, Chris."

He holds a hand mirror up to him. Chris turns one side, then the other.

"It's not the years, it's the mileage," he says, Indy all the way.

*   *   *

The Hovitos arrive. Their moms drive them. Two cars, four kids, stripped to the waist, wearing grass skirts over their shorts. Four eleven-year-old blond Mississippi kids playing ferocious Peruvian Indians out to kill twelve-year-old Indiana Jones. As Elaine and her old friend Billy Bob, an employee at WLOX, sit in the Zala kitchen and try to get a handle on the intimidating two-piece Betamax camera she's rented from Captain Phil's Video, Eric rehearses Chris and the Hovitos. He leads them into the woods and arranges them in position, their bows and arrows and spears drawn, Chris on the ground, their captive. Eric, as Belloq, walks into the scene, taking Indy's pistol—a close-up shot of Chris pulling the gun out of his holster—and then Indy hands over the golden fertility idol he has removed from its altar in the cave. Although the kids display a range of interest and commitment and Eric refers to directing more than three kids at a time as "herding cats," moving them around this first time into their proper places, giving instruction on their movements, facial expressions, and motivation, taking charge—*directing*—feels natural.

*　　*　　*

Eric, out of costume, sits at the kitchen table with Jayson. Eric wags his head, nervous about operating the camera and self-conscious that he's being filmed, the test subject. Elaine hovers over the camera, trying to figure out how this clunker works, one eye on the instruction manual. Billy Bob goes the guy route, ignoring the manual, relying instead on instinct as he pounds all the switches on the face of the console.

"Is it recording?" Eric says.

"I don't know," Elaine says. "Is there a light on?"

"I see a light," Eric says.

"Green or red?" Billy Bob says, thumbing a button.

"Green."

"I think you're recording," Elaine says. "I think this is on."

"It is," Billy Bob says, standing straight up as if he's just done something. "Green means it's on. If it's a blinking red light, then it's off."

"Wait! There it is," Elaine says. "There you are, Eric. And what's this? There's a *zoom*. Oh, wow. Great. Good zoom. I like it. You're gonna love this, Eric."

"Terrific."

"Now, what should this here be on?" Billy Bob says, squinting at the controls. "Let's see. Says here sp. Is that right? I think the slower the speed, the worse the picture."

"It looks pretty slow to me," Eric says.

"Well, then there's lp," Billy Bob says. "What is lp?"

"A record album," Elaine says.

A slow smile burns across Billy Bob's face, then a shake of his head. "Girl, you've gone wild. You need to come back to work."

"I know it," Elaine says. "I know I do."

"I think this is working," Billy Bob says, hunched over the camera.

"Okay, nice," Elaine says. "Now make sure you count down, Eric. You need to count down from five to let the camera catch up."

"I will."

Elaine swings the camera over to Jayson. "Or else you'll record over what you just shot."

"That sounds . . . not good. Okay. Got it."

Lost, Eric looks at Jayson, who's mugging for the camera. He waves, then pokes two fingers behind his head, rabbit ears.

"You want to try it, Eric?" Elaine says.

"You're doing fine," Eric says. "Are you sure you don't want to be our cameraman?"

"Come on, you can do it."

Eric stands, switches places with Elaine and aims the camera, looking to capture Jayson, who's progressed from making faces to spreading his lips apart with his fingers.

"I don't see anything," Eric says. "Oh, wait, there. I think I got it. What do you have there, Elaine? What do you see?"

"I see the wall, Eric. You're shooting the wall."

"Oh. Okay. Let me try this. What about now?"

"Now you're zooming into the wall, Eric. Lovely wallpaper. In extreme close-up. Do you have something against shooting actual people?"

"Elaine, maybe you should be the cameraman. Seriously. At least for today. Please."

"All right. Just for today. Then tomorrow, you're taking over, Eric."

"No," Eric says quietly, but with conviction, the *director*. "Tomorrow Jayson's taking over."

*   *   *

With little fanfare, Eric counts down, "Five—four—three—two—one— *action*." Elaine aims the camera at four shadowy half-naked blond kids, their faces smeared brown to look like Peruvian Indians, their spears and arrows aimed at her son lying on the ground. Savages poised to kill, the Hovitos hover over the fallen Indiana Jones, the only sound a rippling of leaves behind them. Then another kid, dressed in khaki, falls facedown next to them, landing in a bed of soft brush, dead, a cluster of bloody arrows sticking in his back, the "corpse effect" Jayson has created. Finally Eric, dressed as Belloq, steps into the shot and speaks the first words of dialogue they will record: "Dr. Jones, again we see there is nozzing you can possess ¡ . ."

It all feels real and unreal, natural and right: Eric, in charge, shouting directions to the Hovitos as they run after Indiana Jones; Chris, dashing, committed, his voice a kid's unchanged soprano, but cocky, even at twelve, charismatic, the star, pacing while Elaine and Eric struggle to find focus on the stupid camera; and Jayson, fine-tuning everyone's makeup, touching up the corpse's blood, and when Eric hands him the camera at last, feeling like a third partner, especially when he handles the camera with ease and control. At one point, while the Hovitos are regrouping for another take, Eric thinks, *We're in production. We're actually doing this.* It's what he always wanted, and if he's honest with himself, what he sometimes feared. Now that it's happening, really happening, it's better than he could have imagined.

When they finish shooting the scenes in the backyard at Eric's house, actors, director, cameraman, and moms pile into three cars and drive to the woods by the Riverhouse, overlooking the Tchoutacabouffa River. Twenty feet from shore, manning a rowboat with an outboard motor, a kid sits fishing, in costume, in character, playing the part of Jock, Indy's friend and rescuer. With this scene, Eric and Chris have made their first creative compromise, a sacrifice they accept due to skill level, age, and budget. Indiana Jones will not swing from a vine, land in the river, and swim to safety in a seaplane, which his friend Jock will lift off the water, escaping the flying darts shot by the pursuing Hovitos. Instead, they reconceive the scene and replace the seaplane with a dinghy.

"We have to expect to make compromises," Eric says to Chris a few nights before the first day of shooting.

"Yeah. I know."

If possible, Chris sounds even more disappointed than Eric.

"But in order to get this movie *finished*—"

"I hear you, man."

"Not to mention that nobody in their right mind would give a couple of twelve-year-old kids a *plane*."

"I get that. But we're still doing the stunts. I'm still gonna swing from the vine into the river."

"And that alone will be awesome."

It is awesome.

On the fourth take.

Take one.

Eric calls *action*. Chris grabs the rope, starts to swing, fumbles the rope, drops the rope, and nearly falls off the bank into the river.

Take two.

Eric calls *action*. Chris grabs the rope. He pushes off the bank, swings, and bangs balls first into a tree. He sags to the ground.

Take three.

Eric calls *action*. Chris grabs the rope. He pushes off the bank, swings, and lands with a splash in the river. Swimming frantically toward the rowboat, screaming something that sounds like *"Sammmm-yaaaa-yaaaaaaa-seee-seeee!"* Chris latches onto the back of the boat and pulls himself in. Eric hollers, "Cut!" Chris waves, collapses, teeth chattering.

One hitch. Elaine, the camera operator, missed one small detail—Chris swinging by the rope and splashing into the river.

Take four.

Eric calls *action*. Chris grabs the rope. He pushes off the bank, swings, splashes into the river, swims frantically after the rowboat, screams, catches the boat, hauls himself in. Eric yells, "Cut!" And *"Print!"*

The rest of the day's shoot goes even better—Indy in the rowboat with Jock, discovering Jock's pet snake, Reggie, screeching "There's a snake in the boat, Jock!"; Jock and Indy *putt-putt-putting* away in the rowboat; back in the jungle, Indy lashing his whip at Barranca's pistol; a Hovito running toward shore shooting a poison mouth-dart at Indy. But nothing tops the rush the boys feel after Chris's first big stunt, swinging on the rope, splashing into the river, swimming to the dinghy, and hauling himself aboard. What a high!

Unfortunately, in the movie business, the highs don't last very long.

Sitting in an editing cubicle at WLOX—arranged during downtime by Billy Bob—Eric, Chris, and Jayson prepare to watch the footage from the first day. The first shot, the Hovitos standing above Indiana Jones, appears; then the rest of the footage rolls.

It sucks.

Everyone looks dark and grainy, as if the boys shot the film in black-and-white, badly. The acting? Eric can barely watch. The Hovitos stink. They look like scrawny little blond kids holding sticks, stifling smirks. The dart shooter charges the shore with all the urgency of a sleepwalker. The sound? Mostly clear, except for an occasional undercurrent of a woman talking, someone obviously not in their movie but left over from the previous renter's footage. The camera work, overall, looks surprisingly steady, and the shots seem properly framed, thanks to Eric's storyboards. But a large mysterious *A* sits in the left corner of almost every shot.

"What is that?" Eric says to Jayson as if he should know. "Where did that *A* come from?"

"I don't know," Jayson says. "I didn't put it there."

"Don't look at me," Chris says. "I was too busy in front of the camera looking like a dork."

"I think you're good," Jayson says.

"You are good, Chris," Eric says. "The stunts look good. It's the camera. The camera is bad. And that stupid *A*."

The footage keeps rolling. It becomes harder and harder to watch. At one point, Chris slumps down in his seat and covers his face with his hands. "My voice is so high. I sound like a girl. Do I really sound like that?"

"You don't sound that bad," Eric says. "I think the camera distorted it."

"It's brutal," Chris says. "All of it."

"It really is," Eric says. "Totally unacceptable. Guys, we're going to have to shoot this over."

*   *   *

Elaine returns the camera to Captain Phil and one night, with Billy Bob standing watch, "borrows" a camera from the station, a newer, lighter Betamax that's lying around, not in use. Jayson finds that he can mount this camera on his shoulder.

Putting off the jungle reshoot, Eric and Chris decide to tackle the expository scenes next, the sequence in the beginning of the film in which two shadowy government bureaucrats recruit Indiana Jones to go in search of the lost Ark of the Covenant, racing against men hired by Hitler, who covets the Ark as well. These scenes, while not involving difficult stunts or elaborate effects, do require the players—Chris, Billy Kuhn, Jason Ross, and Kurt—to memorize a ton of dialogue and to *act*. Other than Chris, who has acting experience and real talent, Eric discovers that few southern Mississippi ten-year-olds have been blessed with acting chops.

Eric decides to jump ahead a couple of scenes and start with a simple two-character scene between Indy and his friend Marcus Brody. Eric and Chris dress a spare bedroom in the Zala house as Indy's room and stay up much of the night running lines. The actors and Jayson meet at nine the next morning. Eric figures the scene will take a half hour tops, and then they'll move on to a local church to shoot the other scenes of exposition that take place at the college where Indy teaches. Eric has gotten permission from the janitor to use an empty classroom.

Eric badly miscalculates. The bedroom scene takes all morning. The kid playing Marcus stumbles over lines, forgets cues, says things out of order, fights an attack of the giggles and loses. When he's finally gotten his lines straight, with some semblance of believability, and all that's left is Chris removing his gun that's wrapped in a cloth and tossing it into his suitcase lying on the bed, Chris lobs the gun—and misses not only the suitcase but the bed. This sets Marcus off again. Ten takes later, Eric yells, "Print!"

On to the church. Mary drops them off. Eric and Chris dress the set with props to re-create Indy's classroom, and the actors begin the scene that, while necessary to explain the plot, is the most boring in the movie. More flubbed lines, missed cues, and at least two crying jags brought on by sieges of the giggles. To top it off, Jayson has a harder time controlling the camera and focusing on three actors in suits sitting behind a table than on five running and screaming Hovitos. On take *thirty*, Eric, the ability to yell long gone, mumbles, "Print."

"I don't care how shitty it looks," Chris says. "I'm not shooting those scenes again."

*   *   *

"I found it." Chris unfurls a smile.

"Found what?" Eric opens the door to the basement. He ducks inside, Chris at his back. The dampness cools them off instantly, the air smelling of brick and old timber. Eric connects the two extension cords, and a dim fuzzy light scatters over the basement floor.

"I could live down here," Chris says.

"Somebody used to. We may have to rent it out again. What did you find?"

Chris, nonchalant, cranes his neck, pretending to look at something in the rafters. "The boulder."

"The *boulder*. Tell me."

"It's crazy, man. I saw this thing lying in an empty lot in back of my mom's old apartment building. We were driving by and there it was. I nearly shit."

"What is it?"

"A cable spool."

Eric wags his head, pastes on his own smile. "I'm trying to picture it—"

"It's *huge*. Gigantic. It's perfect. I mean, we have to do some work on it, dress it up—"

"A cable spool? Is it round?"

"Round?" Chris rubs his chin. "I wouldn't call it *round*. I would call it round-*ish*. But the ancient Peruvian warriors would definitely have used this for garsching anyone who came into their cave, man."

"Garsching?"

"Yeah, garsching. It means squashing and shmooshing a guy until the guy's guts come gushing out like pudding."

"Garsching," Eric says. "I like that word. I'm gonna look it up."

"I wouldn't," Chris says.

This morning's agenda: the cave.

Eric and Chris return to Chris's grandparents' house and scavenge through the backyard in search of random sheets of plywood. They find a few mostly clean, only slightly wormy pieces and load them into Elaine's minivan. Several sheets of wood short, they prowl through the innards of Eric's basement for stray pieces of plywood Eric remembers seeing around.

They find what they need, lug the plywood into half of the Zala garage, lean the sheets up against the wall, and seal off the garage. Then they spray-paint the plywood walls gray, the color of rock, the color of cave.

Next, they carry ladders outside and prop them against two of the oak trees along the Zala property line. Climbing into the trees, they harvest buckets of the Spanish moss hanging from every branch. They move to a dozen more trees, filling up bucket after bucket with the dry, gnat-filled moss. Back in the garage, using a staple gun they find in the basement, they staple the moss to the freshly painted cave walls. Eric bangs nails into the beams overhead, and he and Chris hang Styrofoam stalactites Eric made the previous night. Finally, learning their lesson from viewing that first grim footage, they convince Mary to drive them to Kmart and buy several cheap aluminum-domed clip-on lamps to light the cave.

Now, the boulder.

*   *   *

Gus's old dusty pickup rattles up the drive, Elaine, in sunglasses and floppy hat, at the wheel. Chris jumps out of the passenger side and races around to the flatbed.

"A little help!"

Eric flies down the back stairs as Chris lowers the metal flap of the truck. He poses like Vanna White pointing at a vowel, gesturing to a lumpy wooden cable spool listing in the back of the pickup. "Ta daaa!"

Eric stares, trying to form the proper words. "It's a spool, all right," he says.

"I told you. It's rad."

"Will it roll? It doesn't look like it'll roll."

"Oh, it'll roll," Chris says. "All we gotta do is cover it with cardboard. Got a whole shitload of it right here. Then we spray-paint it gray and say hello to your terrifying garsching boulder, man!"

On the count of three, they lift the spool off the truck and onto the ground. It teeters and nuzzles into Chris's leg like an adoring puppy. Chris looks down at it. The spool doesn't even reach Chris's waist. Eric's mouth clamps shut. For a while, the only sound comes from the slap of waves from the Gulf and the muffled voices of Hall & Oates singing "Rich Girl" from the radio turned up inside the truck. Eric strains to catch Elaine's eye, hoping she'll come out and reject this ridiculous excuse for a boulder, this silly *spool*, but she's committed to the inside of the air-conditioned cab, sitting this one out.

Eric tilts his head. "Well, it's a bit smaller than one would expect the boulder to be—"

Chris dives onto the ground, aims two fingers up at the spool. "We can shoot it from a low angle, you know, *up*. Jayson's so small he can get below it. Midget cam. You shoot it from below, it will look majorly big and imposing, it'll look *huge*—"

"What's that supposed to be?" Jayson says, squinting from the porch.

"The boulder," Chris and Eric say together.

"Yeah, right." Jayson laughs and heads back inside.

*   *   *

"Roll, mofo, *roll*!" Chris struts around the spool, blasting the cardboard exterior the boys have hammered on with gray spray paint. He circles, weaves, bobs, one hand shielding his face, the other wildly waving the spray can as he douses the spool. The surface covered, he backs away, breathing hard. He shakes the can to make sure it's empty. "What do you think?"

"Very gray," Eric says.

Jayson, shirtless, barefoot, shoots out of the garage, his face lit with urgency. "Nice paint job. I just hope it rolls. Hey, I got two things to show you guys." He barrels back into the garage.

"Is there a problem?" Eric says, catching up to Jayson.

"Not at all. These are good things."

"That would be a pleasant change," Eric says quietly.

"I heard that," Chris says, looping in behind them.

In the garage, Jayson stops short, whirls. "Ready?"

From behind a brick post in the garage, he produces the skeleton head he's been working on—sunken eyes, yellowed bones, rotting brown teeth, a shock of Brillo hair splayed as if this person had been frightened to death. A true horror-movie effect.

"Fuckin' awesome, Jay," Chris says.

"Jayson, this is the best thing in the movie," Eric says.

"Until the boulder," Chris says.

"What's the other thing?" Eric says.

"Scott!" Jayson says.

Kurt's gawky friend Scott Weaver, dressed in a tattered khaki jacket, pants, and filthy T-shirt, the costume for his role as Satipo, Indy's turncoat Peruvian guide, bounces out of a dark basement room and into the hazy light of the garage.

"You guys know break dancing, right?" Jayson says.

"Know about it," Eric says. "Never tried it."

"Tried it," Chris says. "Suck at it."

"Get ready to be blown away," Jayson says. He nods at Scott.

Scott moonwalks across the garage, spins, flips—sort of—drops to the floor, does a reverse push-up, lands on his head and twirls.

"Go, Scott!" Jayson says.

"Ow," Scott says and tumbles over, kicking up a cloud of dust from the garage floor as he clanks into a heap. He sits up, dust flying, and caresses the back of his head.

"Well?" Jayson says.

Eric looks at Chris with a blank stare, then back at Jayson. "Well what?"

"I thought we could work it into the plot that Satipo break-dances."

Eric speaks through a cement smile. "You're suggesting that in the opening sequence Satipo dances on his head?"

"It's different," Chris admits.

"It's—" Eric struggles to form words, then: "Jayson, in *Raiders of the Lost Ark*, Satipo does not break-dance."

"I know he doesn't break-dance," Jayson says. "Not literally. It's symbolic."

"Your creativity is much appreciated, but I don't think we can have Satipo dance, right, Chris?"

"Yeah, yeah, no, we probably should stick with the script."

"Not a problem," Jayson says.

"But you were very good," Eric says to Scott.

"Awesome," Chris says.

"You guys have any aspirin?" Scott says, a lump forming on his fore-head.

*   *   *

"Take fourteen! And . . . *action!*"

Indiana Jones rushes out of the mouth of the cave, the golden idol clutched to his chest. Suddenly, he freezes. Behind him he hears a low ominous rumble. He looks over his shoulder.

Bearing down on him, about to crush him, thunders—

A wobbly three-foot wooden spool covered in cardboard.

Chris, acting his ass off, widens his eyes. The monster rock rolls closer, about to pancake him. Chris sprints. The spool veers off course, tips over. Chris slows to a walk, stops at the garage doors.

"Cut!" Eric shouts.

"Is that a print?" Jayson says, his voice soft.

"Yes," Eric says, his voice flat-lined. "That's a print."

Later, the boys plug the Betamax camcorder into the back of Mary's RCA television in her office and play back the boulder sequence. It's even worse than Eric thought. The spool looks nothing like a boulder. It looks like a weird flimsy homemade cardboard cylinder. Chris plays panicked beautifully. But as Eric watches the footage, he thinks, *Panicked from what? From that thing? It looks like Chris could dodge out of the way anytime he wants. Or if the boulder did catch up to him, it wouldn't even nick him.* Not to mention that the film is tinged with a puke green hue.

"This footage sucks ass," Chris says. "The boulder sucks ass. I suck ass!"

"No, Chris, you don't," Eric says. "You're the only good thing about it."

It's true. Without doing a Harrison Ford impression, Chris portrays the essence of Indiana Jones—his bravado, his toughness, his sly sense of humor. Eric, frustrated by the footage, discouraged by his poor direction, feels as if he's let his best friend down.

"I have to do better," he says.

*   *   *

They turn the main basement room into the Nepalese bar. They work all night. Eric spray-paints a raven on the back wall, duplicating the bar in the original, named the Raven after Marion and her deceased father, Abner Ravenwood. They come across dozens of empty wine jugs and liquor bottles in bins in the basement, courtesy of Eric's dad, for Eric a grim reminder of his father's alcoholism and departure. They hang as many Kmart lamps as they have. Eric spaces them, attempting to find at least a minimum of backlight, hoping to reduce if not eliminate the green hue.

They assign Jayson the job of creating fire. The bar scene turns into a full-fledged gun battle and bar fight with Nazis flailing hot pokers and torches that combust and finally burn down the bar. They need flames that flare up and fizzle quickly. Jayson consults his magic books and comes up with a formula involving isopropyl alcohol and water. He promises blazing fire that's both dramatic and safe. They gather prop handguns and rifles, real torches and fake beards. The next day, they cast the part of Marion Ravenwood, the feisty bar owner and the love of Indy's life. They go through a list of the few girls they knew at CEDS, singling out the one or two who bear some resemblance to Karen Allen, the original Marion. Chris calls Stephanie Ewing, a sweet brunette with a thick drawl, their top choice because he occasionally carpooled with her and she might not laugh at him. He tells her they're shooting a movie and offers Stephanie the female lead. She accepts on the spot.

*　　*　　*

It's a new day. I'm going to make the Nepalese bar scene work.

His nerves frayed from lack of sleep, Eric rehearses the fight scenes over and over with a new sense of determination, a challenge since the Nazi henchmen, played by kids, act like, well, kids.

"Herding cats," he says, under his breath. He works on a complicated moment when Toht, Ted Ross, threatens Marion with a flaming poker. Ted holds the poker an inch from Stephanie's face. She protests demurely. Eric stops them. Wags his head. Not good enough. He has to get her energy up, see if she can lose some of her natural sweetness and find her inner Karen Allen feistiness. Kids screwing around outside, among them Kurt, interrupt. They're laughing and talking so loudly that Eric's sure their voices will be picked up by the camera. He pokes his head out a window and screams, "Hey, shitholes, shut up!"

Silence, from outside and in the basement.

If Chris is acting his ass off, then I'm going to direct my ass off.

Eric's racing against the clock. He counts forty-four storyboards to complete by the end of the day. He'll have to live with Marion's out-of-character sweetness. Nobody will notice, he decides, as long as the fighting looks real and Jayson gets the fire to work. Fire. That's the key.

First take. Eric calls *action.* Toht's poker refuses to light. Eric shouts, "Cut!" Jayson soaks the tip of the poker with isopropyl alcohol.

Take two. Flames shoot up from the poker, scaring the crap out of Ted Ross and nearly blowing his hat off.

"That's a print," Eric says, thrilled.

The fire takes over. They light the bar on fire; they light pieces of plywood on fire. They light the walls. They light the floorboards. On Eric's cue, Chris steps out of a shadow, lashes the bullwhip, and knocks the flaming poker out of Toht's hand. Off camera, Jayson rolls the poker toward the curtains hanging in front of a window. The lip of the curtains catches. Blue flames roar up toward the ceiling.

Now the gunfight. Indy shoots his pistol, ducks. Toht takes cover, shoots back. The bar near him catches fire. Bad guys flip over a table. Wine jugs fly, smash onto the floor, fire licking the table behind. Jayson squeezes himself and the camera onto the narrow ledge where Eric kept his old record player. From this angle, Jayson films the bar fight from below, giving it, in Eric's mind, a documentary feel.

And everywhere—high, low, in the corners, on the walls, like some pagan ritual—fire.

Time running out, more than twenty storyboards to go, Eric abandons his place next to Jayson and prepares for a bit part, the role of the Ratty Nepalese, a rifle-shooting bad guy who, after his back catches on fire, burns to death spectacularly. Eric has conceived this effect carefully. First, for protection, he slips on a second shirt and then buttons a raincoat over that. Over these two layers of clothes, he puts on his costume: a turban, fake beard, and brown military jacket. He calls Jayson over.

"I'm ready," Eric says.

"You sure about this?"

"Absolutely. This is a big effect. It has to really flame up."

"It will."

Instead of isopropyl alcohol, Jayson saturates Eric's back with gasoline.

Jayson scurries away and grabs the camera. Eric stations a ten-year-old friend of Kurt's behind him.

"Remember your cue," Eric says to the kid. "When I aim the rifle, light me up." The kid nods morosely. "Now duck down. Stay out of camera."

The kid hits the floor. Jayson, laconic, counts down and calls *action*.

To Eric's right, off camera, Chris sets a patch of wood on fire. Flames crawl toward Eric. Eric aims the rifle. The kid lights his torch.

VROOOOOSH!

Eric's back explodes in fire.

Replicating the actor who played the Ratty Nepalese in the original *Raiders*, Eric leaps to his feet, frantically waves his arms, and in obvious pain and terror turns his back to the camera and screams for his life.

"Ah! *Ahhh! AHHHHHH!*"

"Cut," Jayson says.

Eric stops flapping his arms.

But the fire continues to rage all over his back.

"*Ahhh!*" Eric says. "*AHHHHH!*"

"Fire extinguisher," the ten-year-old kid behind Eric says, getting to his feet, standing there and doing nothing. He may as well have said, "When's lunch?"

Another kid approaches Eric, a blanket in his hand, and gently pats Eric's back, fanning the flames. Dumbfounded, the kid steps away and stares. The flames roar across Eric's back like a brush fire. The flip at the bottom of Eric's long hair begins to burn.

"Guys," Eric says.

"Jesus," Chris says.

Acting like Indiana Jones—*becoming* Indiana Jones—Chris hurdles the kid in front of him, jerks the blanket out of his hand, dives onto Eric, and smothers his burning back. Another kid trots over holding a fire extinguisher.

"No," Eric says.

But the kid blasts away, covering Eric with a gust of white powder that sticks like snow.

"Damn it," Eric says. "That stuff's expensive."

"You okay?" Chris says, hopping off Eric's back. He has snuffed the fire. The smell of gasoline mixed with Eric's singed hair fills the basement.

"Jayson, did you get that?"

"Yeah."

Eric smiles at Chris. "I'm fine."

*   *   *

Later Eric, Chris, and Jayson watch the Nepalese bar scene in the editing room at WLOX. As the playback comes up, Eric cringes, squirms. The footage still looks grainy and green. But after a few seconds, Jayson's camera work steadies and the composition of the actors seems right, and Eric relaxes. He admits he's thrown off by Stephanie's performance and deep drawl. It's as if she's acting in a different movie. He'll have to work with her.

Then Ted Ross as Toht enters the bar with his henchmen and the action picks up. Toht threatens Marion with the burning poker, Indy jumps out of the shadows and flicks the poker out of Toht's hand with his bullwhip, the basement walls start to burn, and the boys laugh. Damn! This looks *good*. And when Eric catches on fire, for real, and screams exactly like the Ratty Nepalese in the original, they howl. Their movie has gone from unquestionably feeble to unmistakably cool. Eric, gripped by a rush of accomplishment, smiles. "I feel like we're on our way."

They rewind the footage, watch it a second time.

Behind them, Billy Bob, drawn by the laughs in the edit room, watches from the doorway.

When flames crawl along the basement floor and climb up the curtain over the window, he folds his arms across his chest.

When fire engulfs Eric's back, he retreats from the edit room, slides into his cubicle, and dials the phone.

*   *   *

After dinner, Eric sits at the kitchen table and spreads the rest of the bar scene's storyboards in front of him. He thinks about how he will shoot the rest of the gunfight, rearranges the order of the shots, jots a note to himself. As he writes, a car rumbles up the driveway and stops. Doors open, slam shut. Approaching footsteps slap pavement. Strange. He, his mom, and Kurt rarely receive visitors after dinner, and his dad would never make an unscheduled appearance. He heads to the back porch and sees Chris and Elaine slowly climb the stairs as Mary rustles into the kitchen. She wipes her hands on a dishtowel.

"Elaine called me," Mary says. "We all need to talk."

She leans past Eric, swings the porch door open for Chris and Elaine. "Thank you for coming."

"What's going on?" Eric says.

"Got me," Chris says. "My mom wouldn't tell me."

"Let's all sit down," Mary says. She gestures toward the table in the living room. "Would you like some tea? Or—"

"We're fine, Mary, thank you." Elaine nods at Chris, waits for him to move by her and take a seat at the table. Eric hangs back, sits next to Chris. Elaine sits on the edge of a chair, across from Mary.

"I feel like I'm in the principal's office," Chris says.

"You would know," Elaine says.

"Elaine called me this afternoon," Mary says. "She said, 'I'm really upset. My friend at the TV studio—'"

"Billy Bob," Elaine says.

"Yes. He saw the film you've been making and he said, 'Eric's on fire.'"

"How did he see it?" Chris says.

"That doesn't matter," Elaine says. "What matters is you *set Eric on fire.*"

"It's in the movie, Ma," Chris says.

"It may be in the movie," Elaine says, "but it is not going to be in *your* movie."

"After Elaine called, we met this afternoon," Mary says. "We agree. There is to be no more fire. Or you won't be able to continue."

"Nonnegotiable," Elaine says. "No discussion."

"It's too dangerous," Mary says.

"Mary is being awfully nice about this, awfully calm," Elaine says. "You two could've burned this house down."

"We were careful. For the most part we used isopropyl alcohol," Eric says, leaving out any mention of gasoline. "And I wore a flame-retardant raincoat."

Elaine crashes back in her chair. "We don't really care what you used. Or how careful you were. We're talking about fire. Let me repeat this for you both, but I will direct this to you, Christopher, since you sometimes have a tendency to hear what you want to hear. *No. More. Fire.* Are we clear?"

"Eric?" Mary says.

Eric speaks into the table, his voice cracking. "We're not finished shooting the bar scene. That's the scene with all the fire. We still have twenty-four storyboards to go."

"I'm sorry, Eric," Mary says.

"Why does it have to be fire?" Elaine says. "Can't you change things up? Why can't Indy hit the bad guys with a bag of leaves?"

"A what?" Chris says.

"A bag of leaves," Elaine says.

"Yeah, that's a good idea, Ma. Indy, you ready to take on the Nazis? Yep, got my whip, got my gun, got my bag of leaves—"

"Okay, fine," Elaine says, dismissing the idea with a flick of her fingers.

"If we can't have fire," Eric says, his voice going even quieter, "we can't shoot any more scenes."

"Then that's the way it has to be," Mary says, and again says, "I'm sorry."

"May we be excused?" Eric says.

"Just for a moment," Elaine says. "I have to fix Jimmy dinner. He's on his way home."

Upstairs, the boys don't say much. Eric paces, wags his head, runs his hand through his hair. Strands near his neck feel brittle as straw and still slightly warm. "Now what?" he says.

Chris, lying on Eric's bed, follows the slowly revolving ceiling fan. Even though he can escape the thick Mississippi heat the moment he steps into the blast of the air-conditioning at the Riverhouse, he'd rather sleep here in Eric's room. He'd rather spend all his time here.

"We don't have the boulder," Eric says. "We'd have to build the Well of Souls or something and shoot out of sequence. I guess. I don't know. I'm not sure we have enough time this summer."

"This is fucked," Chris says.

"Yes," Eric says. "It is fucked."

*   *   *

Lying in the bottom bunk in his strange isolated room, in this icy sprawl of a house, Chris curls into his pillow. Suddenly, his body jerks. His eyes snap open. He senses a presence at the foot of his bed. A fist of fear plunges into his chest. *It can't be.* He has been out of Chris's life for ten years. Chris has thought about him, sure, even tried to dredge him up on occasion, just to be certain that he will no longer come. He assumed he'd outgrown him, never realizing until this night that he couldn't outrun him. He feels the green mist float into the room from the open doorway. He waits. He waits for the green clown.

A heavy footstep. A grunt. Chris sits up. He wants to scream, but his voice is stuck in his throat. A figure rams into the bed frame, swears, bucks forward, comes closer. A man's hand reaches for Chris, hot salty breath blowing on his cheeks like a kiss, the smell of liquor strong enough to make Chris flinch. Then the hand jabs past Chris's face, grabs the headboard and hangs on.

"You stupid—"

His stepfather. Jimmy Love III. His voice slurred like a cartoon drunk's. "You stupid *shit.*"

Jimmy Love III pushes off from the headboard, teeters backward and punches his fist into the mattress. He hunches over. Chris calculates what he might do next—take a swing at him, hurl, pass out on the bed.

"If you were my kid—" He stands erect as a sergeant. "You listen to me."

Chris has seen drunken people before, many times. Loud, obnoxious, slurry, goofy, clingy drunks. But he has never seen anyone this drunk, this way.

"You ever do something like that again? *Ever.* Set fire. Anything. You will answer to *me.*"

He backs up unsteadily, his arm slicing the air. For a moment, Chris thinks his stepfather will fall. Then Jimmy Love III lowers his shoulder and slouches out of the room. Chris gasps and air rushes out of his mouth. Only then does he realize that he's been holding his breath.

YEAR THREE

"Perhaps the girl can help us."   —Gobler

1983–1984.
Pre-production.

Eric, fourteen, begins eighth grade at Ocean Springs Junior High. He sees his dad when it's arranged, their visits cursory and cool. Eric has little to talk to him about. As the school year progresses, his mom pushes herself, stays up late trying to line up new clients for Mutual of Omaha. With money tight, the house falls further into disrepair. During high winds and hurricane rains, leaks spring from the shaky roof, and windows in their rotting frames threaten to crack. Eric wants to comfort his mom, wants to help. When he asks what he can do, Mary says, "Work hard." He and Kurt do. Both earn all A's.

Meanwhile, Chris, thirteen, leaves southern Mississippi and starts seventh grade at the Knox School on Long Island, paid for by his stepfather, Jimmy Love III.

"He sees something in you," Elaine says.

Promise, perhaps. Or maybe Love recognizes that Chris's rebellious delinquent side needs to be contained. Or Love might imagine Chris as a male Eliza Doolittle, hard edged, low class, whom Love's inner Henry Higgins determines to educate, to refine, to turn into a gentleman. A project. He would never admit this to anyone, but perhaps his pet project. He sees a chance to turn Chris into a man's man like himself, a man with culture and breeding, a man he can someday sail with and then lunch with afterward at the club, slamming shots of expensive Scotch. A Southern gentleman like himself.

"You throw enough money at a problem, maybe you'll fix it," Elaine says years later.

As for the movie, even though their moms abruptly halted production and Jimmy Love III shipped Chris a thousand miles away during the school year, Eric and Chris's dream of remaking *Raiders* has not ended. It has been put on hold. They are on hiatus.

Eric uses the time to rethink his role as director. Directing the first year, he felt frustrated. He had difficulty adjusting to the cranky cameras, moving the actors to match the positions in his storyboards, achieving consistent performances, getting used to the constant stopping and starting. In other words, he didn't have a handle on what he was doing.

The key, he believes, is preparation. He bikes to the mall and, using allowance he's saved up and Christmas and birthday money, buys two books on filmmaking. He studies them, picks up tips on backlighting, camera placement, and blocking actors. He reads how directors have to be forceful, always in charge, to appear to know what they're doing. In several photographs, he sees the director wielding a megaphone. *That's what I need. A megaphone.*

At the mall one day, he bumps into Stephanie Ewing. He reminds her that they'll be shooting *Raiders* again over the summer, picking up the bar scene where they left off.

"Eric, I'm sorry," she says, her drawl even thicker than he remembered. "I can't do it."

"That's too bad. Why?"

"We're all moving to Alaska."

"Wow. Well, okay then. Take care."

Eric's initial reaction—relief. *Good-bye, Stephanie. And good luck in Alaska with that grating monumental drawl.* Then reality hits. They need to find another Marion, and they need to reshoot the entire bar scene.

Great. Two years in and they're starting from scratch.

*   *   *

One day during winter break, Chris brings over his Christmas present from his dad: a genuine leather jacket and authentic lace-up army boots.

With Chris's leftover cash, they hit the mall and find a real Indy-type wide-brimmed fedora. The day after Chris heads back to boarding school, Eric stays up past 2:00 A.M., buffing the leather jacket with a metal bristle brush, giving it the proper "distressed leather" look. In the end, Chris will never progress past beat-up brown corduroy pants, but from the waist up, his costume is now complete. And as Eric learns from one of his filmmaking books: *If the audience is looking at the pants, then everything else must stink.*

*   *   *

In spring 1984, Eric starts spending time with Peter Keefer, the actor who appeared in *Dawn of the Dead*. One day after school, Eric is about to walk up the back porch steps when Peter, wearing a floppy sunhat, a T-shirt, and cutoff jeans, trailing his dog, Lucy, a Bud in one hand, smiles at Eric under his walrus mustache.

"Hey," Peter says. "I'm Peter. Cottage three."

Of course, Eric knows who he is. He's been starstruck ever since Peter moved in a few months ago.

"Eric," he says. "I'm Eric."

"Gotcha. This is Lucy."

"Yeah. I've seen Lucy around."

Peter pops open the Bud, drains half the can. "Your mom told me you're shooting a movie."

"Yeah. My friends and I are remaking *Raiders of the Lost Ark*."

"Ambitious." Peter downs the beer. He crushes the can, pulls a fresh Bud out of his pocket.

"We don't have much to show for it so far."

Peter combs a couple of fingers through his mustache. "Movies take time. I've done some movie acting. I was in *Dawn of the Dead*. George Romero? The director? In. *Sane.*"

"I heard. I mean, about your acting career."

"Yeah. Well. I'm between gigs right now. Taking a little R and R. Me and Lucy. But, hey, you ever need any help? Or a stand-in. Or whatever. I'm pretty much always around. Knock on my door. Just not too early."

"Really? Cool. I will."

Eric sees Peter a few times after that, and when Chris returns from his year in boarding school, he introduces him to Peter. One night, as Peter regales the boys with backstage tales from *Dawn of the Dead* and other inside Hollywood gossip, an idea worms its way into Eric's head.

"Peter, remember you offered to help with our movie?"

"What do you need?"

Eric gives Chris his *why didn't I think of this before* look.

"A favor."

*   *   *

Eric and Chris and Peter gather with Mary on the back porch. Chris, who's added a few extra pounds over the winter at boarding school, throws on a salesman's *trust me* grin he's practiced in the mirror. He shifts his weight from foot to foot, a bottle of isopropyl alcohol in one hand, an old blanket tucked under his arm. Eric wears a thick industrial glove on his left hand.

"Well, Mom, it's that time again. Chris and I are preparing to resume filming *Raiders*." Eric holds, waits for Mary to react. "Good. Excellent. So far, no objection."

"Go on."

"As you know, the film calls for scenes that contain a certain amount of fire. In fact, since we have to recast Marion, we'll have to reshoot all the previous scenes, which contained fire as well."

"Keep going," Mary says.

"We've brought you out here to demonstrate that after last year, we've learned our lesson. We understand your concern about the fire. We share your concern."

"That's a relief," Mary says, although she doesn't look all that relieved.

"To prove how responsible we've become, we've incorporated two significant safety measures. First, Peter has agreed to serve as our chaperone. Our fire marshal, if you will. We recognize that we're kids and that we need an adult on the set."

Peter, looking a little drunk, tips his sunhat. "I'll be there at all times. I'll supervise the fire. I have experience on movie sets. Especially with special effects. All that technical gizmo gadgetry and whatnot." He stifles a burp. For the first time, Mary looks doubtful.

"In addition, Mom," Eric says, "I'm going to demonstrate that the fire we will use from isopropyl alcohol is perfectly safe. Chris?"

Chris puts the blanket on the ground, steps forward, uncaps the bottle, and drizzles isopropyl alcohol over the glove. Eric nods again. Chris places the bottle of alcohol on the ground, pulls a pack of matches from his pocket, strikes a match, and lights the glove. Flames spurt, engulfing Eric's hand.

"As you can see, my hand is on fire."

"Yes, I see that, Eric," Mary says.

"I feel a warm sensation inside the glove, growing slightly warmer, but I am in no danger."

"Absolutely none," Chris says.

"Zero," Peter says.

"This is a wonderful demonstration, Eric. Now put out the fire."

"Are you sure? Because I can continue to allow the fire to burn the glove, and while I do feel a warmish, not quite hot, sensation inside the glove, I am not in any harm."

"None whatsoever," Chris says.

"Zero," Peter says.

"Put the fire out, Eric," Mary says.

"Warm in here, but I'm fine," Eric says, waving his flaming hand.

"Just a little warm, that's all," Chris says.

"Toasty," Peter says.

"Eric!"

"Yes, Mom." Eric nods at Chris. Chris picks up the blanket and presses it over Eric's burning glove until the fire sizzles and smokes out. Eric removes the glove and wiggles his unblemished fingers.

"So?" He looks eagerly at his mother. "Do we have your permission to resume shooting *Raiders*, with fire?"

"Peter? You'll be there?"

"Huh?" Chris nudges Peter's knee with his foot. "Oh, yes, ma'am."

Mary squints as if she's looking into the sun, but the afternoon is cloudy, rain threatening. "I do like having all you kids around here."

"Better than going to camp. And a lot less expensive."

"Totally," Peter says.

"All right. But be careful. Be *responsible*, Eric."

"We will. I promise."

"Yes!" Chris shouts.

"Thanks, Mom," Eric says, hugging her.

Peter tips his floppy hat.

*   *   *

Eric sees her for the first time in church. After the 9:00 A.M. Sunday service, while Mary sips coffee and schmoozes with friends in the parish hall, Eric watches the girl drift away from the cluster of churchgoers and lean against the wall at the far end of the hall. Auburn hair, close cropped. Slightly older, fifteen maybe. Aloof and pretty. Sultry even. But with an edge. She sends Eric a look informing him that she's bored and out of his league. He has no doubt. She would be perfect for Marion.

"I ask only one thing," Chris says when Eric tells him about her. "She has to be shorter than me."

The next Sunday, Eric again watches her assume her position against the far wall. He hesitates. All week, he's been silently rehearsing what to say to her. His sales pitch. He wishes Chris were here to ask her. Eric's shy around girls, awkward. When it comes to talking—when it comes to most things—Chris seems to have no fear.

A part of Eric wants to run outside and wait in the car, but he promised Chris. And now that they've gotten Mary's permission to start production, he has to do this. He's the freaking *director*. It's his job. He locates a small reservoir of courage and forces himself to move toward her.

"Hi."

"Hello." A half smile. Not unkind.

"Um," Eric says.

He pauses. Forever. Feels like a week.

"Yes?" she says. A wider smile. You might even call it encouraging.

"I was wondering." He stops. This is not what he rehearsed. He starts again. "Some friends of mine and I are making a movie?"

"Really?"

"Do you want to be in it?"

Wow. I sound like an idiot. Say something else before she runs away. Quick! Save this!

"It's not just any movie."

When did my voice get so deep?

"No?"

"Oh, no, no. We're doing a remake of *Raiders of the Lost Ark.*"

Now she's staring.

"You'd be Marion. The part Karen Allen played. The female lead."

Now how did my voice go so high?

"Okay. Sure."

Eric's not sure he's heard her right.

"Really?"

"Yeah. Sounds like fun."

"Okay, cool. Very cool. Great. Terrific." He puts a hand on his hip and for a moment goes Hollywood. All that's missing is the sunglasses, the deck shoes, and the cashmere sweater laced around his neck. "So, I'm typing up the script at home. I'll print out all your scenes and bring them next Sunday so you can have them to memorize. I'll call you with the shooting schedule."

She tilts her head, digs her stare into Eric's eyes. Is this guy for real?

"I'm Angela." She extends her hand. Eric swallows before he takes it, presses her fingers clumsily, and crash-lands from his Hollywood fantasy back to southern Mississippi.

"Eric. I'm Eric."

"Nice to know you. Who's playing Indy?"

"My best friend. Chris. Great guy. Funny. You'll love him. He's taller than you."

*   *   *

Once again, they turn the basement into the Raven Bar. This time they build an actual bar from scrap wood. They dress the set with trays of shot glasses and a more diverse selection of empties, artfully arranged instead of the haphazard way they were set up before. They hang a few more Kmart lights for backlighting. Chris contributes two breakaway bottles he bought at a specialty shop while visiting New Orleans. Jayson, for his part, has spent the off-season experimenting with gunpowder that he plans to use to approximate gunshots ricocheting off the walls, in addition to a new commitment to making blood spurt. He promises that on cue Kurt, a Nazi—one of the many roles he will play—will get shot, writhe in pain, slam his hand into a condom filled with fake blood concealed in his overcoat, and fall as blood spouts from his chest.

On the day Angela arrives, Chris paces in the bar. He's entered an unprecedented tubby phase, and he's annoyed that his new official Indiana Jones leather jacket fits a little snug. Right on time, a boxy little car the color of a banana barrels up the driveway and skids to a stop outside the back door. Eric bolts out of the basement, leaving Chris behind trying to tug his jacket tight around his expanded midsection. For some reason, this new Marion, sight unseen, makes Chris nervous.

"Hello, Angela," Eric says as she exits the car. "Welcome. Thanks again for helping us out."

"No big deal." She waves at the driver of the banana-colored car, her mom, Eric guesses. The mom tinkles a wave back and guns the car down the driveway as if she's glad to get out of there.

"Some house," Angela says.

"Oh, thanks. I'll give you the tour later, if you want. So. Are you ready to start?"

"Why not?"

"Great." Like a greeter in a hotel, Eric beckons her into the basement.

She takes one step into the dank hazy maze of unfolding underground rooms and stops. "This is freaking awesome. The bar is so cool."

"Hi. I'm Chris." Sweaty hand thrust forward. Gut sucked in.

"Angela." She passes her eyes over him, then accepts his hand. She smiles. The full-wattage version. Chris flushes.

"Okay," Eric says. "Let's start right at the beginning. This is where Indy sees Marion for the first time in years. She's not happy to see him at all. In fact, she belts him."

"Nice start," Chris says, eyes prowling all over Angela. "I've known you for a total of five seconds and you get to beat the crap out of me."

She giggles. "I'll try not to hit you too hard."

"Appreciate that," Chris says, rubbing his chin Indy-style.

Eric taps his copy of the scene. "Angela, did you get a chance to look at your lines?"

"Yeah. I memorized them." She balls her hand into a fist. Looks like she can throw a punch. "When do I hit him?"

Chris laughs so much that he forgets to hold in his stomach.

*   *   *

It takes Eric thirty seconds to see it.

Chemistry.

In the bar, in the basement, every moment between Chris and Angela sizzles.

Angela—feisty, sexy, at ease with herself while inhabiting Marion—chills Chris out. He forgets his baby fat and channels Harrison Ford's charm and toughness. You buy them as young Indiana Jones and Marion Ravenwood and believe, without a doubt, that they have the hots for each other.

The same way you don't buy twelve-year-old Ted Ross as Toht the Nazi.

Toht, his four henchmen in tow, steps into the bar. Outside, a Himalayan blizzard rages. Off camera, a kid dumps a canister of baby powder in front of two whirring portable fans to simulate snow.

"Good evening, fraulein," Ted says without a trace of German accent or acting.

"The bar's closed."

Wow. Angela's so good, Eric will live with Ted's flat line reading.

"We. Are. Not. Thirsty."

Damn, Ted, I know you're not a professional actor—I know you're just a kid—but give me something.

"What do you want?" Angela says.

Even that, Eric thinks, a nothing line, rivets you, makes you want to watch her. Eric prints the scene.

The next shot calls for Angela to light a cigarette, step right up to Toht, and blow smoke into his face. A couple of days ago, Eric pilfered a pack of his dad's Parliaments and his lighter. He sees this as Angela's first big test. Will she accept the cigarette Eric offers and light up?

"No, thanks," she says.

Eric's heart sinks. Angela's refusal to smoke will kill a highlight of the scene. No way to make it work if Marion doesn't smoke.

"I brought my own," Angela says. She digs into her bulky purse and pulls out a pack of menthols. She taps one out and fires up. She inhales deeply, then exhales out of each nostril. She scratches her lip with the tip of her pinkie. Eric and Chris catch each other's eye.

Whoa, Eric thinks, *I've found the perfect Marion.*

Whoa, Chris thinks, *I'm in love.*

* * *

At the end of the long shooting day, the first half of the bar scene completed and printed, Angela's mom bombs up the driveway in her banana-colored little car and whisks her away. Chris and Eric wave good-bye and then head into the basement to clean up and unplug the warm lights hanging over the bar. Chris grabs a broom. "I've been thinking. I know we've got the redo of the college scene scheduled next, but—"

"Uh-huh." Eric unclips a lamp, says nothing. He has an idea where this is going.

"Instead of moving everything, why not stay here and shoot the cabin scene next?"

"Shoot out of order?"

"It's a thought," Chris says. "I mean, as long as we have a new Marion, and she's so great—"

"She's terrific."

"Definitely. So maybe the smart thing to do is hit her scenes first, start knocking her up."

"Knocking her up?"

"What?"

"You said 'knocking her up.'"

"No, I didn't. I said knocking them *out*. The scenes."

"You said *knocking her up.*"

"Whatever," Chris says. "Anyway, what if she bails on us? Or becomes unavailable? Or moves to Alaska or some shit?"

"Unlikely for lightning to strike twice, don't you think?"

Chris shakes his head, leans into the broom, and begins sweeping the floor with short sharp jabs of the bristles.

The cabin scene, Eric thinks. *Where Indy and Marion kiss. Oh. I get it.*

"Let's do it," Eric says.

*   *   *

They shoot at night. They turn the tiny empty upstairs bedroom, formerly his sister Cynthia's room, into the private cabin of Captain Katanga, the pirate leader who hides Indy and Marion aboard his tramp steamer, the *Bantu Wind*. Duplicating the storyboards, they place lit candles around the bed, fill a bottle of rum with apple juice and put it on the nightstand, dress the window behind the bed to look like a ship's porthole. They drag in a full-length mirror they find, and Eric, using his thumb, smears the glass surface with toothpaste. The mirror must look smudged to justify Marion flipping it around to see herself, accidentally banging Indy square on the chin.

Angela leaves the room to change into her costume, a satiny purple nightgown. Jayson sets the camera on a tripod. Kurt plops down onto the bed.

"What are you doing?" Eric says.

"Waiting for Angela," Kurt says.

"This is the love scene," Eric says.

"I know."

"This is a closed set."

Kurt glares at Eric. "What does that mean?"

"It means get out."

"This is my house."

"This is my movie. Leave, Kurt. Go somewhere else."

"No."

"Kurt. I'm the director. This is a closed set!"

Kurt tilts his head toward Jayson. "Why are you letting him stay?"

"He's the freaking *cameraman!*"

"I'm gonna wait outside," Jayson mutters. "Got some things, to, ah, yeah." Jayson ducks out of the room.

Kurt keeps his eyes locked on Eric. He amps his glare. Eric shoots back a high-beam stare of his own. "Kurt, I don't want to *make* you get out."

Kurt backs down. "Fine."

He rolls off the bed, shuffles out the door, and closes it behind him harder than he needs to.

"He can be such an obnoxious little pain," Eric says.

"He's your brother," Chris says. "That's his job."

"Let's get rolling," Eric says, starting for the door. "I'll call in Jayson and Angela."

"Wait. Give me a minute."

Eric picks up something new in Chris's tone, a tremor he hasn't heard before. "You all right?"

"Yeah. Fine. I'm just a little, I don't know, nervous."

"About the kiss?"

"No. Not the kiss. About *this*." Chris plows his hands into the flab around his stomach and grabs two fistfuls of flesh. "Last night I took off my shirt and looked at myself in the mirror. I fucking freaked out. Look at this, man. It's embarrassing."

Wow, Eric thinks. *No way I'd take my shirt off and kiss a girl on camera. No way. Especially if I had Chris's meaty gut.*

"You look great," Eric says.

"I look like a fat pig," Chris says.

"No way. Plus the camera takes off five pounds. You know that, right? Or is it ten?"

"Really? Are you serious?"

"Yes. I read that in one of my filmmaking books. Can't remember which one. It might have been the one where Spielberg is quoted extensively—"

"You made that up. You're full of shit."

"I shit you not."

Staredown.

Chris so wants to believe Eric.

Eric so wants Chris to believe him.

"You're just trying to make me feel better," Chris says.

"Did it work?"

"Yeah," Chris says. "It did."

*   *   *

Jayson, perched behind the tripod, follows Angela with the camera as she enters, whistling the *Raiders* theme—Jayson's idea—an inside joke they will keep private until years later. Even though both Chris and Eric think *Holy shit* when Angela reveals her clingy nightgown beneath the blanket draped over her shoulders, the actors approach this scene as if they are two respectful professionals.

At first, though, Chris feels out of synch. He stops the scene, tells Eric to start again. He concentrates harder, pushing himself into a deeper emotional place. His nerves fly away—at least he keeps his terror in check—and he commits to every moment.

Angela, meanwhile, shows no inhibitions. She's confident, calm, sexy, and her confidence puts Chris at ease. Performance-wise, Chris kills. He plays the physical comedy of being clunked in the chin by the mirror without forcing the moment, banters with Angela without pressing.

Then the kiss.

Indy complains that he only wants to sleep, that he doesn't want Marion to be his nurse. She asks him where it hurts. Everywhere, he says. Where doesn't it hurt? she asks. Chris points to his elbow. Here. Angela kisses his elbow. Forehead. Angela kisses his forehead. Here. Chris points to his eyebrow. Angela kisses his eyebrow. And then Chris points to his mouth.

Angela leans down and kisses Chris. They hold the kiss. It's real. It's sweet. It's hot.

It's Chris's first kiss.

"And cut," Eric calls.

They don't cut.

They keep kissing.

"And . . . *cut*," Eric says again, louder.

They keep kissing.

"Uh. Guys?"

They break the kiss.

Their kiss becomes one shared goofy grin.

Eric clears his throat. "How was that, Jayson?"

"Fine. Well. Except."

Everybody looks at him.

"You couldn't hear them because of the frogs croaking in the swamp."

"You couldn't hear any of the dialogue?" Eric sounds stricken.

"Not really," Jayson says.

"Sorry, guys," Eric says. "We're gonna have to do it again."

"Darn," Angela says with a smile.

"Oh, well," Chris says, smiling back.

"Not your fault," Eric says. "The scene was really good."

"I thought so," Angela says.

"Me, too," Chris says.

"We'll just wait a sec for the frogs to stop their mating call. Oh, and when I say 'cut . . .'"

Angela looks down at the floor. Chris reddens.

"Never mind," Eric says.

*   *   *

They nail the love scene. Jayson whistles the *Raiders* theme as he unhitches the camera from the tripod. Chris and Angela jostle each other by the doorway. He whispers something. She giggles. She waves to Eric and Jayson and heads downstairs to meet her mom. Eric, happiest of all, strikes a fat red *X* through the cabin scene storyboard. Chris bounds back into the room, shirtless.

"We rock, man!" Chris slaps his flabby belly.

Eric caps the red marker. "You got all that, right, Jayson?"

"Yep."

"No frogs?"

"Nope. Clear."

"She's hot, man," Chris says.

"Indeed," Eric says. "A very attractive older woman."

Jayson lugs the tripod out of the bedroom. Chris and Eric blow out candles, clear away the props.

"We're on a roll," Eric says. "Next, we finish the bar scene, then redo the college scene. Hey, you want to sleep over tonight?"

"Can't," Chris says. "I have *plans.*"

"Seriously?"

"Angela's coming over to the Riverhouse. We're gonna hang out. Maybe order in a pizza, watch a movie. You know."

"Wow. So, it's like the two leads want to keep the romance going off camera. I've heard about such things. You want to continue the cabin scene."

"Nah. We just want to hang out, man."

He flicks his tongue like a snake.

Good for you, Chris. Besides, I have plans tonight, too.

*   *   *

The image haunts him: Indiana Jones running through the cave, the giant rock bearing down on him, about to flatten him into dust.

That's why we can't skimp on the boulder. The boulder has to have size and heft and weight and menace. The boulder has to be a monster. The boulder has to tower over Chris. The boulder can't come up to Chris's waist and waggle like a spool.

A few months ago, Eric remembered an ad he once saw in some comic book for a gigantic round boulder-type thing. He dug out his boxes of old comics and feverishly flipped through the pages. He skimmed past ads for joy buzzers and whoopee cushions and dribble glasses and Charles Atlas bodybuilding courses and there it was—a postage-stamp-sized ad for an inflatable weather balloon. Eight feet in diameter! In the ad, the balloon dwarfed a six-foot man standing beside it.

"Perfect," Eric said.

One problem. The price. Thirty dollars.

He convinced his mom to advance his allowance and sent away for the weather balloon.

Today, the package has arrived. A bulging box from Battle Creek,

Michigan, sitting on the back porch. Eric tears into the cardboard and yanks out a lumpy folded-over blue weather balloon.

Eric blocks off the whole weekend. Friday night, as he watches *Night Tracks* on TBS, featuring the latest music videos, he gathers a month's worth of newspapers and tears them into strips. Ripping to the rhythm of Duran Duran and the Thompson Twins, he fills box after box with torn newspaper.

Saturday morning, he rides his bike to the local library and picks up a hobby-and-crafts book he's put on hold. He races home, consults the book, parcels out the ingredients he needs, and follows the directions for making papier-mâché. He then carries his mom's canister vacuum to the back porch, where he's placed the flat blue weather balloon inside a corral of porch chairs. He inserts the scratched chrome metal hose into the balloon's opening and—*vroom*—blows up the balloon.

Tying it off and stepping back, he ogles the eight-foot orb captured inside the porch chairs. It's huge. Bouncy. Kind of cute. A big round baby. The nasty papier-mâché exterior he's about to paint on will change that.

He carries his vat of paste and boxes of torn newspaper onto the porch. For the next two hours, he lathers on the strips of newspaper until he's covered the entire surface of the massive balloon. Gummy, sweaty, smelling of paste, he crouches and admires his work. He'll allow the balloon to dry overnight and tomorrow lather on a second coat. Chris will absolutely *freak*.

Sunday morning, he wakes at six and barrels down the stairs, paintbrush in hand, ready to apply the balloon's second coat of papier-mâché. He hits the porch and skids to a stop. Instead of an eight-foot weather balloon with a crusty, rocky surface, he finds—

A five-inch mound of mushy newspaper.

The weather balloon is a thirty-buck bust.

He slumps onto the porch steps, defeated.

This freaking boulder!

*   *   *

Floppy hat tipped back, Bud in hand, Peter works the camera. He squints through the viewfinder, nearly spills his beer.

"That's good," he says. "Now pull that light back."

Eric calls *action*. Chris appears around a corner, shoots a blank from his pistol, Indy scowl locked in.

"Cut!" Eric says. "That's a print."

"Now let's trash this place," Chris says.

Kurt runs into the bar set and he and Chris dive in, kings of destruction. They lob wine bottles onto the floor. Chris, crazed, flings jugs against the basement wall. Glass shatters and sails.

"Jeez, Chris," Kurt says, throwing his shoulder up to block a shower of glass shards.

"Watch it, you guys," Eric says. "Watch the glass."

Camera rolling, something happens to Chris. He morphs into a frenzied maniac, his face red as fire. He tromps through the set, smashes bottles onto the floor, hurls empties at the wall, screams, "This goddamn bar! I hate this place. I HATE THIS FUCKING PLACE!"

Then Eric bursts onto the set, lights a match to a tight roll of newspaper he's doused in alcohol. He fans at flames that begin shooting up from random pieces of wood. Around the destroyed bar, glass everywhere, fire spreads. Each corner of the basement bar flares.

"How's that?" Eric asks into camera. Peter, through the viewfinder, shakes his head, his satellite of a hat flapping.

"Nah. More. More fire," Peter the fire marshal and adult chaperone orders. "Behind the bar. In the corner. Boy, it's getting hot in here. More. On the table. More. How about on the front of the bar?"

Eric lights every spot Peter suggests. Within seconds, fire engulfs almost the entire basement room.

"That's it!" Peter says. "That's perfect!"

His voice caroms off the walls, an ecstatic firebug watching the building he's just torched burn.

"Let's do it!" Eric shouts. "Fast. Three—two—action!"

Chris and Angela, his arm around her—Indy and Marion—rush out of a wall of flames, barely escaping the inferno.

"One more time!" Peter says.

Chris and Angela duck back into the burning basement, hit their marks, Peter yells, "Go!" and they rush out, fire surrounding them.

"Yeah!" Peter says. "That'll work."

He downs the rest of his Bud, saunters toward the fire. With Eric wildly slamming his blanket on pockets of flames, Chris spraying the fire extinguisher, the fire peters out.

They peer into the puffy gray smoke lingering in the remains of the Nepalese bar set, watch the smoldering ash, daring the fire to return. And then they scream.

"Whoaaaaa!" Chris plows through the room, a wild man, hollering himself hoarse.

They run outside, Peter following, the camera still rolling.

"We did it, man," Chris says. "The heat was intense. But we did it!"

"Woo hoo!" Eric shouts.

"Movie magic! Right here. Two scenes done. Two of the hardest scenes. *Done!*"

"Congratulations, man," Eric says to Chris. He offers Chris his hand.

"We did it, man," Chris says again. He steps past Eric's hand and throws his arms around him in a bear hug.

Clinging to his friend, clapping him on the back, Eric says, "Yeah, man, we did it."

*   *   *

He clowns around; she laughs. She complains of tightness in her neck; he massages her shoulders. She tucks a cigarette into the corner of her mouth; he flicks open her lighter. She cups his hand with both of hers; he gallantly lights her cigarette. One day, she offers him one. He takes it. Soon he's hooked, and not just by the nicotine. By the cool. A smoke dangling from his fingers, he leaves that loud chubby Greek kid in the dust. He's become Indiana Jones—tough, swashbuckling—and like Indy, he gets the girl.

As Eric prepares the storyboards for the tent scene, he watches the two of them goofing off, flirting, giggling.

He seems excited and happy, that's for sure. And, damn, she's an older woman. I'm not even brave enough to ask out anybody my own age. Where does he get the confidence?

He believes he's Indiana Jones. That's where. He's *living* his fantasy.

That's terrific. Except that he's not thinking. Or he's blind. He doesn't see that he's putting our movie in jeopardy. What if they have a fight? Or worse. What if they break up and they hate each other and refuse to be in the same room together? The movie would be doomed.

What should he do?

What *can* he do? Tell Chris to dump her for the sake of the movie? What kind of friend would that make him? No. That's just . . . wrong. Eric knows there's only one thing to do.

Press on. Move forward.

They've completed the romantic cabin scene and finished the dicey bar scene, basement ablaze, viewing what they've shot on Mary's TV when she leaves for a meeting at a client's house. This time, they make sure their moms never glimpse so much as a second of the footage. They've wrapped the college sequence, too, putting the boring exposition to bed once and for all, again after a million takes. Now, with Eric pushing, they determine to shoot at least a portion of one more scene before the end of the summer.

They decide on the tent scene in which the scummy French horndog Belloq—Eric—attempts to put the moves on Marion in his lavish desert tent. He forces her to change into a slinky white cocktail dress for what he hopes will be a seductive dinner. Before the main course, Belloq trades glasses of wine with Marion, unaware she can drink him under the table and has hidden a knife up her sleeve that she will draw on him in an attempt to escape. Eric and Chris identify the small upstairs sunroom as the best location for the scene and cover the walls with bedsheets that Eric pins together to achieve a billowing tent wall effect.

Creating Marion's costume, Eric hits a snag: He sucks as a seamstress. Angela's mother comes to the rescue. She volunteers to sew the cocktail dress. Eric provides her with photographs of the original. Shortly Angela's mom presents them with a stunningly accurate replica of the dress Karen Allen wore, complete with polka dot netting that frills the shoulders and skirts the dress from the waist down to the tulle tail in the back. She seems to have missed only one detail—the plunging neckline. She opts for parenting over accuracy. Angela's mom's chaste version comes with a high collar, kind of a combination cocktail dress and turtleneck.

The tent scene seems simple enough on paper—two actors, fast-paced dialogue, no special effects, and no stunts. The scene does contain, to everyone's nervousness, a smidge of nudity. In the scene, Belloq hands Marion the cocktail dress, which she agrees to put on behind a screen. Thanks to a strategically placed mirror, slimy Belloq watches her undress. We, the audience, never see any frontal nudity; we see only her naked back. But no doubt. From the waist up, she *is* naked.

The day they shoot, the crew feels the heat, and not just from the throbbing August afternoon. Eric starts with a camera run-through for the crew—Jayson, Kurt, and Chris. The actors walk through the action, hit their spots, and when it comes to the moment of truth, Angela mimes taking off her shirt. Jayson wants to try something and climbs out on the roof to shoot the scene through a window opening. Nice touch. A little added visual artistry. Should work well as long as Jayson doesn't slide off the roof.

Eric calls *action*. The scene begins. As they approach Angela's nudity, the same question threads its way into everyone's head: *Will she do it?*

Eric gives his cue in Belloq's faux French accent, Angela steps in front of the mirror, and professional that she is—to the crew's shock—pulls her shirt over her head. Silence. And . . . cut!

Eric murmurs a silent prayer to the god of cinematography.

Jayson, please tell me you got the shot. I can't ask Angela to take off her shirt again.

"Jayson, how was that?"

"Good. Great."

"Okay, cool, that's a print. Moving on."

Relief all around. And then a gasp flutters through one of the bedsheets like a tiny wind. Later that night, production shut down for the year, Kurt confides in Eric that he was the one who gasped. During the mirror scene, he found a gap in one of the bedsheets and caught a brief flash of nipple.

1984. A great year for *Raiders*.

YEAR FOUR

"Very dangerous. You go first."   *—Sallah*

1985.

A ninth grader now, imprisoned in fifth-period math, his teacher's drone the perfect white noise by which to work, Eric, fifteen, ponders the locations he needs to scout and props he needs to procure for next summer's shoot. Jotting key words in his *Raiders* notebook hidden inside the open pages of his pre-algebra book, he pores over what he's written: *airplane, submarine, two trucks, downtown Cairo, the Sahara Desert.* The work ahead seems monumental. Staring at these words, he feels light-headed, as if he's about to hyperventilate. He considers dumping out the contents of his lunch and breathing deeply into the crumpled brown paper bag.

We also have to reshoot the opening chase, turn the big basement room into the Well of Souls, find seven thousand snakes, finish the tent scene, build an ark, train Snickers to play a Nazi monkey, and don't forget that freaking BOULDER.

He sighs loud enough for his math teacher to stop lecturing and nod gravely. "I sympathize, Mr. Zala. Not everyone gets pre-algebra."

Eric shoots a sheepish smile, closes the *Raiders* notebook, and slips it under his math book.

Relax. Breathe. Take it one step at a time.

Step one. Finish the tent scene. They'll have to pick up after Angela takes off her shirt. No way will Eric ask Angela to do that again. But first they'll have to build a new set that looks something like a *tent.* When they viewed the mirror scene footage right before Labor Day, they saw that the upstairs sunroom just did not work. Even with Eric's resourceful bedsheet solution, the extravagant tent he envisioned looked like the inside of a shoe box. Only smaller. And not as lavish.

Eric finds the perfect place for the tent right under his nose: the living room. He asks his mom's permission.

Mary's face darkens. "What exactly are you planning to do to the living room?"

"I'm going to make a big tent using cheap fabric I plan to buy at Josette's costume shop. I'll sew everything myself on your sewing machine, if that's all right."

"That's fine. You can use that old clunker all you want."

"I won't ruin anything or break anything or burn anything, I promise."

"The walls are already a disaster. You couldn't hurt them any worse." But Mary still looks troubled. "How long do you plan to turn our living room into a tent?"

"Not long. A few days. Maybe a week."

Eric slightly miscalculates. Trying Mary's good humor and immense patience, he turns the living room into a tent for the next year.

*   *   *

Although separated by a thousand miles during the school year, Chris and Angela remain an item. When he comes back to Mississippi for holidays and school breaks, they hang out, mostly at the Riverhouse. One night in his room, as she eyeballs Chris's expanding camouflage gear, weapons, and survival knife collection that has spilled over from bookshelves onto windowsills, Angela says quietly, "Chris, you live in a fantasy world."

He starts to object, then stops himself, because he realizes that she's right.

As summer approaches and they jump back into production, their relationship intensifies but never gets intimate. In fact, whenever Chris makes a move to kiss her, she stops him. *It's crazy*, Chris thinks. *She likes to make out with me on camera, but not off.*

Nowhere is this more obvious than during the continuation of the tent scene. In the scene, Indy enters the tent—now taking up most of the Zalas' living room—and sees Marion gagged and tied to a stake. He pulls the gag off and is about to untie her when he decides they'll be better off if he leaves her there, a captive, and goes off on his own. He kisses her and stuffs the gag back into her mouth. She objects, her muffled cries following him out of the tent.

The storyboard—Eric has copied it from the original—calls for Indy and Marion to kiss quickly before he scoots out of the tent.

Action!

Indy runs in, finds Marion gagged and lashed to the stake. He yanks off the gag and they kiss. And kiss. And *kiss*.

"Cut," Eric says. "How was that, Jayson?"

"The camera sort of moved."

"Let's take it again. Okay. Five—four—three—and *action*."

Indy in, gag off Marion, and heavy making out.

"Cut."

"The lighting was off."

"Again. And . . . action!"

Now the kiss comes and it doesn't look like Chris and Angela are stopping anytime soon.

"Cut! Jayson?"

"That was good."

"I didn't feel right," Chris says.

"Yeah. I felt off," Angela says.

"Can we do it again?" Chris says.

"Sure. Fine," Eric says, thinking, *Get a room.*

They get it right this time—the lighting works, the camera doesn't waver, the actors nail every line, the kiss looks hot and long.

"That's a print," Eric says. "Moving on."

Chris cracks a joke, Angela giggles, but Chris, even at fourteen, can't help wondering: *Is she my girlfriend? Are we ever going to make out in my room? What the hell is this?*

*   *   *

They need alleys. One day, they walk from Manyoaks to the center of tiny Ocean Springs and roam through what everyone calls downtown. Behind

Lovelace Drug Store, they find a clump of tin shacks with a couple of short narrow alleyways slithering between them.

"What do you think?" Eric asks. "Could this pass as Cairo?"

"Seems a little tight," Chris says.

"Let's think about the scene," Eric says. "Arabs carrying wicker baskets, a crowd gathers, you shoot the big swordsman, the fight, lots of running and chasing around corners."

"I see one corner," Chris says.

"We'd have to reshoot that one corner like eighty times."

"Seems a little tight," Chris says again.

*   *   *

On a Saturday afternoon, they load Elaine's minivan with Arab costumes sewn by Eric, fake beards bought at Josette's, the costume store in Biloxi, bedsheets, trinkets, oranges, pots, pans, card tables, all loaned by the moms, and wicker baskets high enough to conceal Angela, bought at World Bazaar in Edgewater Mall. Elaine drives them through Gulfport's business district, a collection of low buildings tucked together, behind which traverse several workable alleys. Behind a diner, they spot an alley that runs into a cul-de-sac. They've found it. Cairo.

"Good angles," Eric says, as he and Chris unload the minivan. They pile their stuff against the side of a brick building, and Elaine drives off, promising to pick them up in a few hours.

The storyboards their blueprint, the boys begin turning the alley into a replica of the Cairo street from *Raiders*. They work without interruption since most businesses close early on Saturday. And because everything shuts down on Sunday, they plan to dress the set completely, leave everything in place covered with blankets and sheets, and return early tomorrow for the shoot.

Eric, his view obscured by an armload of wicker baskets, doesn't notice Chris gazing off toward the end of the alley. Chris taps him on the shoulder. Eric lowers the baskets onto the concrete.

A man walks toward them. Over a T-shirt, he wears a filthy apron, which flaps over his flouncing beer belly.

"Hey, there," Chris says. "How you doing?"

"Hello," Eric says.

The man wipes his hands on his apron. "What are you boys up to?"

"Actually," Eric says, "we're shooting a movie."

"Shooting a *movie*."

"Yes, sir," Eric says. "We're doing a remake of *Raiders of the Lost Ark*."

"Is that right?"

"We really are." Chris laughs. "Eric here is the director, and I'm playing Indiana Jones. I'm sure you can see the resemblance."

A bigger laugh. Trying to pull the guy in.

"We know businesses are closed Sundays, so we're setting up today and shooting tomorrow," Eric says.

"Unh-uh," the man says, his eyelids violently fluttering. "No, you are not. Unh-*uh*."

He breaks into a run, heads up the alley around the corner to the street. The boys hesitate, then chase after him. The man turns into a scabby-looking diner, still open but empty. The place smells of bacon and sweat.

His fingers flying as he dials his phone, the man cranks his head toward his deserted counter, then swivels away, his fleshy back to the boys. He spits into the mouthpiece. "Police? I want to report a *crime*. Right outside my business establishment. As we speak."

The boys, struck mute, stand immobilized, their legs heavy as cement.

The diner owner raises his voice. "Two young men. Moviemakers, they claim. I have strong suspicions that they are engaged in child pornography."

"What?" Chris starts to rush the counter. Eric grips his arm.

"Sir," Eric says. "We're remaking *Raiders of the Lost*—"

The diner owner enunciates his address twice, says, "Thank you," and lays the phone down gently. "Police are on their way. You won't be shooting *shit* tomorrow."

Eric brushes by Chris, follows the diner owner, who waddles toward his kitchen. "Sir, please, we're fifteen years old. We're really making a legitimate—"

The diner owner plows into the kitchen door with his stomach and disappears inside. Chris bangs the counter with his palm. "You fucking believe this?"

"Let's go," Eric says.

"Yeah, Capone," Chris says. "Let's wait for the cops."

Outside, they plunk down on the curb and await Gulfport's finest to shut them down, ticket them, or, worst case, cuff them and arrest them.

"Child pornography," Eric says, a wag of his head. "Where did he get that? We didn't even bring a camera."

"Or a child."

"This does, in fact, suck," Eric says.

Chris raises his head toward a rustling at the opposite side of the alley. A younger man, slacks, tie, long unruly hair dusting his ears, plastic garbage bag slapping against his leg as he walks, lobs the bag into a Dumpster. He sees Chris and Eric sitting on the curb and slowly approaches.

"You boys look lost."

Chris blurts, "No, we're just waiting for the police."

"What'd you do?"

"Nothing," Eric says, and bends his head toward the wicker baskets, tables, and props. "We're setting up to shoot a movie tomorrow. The owner of the diner called the cops on us."

"He thinks we're making a porno," Chris says.

The man looks the boys over. "Well, are you?"

"We're remaking *Raiders of the Lost Ark*," Eric says in a monotone.

"You gonna do the boulder and everything?"

"Everything," Eric says.

"Co-oo-ol." The man drags the word out to multiple syllables. He waves at the stuff the boys have crammed in the alley. "What's all that?"

"Props. We're planning on shooting the scene in Cairo here. There's an elaborate chase scene when Indiana and Marion—" Eric shoots to his feet, causing the man to step back. "Sir. Mr.—?"

"Neville. Conrad Neville. That's my furniture store."

"Mr. Neville, sir, could we have your permission to shoot in your alley? We can't pay you. But I promise when the movie's finished, we'll thank you in the credits."

The man sticks his tie into his belt. "I know something about show business. I was in the drama club in high school. Played a featured role in *Our Town*. So." He holds. "Sure. Go ahead. But you don't have to thank me—"

"We insist," Chris says.

"That's Neville with two *L*'s."

"Thank you," Eric says over his shoulder because he's sprinting toward the card tables, Chris a step behind.

*   *   *

As they finish carrying the last of the props to Neville's side of the alley, the first squad car arrives. With a cowboy swagger, a toothpick planted in his mouth, and one hand resting on his holster, a cop, his face raw red and all jaw, strides through the alley. He blankets them with his shadow.

"Got a call someone's making a porno," the cop says, his toothpick hopping against his cheek. He looks over Eric and Chris, dismisses them. "Who's in charge here? Where's your boss?"

"That would be us," Eric says. "We're the ones making the movie."

"It's not a porno," Chris says. "It's *Raiders of the Lost Ark*."

"And Mr. Neville has given us permission to shoot in the alley," Eric says.

"Permission?"

"Yes, sir," Chris says. "You can ask him."

"*Raiders of the Lost Ark*?"

"Yes, sir," Eric says.

"That's been done."

"We know," Eric says.

"What's this, the porno version?"

"No!" Eric and Chris shout.

The cop eyes them. "You don't look like porn stars."

"We're not. We're in junior high," Chris says.

The cop grins, tongues the toothpick so that he swallows it whole. After a second, the toothpick dances back onto his bottom lip. "I will talk to Mr. Neville. First, I'm gonna have to search this stuff. For contraband. Drugs. Porno material." But now he's covering a laugh. "Where's your camera?"

"We didn't bring it. We're not shooting until tomorrow."

He pats his holster, crosses the alley in two steps. He passes his eyes over a table covered with pots, pans, and props. "Who's playing Indiana Jones?"

"I am," Chris says.

The cop, a frying pan in his hand, slides the toothpick across the length of his mouth, looks at Chris. "I can see that."

The cop roots through everything on the table. He scrunches his maroon forehead and picks up a curved Gurkha knife the boys acquired at an antique store for two dollars. He holds the knife up as if he's found a prize. The blade glints in his hand. "Well, well. This here is a concealed weapon."

Something sour rises into Eric's throat. Chris stares at his shoes, shifts his weight. *Are we busted? Are we going to jail?*

The cop turns the curved knife blade over, runs his thumb along the edge. "Dull as a noodle. This thing couldn't cut wind."

"It's a prop," Chris says.

The cop lays the knife back on the table. He clicks his tongue twice, easily translated as *what a waste of time this is.* "Can you give me the name of somebody who will verify that you're really out here making *Raiders of the Lost Ark?*"

"Technically, it's a remake," Eric says.

"Our moms," Chris says. "I'll give you both numbers in case one's not home."

The cop shimmies a pad and pen out of his shirt pocket and writes down both phone numbers. He points the pen at the boys. "Don't move. I'm going to talk to Mr. Neville."

As he starts toward the furniture store, a second squad car screeches to a stop in front of the alley. Two uniformed cops pop out, leaning forward as they walk.

"Got a call someone's making a porno," Driver says.

"False alarm," the first cop says.

"What's all this?" Shotgun says, waving at the prop table.

"They're making *Raiders of the Lost Ark.*" A look at Eric. "Technically it's a remake."

"That was a good movie," Shotgun says. "How they gonna pull off the boulder?"

"I'm gonna check it out," the first cop says, as a third car, a nondescript Dodge, pulls up. A plainclothes cop in a rumpled suit bounds out. "Heard someone's making a porno."

Shotgun hitches his thumb at Chris and Eric.

"Them?" Plainclothes says. "They're kids."

Driver shrugs.

"They in it or they making it?" Plainclothes asks.

After a few minutes, the first cop strolls out of the furniture store, a fresh toothpick in place.

"You check out," he says. He nods in the general direction of Chris and Eric. "I spoke to somebody's mom. She confirmed it."

"So we can shoot here?" Eric says.

"Yep. The guy in the furniture store gave his permission. He said he's the producer."

"Wow," Eric says, too stunned to correct him. "Thank you, officer."

"Yeah. Thanks a lot," Chris says. "And sorry for the misunderstanding."

"So, you're doing *Raiders of the Lost Ark?*" Plainclothes says.

"Well, it's a remake," Eric says.

"I'm Indy," Chris says before anyone can ask again.

"I got a kid your age," Plainclothes says. "Can't get him out of the house. He just watches TV, eats junk food, and lies like a lump on the couch. Least you're doing something. Got a project."

"Takes up a lot of time, that's for sure," Eric says.

"Years," Chris says.

"Well, stay out of trouble. Hey. How you gonna make the boulder?"

*　　*　　*

Nothing like a run-in with the law to motivate the guys to burn through the Cairo street scene in one day.

They meet in the alley before eight for rehearsal. The day's storyboards call for chases, fights, twenty kids playing Arabs and Nazis, and Chris's dog, Snickers, taking on the role of a Nazi monkey. Again Eric feels as if he's herding cats, but today the kids sense his urgency. The cast members stay loose, but they pick up a different vibe and they're careful not to cross a line.

Eric directs with full-blown confidence, perhaps born from his sense of dread that the cops will change their minds, swoop in, close them down, and round them up. Or Eric's confidence may come from his new perception of Chris. Tighter now with Angela and channeling his inner Indy more than ever, Chris as Indy fights, flirts, and oozes a cool bordering on cockiness. Maybe Eric wants to match that with a cockiness of his own.

From beginning to end, the boys are on fire. Eric X's out completed storyboard after storyboard. Between takes, Chris and Angela flirt like a cliché of leading man and leading lady who've become an off-screen couple, hands all over each other, Chris lifting her, dipping her, Angela giggling, locking her legs around his waist, Chris raising his eyebrows, flicking his tongue, mugging for the camera. When they're not groping each other, they pause for a smoke. On this day, Gulfport passing for Cairo, occasional passersby stopping to gawk, local kids approaching the actors to ask about the movie, Chris feels a headiness he has never felt before and rarely since. For this Sunday at least, he has buried that insecure chubby Greek kid and become a star.

*　　*　　*

Lying in bed at night, Eric fixes his gaze on the ceiling fan whirling slowly and imagines that it's the blades of a propeller. He pictures the airplane scene. He envisions the muscular German skinhead screaming in close-up and the propeller spraying blood onto the fuselage of the plane.

How will we create that blood-spattering effect on no budget? Who will believe some scrawny thirteen-year-old kid as a scary muscular German? How can I convince that same scrawny thirteen-year-old kid to shave his head? Where are we ever going to find a plane? And if we find a plane, how are we going to blow it up?

He devises a plan involving four people.

Jayson. He'll figure out the blood-spattering effect, no problem. Blood-spattering effects are his life.

Peter Keefer. They'll recruit him to play the scary skinhead German. They'll have to break their kid-only rule just this once. They'll bribe him with Bud if necessary. He won't even have to shave his head. They'll buy him a bald wig at Spencer Gifts.

Elaine. He recalls her saying she knew someone who owned a single-engine plane that he kept at Keesler Air Force base in Biloxi. They'll ask permission to use it for the exploding airplane scene. On second thought, maybe they should go guerrilla-style on this and sneak Angela into the cockpit when nobody's looking. And they won't blow it up. They'll photograph it, build a scale model, and blow that up. Better.

Henry Jack. A weird kid who sits a row over in homeroom. Henry wears a torn Indy-type leather jacket year-round. According to school gossip and rumor, Henry shows up at junior high when and if he feels like it. He devotes most of his time to working on his career: breaking and entering, stealing, fencing, and mayhem. One day, Eric overhears Henry bragging that he knows how to make a pipe bomb. Eric finds Henry's phone number, calls him, tells him about *Raiders,* and asks him for the pipe bomb recipe. They meet the next day outside Lovelace Drug Store, and Henry hands him a smudged sheet of notebook paper with written instructions and a list of ingredients. Eric promises to put him in the credits.

After Chris leaves to spend the evening not making out with Angela, Eric and Jayson head to Ocean Springs Hardware to purchase the ingredients to make the bomb: a sack of manure, a spool of electrical wire, a foot-long length of pipe, and screw caps to cover both ends of the pipe. The next day in the basement, the three boys follow Henry Jack's instructions and build the bomb. That afternoon, the bomb hidden under a beach towel in the back of Elaine's minivan, they go to Chris's grandparents' house for a combination sleepover and bomb test.

They carry the bomb through the backyard to an isolated spot in a dusty clearing. They place the bomb in the dirt. Jayson fiddles with the fuse, then pulls out a book of matches and tears one off. Hands shaking, he strikes the match. The matchbook sails out of his hands.

"Nervous?" Chris says.

"N-n-no," Jayson says.

"This has to work," Eric says. "How else are we going to do the scene?"

"I-I-I don't know." Jayson retrieves the matchbook, tears off another match, tries to light it and whiffs.

"Give me that," Chris says.

He strikes the match with a flourish and lights the fuse. The fuse sizzles, crackles, and wiggles toward the center of the bomb.

"Run!" Eric screams.

He and Chris sprint toward a downed tree. Jayson, his knees clattering, stands over the bomb, frozen.

"Jayson!" The boys skid, pivot, and race back for Jayson. They each grab an elbow and pick him up.

They bolt for the tree, the fuse snaking on the ground behind them, flicking two inches away from the bomb. They roll over the dead log and fall onto the hard dirt behind it. They squeeze into three matching fetal positions and curl into the rotting wood. They ram their eyes shut and clamp their palms over their ears.

Pfff.

Eric and Chris poke their heads over the top of the tree.

"You can come out now," Eric says to Jayson.

"What?"

Eric pulls Jayson's hands off his ears. "It's safe."

"It didn't go off," Chris says. "No bomb. No explosion. No nothing. It was a dud. You fucked up."

"We followed Jack's directions, didn't we, Eric?"

"To the letter."

"Why would you trust that dirtbag?" Chris says. "He's a fucking felon. He's got a record longer than my dick."

"I'm relieved," Jayson says.

Eric and Chris look at him.

"I don't like bombs," Jayson says. "Not my métier."

"You met who?" Chris says.

"It's French," Jayson says.

"Jesus," Chris says.

"What are we going to do?" Eric says.

"The truth is . . . we blow up a model plane? It's gonna look cheesy," Jayson says.

"He's right," Chris says. "It's gonna look like shit."

"I'm open to suggestions," Eric says, straddling the tree.

"I have a suggestion," Chris says. "You won't like it."

"I have an open mind."

"Cut the scene."

"No. Absolutely not. Forget it. We have to stay true to the original. We've already taken license substituting the motorboat for the biplane. End of discussion."

"As long as you have an open mind," Chris says.

Jayson stretches, rolls over the tree, slides to a sitting position on the grass. "We don't need the scene," he mumbles.

After a moment, Chris says, "You really don't. Think about it."

Eric peers at the impotent bomb fifty yards away, now nothing but a piece of chrome pipe bouncing sunlight into their eyes. "How would it work?"

"Easy," Chris says. "You go from Indy and Marion escaping the Well of Souls—"

"And cut to the truck scene," Eric says.

A long pause. Finally, Chris says, "It could work."

"Plotwise, the scene is extraneous," Eric says softly.

"It's a very creative solution," Jayson says.

"We wouldn't have to find an actual plane," Chris says.

"Or blow one up," Jayson says.

Eric stands, paces, slings his hands onto his hips.

"All right," he says. "Let's cut it."

The moment he speaks, Eric feels relief. He might even go so far as to admit that cutting the scene is not only an inspired solution to their airplane problem but the smart thing to do.

What he doesn't know is that cutting the airplane scene will haunt his dreams for the next ten years.

*   *   *

Most nights, Chris stays over at Manyoaks. Since he and Eric begin shooting the movie early every day, staying over saves his mom the hassle of picking him up in the evening, driving to the Riverhouse, then bringing him back to Manyoaks by eight o'clock the next morning. In truth, Chris prefers staying at Eric's house. In the cold isolation of the vast Riverhouse, he feels like a visitor, or sometimes even a stranger. The Riverhouse reminds him of a mausoleum, without the warmth. And Jimmy Love III—wandering the halls or occupying an armchair in one of the hangar-sized formal rooms, a scowl etched into his face, a Scotch attached to his hand—reminds him of the crypt keeper. When Jimmy speaks to Chris, he talks in clipped sentences, his Southern patrician drawl oozing out hushed and slurred. Sometimes late at night, when Chris lies sleepless in his bed in his converted attic room, he hears the opposite of the buttoned-up Southern gentleman. He hears his mom and Jimmy screaming, doors slamming, a bottle smashing. When he sees Jimmy Love III the next morning or evening, his stepfather will acknowledge Chris with a slight nod or engage in bland conversation. Unlike Elaine, who wants to be told what's going on with the movie in detail, Jimmy never asks about *Raiders*. As August begins, Chris admits to Eric that for the first time in his life, he's actually looking forward to going back to school.

They end the summer at the beginning. Since the footage they shot of the opening turned out to be useless, they decide to reshoot the sequence, this time using the woods across the street from the Riverhouse as the jungle. One problem. They need a new motorboat. The motorboat they borrowed before turned out to be a one-time favor. As they gather actors to play the bloodthirsty Hovitos who chase Indy out of the jungle, Elaine breezes across the street and announces that she has convinced Jimmy to lend them his motorboat.

The shoot goes well. The kids playing the Hovitos look older and more threatening. Dripping with bravado, Chris swings skillfully from the bank of the river, splashes into the river, swims to the motorboat, and climbs aboard with a stuntman's flair. The filming goes so well that people out for a leisurely boat ride on the river stop and watch. Chris bobs to the surface from the river and doffs his sopping fedora.

Then disaster.

Just as they are about to finish the last shot, Chris lifts himself into the motorboat and watches with horror as the outboard motor rips away from the boat and drops into the water.

"Uh-oh," Chris says. He dives into the river after the motor. He surfaces a few seconds later. "I don't believe this. The fucking motor's gone."

"What happened?" Eric shouts from shore.

"I don't know. The motor just fell off."

"Shit," Eric says.

Chris slaps the water. He sucks in a huge breath and dives in again. He surfaces, splashing violently, slamming his fists over and over into the murky river.

"You're never going to find it, Chris," Eric says. "I'm sure it sank to the bottom."

"He's gonna get so far up my ass," Chris says. "I'm gonna have to pay for the fucking thing."

"I'll chip in," Eric says.

"I'll tell you what," Chris says. "I'll pay. You tell Jimmy."

That night, Chris heads directly to Jimmy's study. He doesn't plan what he's going to say. He knocks on the door, enters, and tells his stepfather that he lost the outboard motor. Chris takes total responsibility. He braces himself for Jimmy's reaction.

Jimmy drains his Scotch, pours another.

"Your movie," he says, after a sip. "Your little folly. It's child's play. A waste of time and a waste of money."

Chris says nothing, but he feels his face burn with anger. Jimmy swallows another sip. "I want the motor back. I'm going to give you the name of a former navy diver. You call him and pay him to find it."

Chris stares at Jimmy. "How much does he cost?"

"One hundred dollars."

The next day, Chris withdraws the money from his savings account, leaving him nearly broke. The diver Chris hires spends two hours in the river searching for the motor. He finds nothing.

Feeling a mix of relief and guilt, Chris returns to Long Island. He's relieved to be out of southern Mississippi and to spend the next nine months disguised as a uniform-wearing preppie in a highly rated, extremely expensive East Coast private school, far away from his distant and cold stepfather. He's racked with guilt because his stepfather pays all his bills.

*   *   *

I'm overthinking the boulder, Eric thinks. *I need to simplify. Okay. What would be the easiest, cheapest material to use?*

Chicken wire.

So obvious.

Mary drops him at Ocean Springs Hardware, and Eric purchases the largest roll of chicken wire he can afford. Back at Manyoaks, he sets up on the front porch. He plans to bend and shape the entire roll into a massive sphere and again cover the surface with papier-mâché. The beauty of chicken wire is that it can't pop, deflate, or smash apart. Why hasn't he thought of this before?

As a stiff wind kicks off the coast, he settles onto the floor of the porch and twists the chicken wire into a huge circle. An hour in, when a stretch of wire snaps back and slices his hand, he realizes he should be wearing gloves. Too late now. He can't take the chance of losing the shape and starting over.

Finally, he finishes. He again corrals the gigantic sphere inside a square of porch chairs. He steps back and admires the huge wire globe. Once he slaps on the layers of papier-mâché, he'll have succeeded—at last—in building the boulder. He wishes Chris could see it. The wind bangs the screen door shut, jars him. He heads inside, the chicken wire boulder safe on the porch. First thing tomorrow, he'll work on the papier-mâché.

The howling gusts of Hurricane Elena wake him in the middle of the night. Horizontal sheets of water pound the house. A serious storm, a Category 3, but not out of the ordinary for the Gulf. Nothing Eric hasn't experienced before.

We're not in any real danger. I doubt we'll sustain any significant losses. Except—

Eric charges downstairs.

He presses himself against the windows in the living room, the wind cracking hard against the house, the rain piercing his vision. Right in front of him, right in his *face*, as if mocking him, a wall of wind spirals onto the porch, lifts the chicken wire boulder, pushes it along the wide front lawn, bats it like a beach ball, and carries it across the road and into the Gulf.

Eric watches the boulder bob on the water like a child's toy.

It floats away, forever.

YEAR FIVE

June 1986.

Eric, sixteen, sits at the kitchen table after dinner and doodles in his *Raiders* notebook. He lowers his chin onto the lacquered finish and writes in bold cursive script *The Well of Souls,* then in frustration rolls his pen to the far rim of the table. He once again feels overwhelmed by the amount of work they face, but this year he feels time closing in and whizzing by. He feels this way partly because Chris, fifteen, after spending spring semester as an exchange student in England, has taken an extra two weeks to bum around London. He feels slammed because of the problems he has to solve— how to create the Well of Souls, where to shoot the Sahara Desert, how to procure a submarine, how to build the Ark, where to locate a truck they can wreck. Mostly, though, since Chris isn't here, he feels the burden of having to solve these problems himself. He feels alone.

He stretches his pinkie across the table and retrieves the pen. He twirls it through his fingers, then spins it slowly. He's only peripherally aware that Mary has come in and pulled up a chair.

"I've been thinking about the boulder," she says. "I have a suggestion."

"I'm open to anything."

"Fiberglass," Mary says.

The pen falls out of Eric's fingers and clatters onto the tabletop. "Wow. I never would've thought of that."

"I have a client named Mic Sajway out in Vancleave. He does custom fiberglass work on boats. Maybe you should call him."

Eric snatches up the pen and taps it thoughtfully into his palm. "I don't know much about fiberglass, but it would seem to be pretty light and flexible and certainly waterproof."

"It's sturdy, too," Mary says. "Here. I wrote down his number for you." She snaps her business card on the table.

"Thanks, Mom."

She smiles, stands, musses his hair. "You got me thinking about the movie, too."

The next morning Eric bikes to the Ocean Springs Public Library and holes up in the stacks for most of the day. He discovers that fiberglass is thin as cloth. In fact, it *is* cloth. When soaked with its resin and left to dry, it forms a hard, durable surface. Diving into his pile of books, writing notes furiously, Eric concocts a plan.

He'll dig a hole in the ground, form it into a perfect half-sphere, and coat the walls of the hole with fiberglass resin. He'll allow the fiberglass to dry, and when it's hard he'll pop it out of the hole and repeat the process. He'll then join the two halves, forming a sphere, and seal the whole thing with more fiberglass. This could actually work.

But.

He'll have to carve out the hole perfectly. Otherwise, the two halves won't fit.

He bikes home knowing that he's close. He just has to figure out how to make two hemispheres that are exactly the same so the halves fit seamlessly.

He can't sleep. A movie clip runs through his mind. A trailer from their future *Raiders*. Chris, as Indy, runs out of the cave, the giant boulder rolling behind him. Suddenly, the boulder groans and splits in two, the pieces plopping over like two halves of a giant plastic grapefruit. Eric opens his eyes and sits up. Forget this idea. Forget fiberglass.

But . . . wait . . . this may not be a question of the substance but of the execution. He's nagged by the issue of precision.

How will I ever be able to dig a perfect half-sphere?

He hits the library again. He rummages through reference books, plows through encyclopedias, not quite sure what he's looking for. Something catches his eye. He riffles back toward an image he saw. He stops at a picture that practically leaps off the page.

A color drawing of an ancient Egyptian.

The Egyptians built the Pyramids.

The Egyptians employed primitive yet innovative methods of architecture and construction.

Maybe the ancient Egyptians hold the key to the boulder.

An hour later, he finds it.

It's called a plumb line.

Sketching frantically in his notebook, Eric draws the plans to make the boulder.

He needs to make the boulder six feet high. The hole he will dig must be precisely three feet deep. Once he digs the hole, he'll use the plumb line to create the exact measurements.

For the plumb line, he will nail two boards together to form an X. He will drill a hole in the center of the X and thread a rope through. He will tie a knot at one end to keep the rope in place. Onto the other end of the rope, he will tie a metal spoon. Along the length of rope he will measure a distance of exactly three feet from the X to the tip of the spoon.

To make the mold for the boulder, he'll dig a hole large enough for him to fit in, then place the plumb line over the top with the rope hanging dead center. Crouching or lying beneath the plumb line apparatus, he'll scrape the sides of the dirt with the spoon, in every direction, until the spoon can reach no farther. He'll scoop out any loose dirt pooling at the bottom of the pit, maintaining the three-foot measurement at every point. Then he'll crawl out carefully and line the walls of the hole with the fiberglass mixture.

He finishes his drawing, stares at it. He considers the ditch, the plumb line, and the idea of fiberglass. Seeing no flaw, he commits to the idea. He bikes home and calls Mic Sajway, who offers him a deal. Mic wants one hundred dollars—which Eric doesn't have; he'll ask his mom for a five-month advance on his allowance—for materials and the use of his land to dig the hole. In addition, after they finish shooting the movie, the boys must return the boulder as a souvenir and example of Mic's wonderful world of fiberglass.

The more Eric studies his plan, the more he believes it will work.

While nailing together the plumb line pieces, he also realizes that this is a two-man job. He needs someone to get down into the trenches with him, literally. Someone committed and quirky like him, who won't mind spending two entire days digging a hole in the hot Mississippi sun.

"Sounds like fun," Jayson says.

Early one morning, Mary drives the two boys along the Gulf for what seems forever, then finally turns down a two-lane highway that disappears into a pine tree wilderness. After backtracking from several dead ends, she blindly chooses a dirt road that takes them even deeper into the woods. Mary's about to give up and burrow her way out of the pine tree maze when the woods open into a clearing. A trailer on a slab sits at the far end of a wide patch of land, rock music pumping out of a screen door cracked open.

"We're here. I think," Mary says.

A grinning guy with a mullet springs out of the trailer, his bare tattooed arms stretched toward them through his cutoff tee as if he's about to embrace the whole car in a hug. "Any trouble finding me?"

"None at all, Mic," Mary says, her head out the window.

"Well, you're the first," Mic says. "Awright. Let's get this party started."

"I'll pick you boys up at six," Mary says, taking in Mic, his trailer, and the clearing with a quick scan of her Mom-radar, concluding they'll be fine.

Eric pops the trunk, and the boys pull out two shovels and the plumb line apparatus. They wave to Mary as the Accord fishtails away.

"Damn," Mic says. "Is that a plumb line?"

"Yes, sir," Eric says.

"Never met anybody who heard of a plumb line, never mind used one."

"You never met Eric," Jayson says.

Mic sets them up thirty feet from his screen door. He goes into his trailer to conduct some business, and Eric and Jayson start digging. Three hours later, their shirts off, sweat running up their stomachs and down their backs, their vision blurry from the heat, they climb out of the hole and take a break. As if he's been watching them, Mic shoots out of the trailer. He hands them each a Coke and peers into the hole. "You're getting there."

"Yeah?" Eric says. "Hard to tell."

"You're close. Time to use that plumb line. Knock on my door when you're ready."

They climb back into the hole and lay the plumb line apparatus over their heads. Cramped together, crawling on their hands, knees, and bellies, the plumb line's boards forming the shadow of the X over them, they begin phase two, the more precise digging of the crescent. Eric scrapes all sides of the trench with the spoon, stretching it as far as it will go. Jayson scoops handfuls of loose dirt off the bottom, flings them out of the ditch. They work in silence. To Eric, they are artists, craftsmen, gravediggers.

Later, exhausted, filthy, exhilarated, Eric taps on Mic's screen door. After a moment, Mic nudges his shoulder into the screen and comes out, his arms clutching his tools and a bucket. He looks into the crater, whistles through his teeth, and begins his magic. He coats strips of white woven fiber in the bucket, filled with a syrupy resin, and layers the wet strips inside the hole. The boys watch as Mic lines the entire trench and creates a huge cloth bowl.

Mary arrives as Mic packs up. "How did it go?"

"We just finished," Mic says. "It'll dry overnight, then tomorrow we'll lift out the first fiberglass mold."

"I'm holding my breath," Eric says.

A violent summer shower wakes Eric in the morning. He checks his bedside alarm clock: 7:45. He waits fifteen minutes and calls Mic. His voice cracks. "Hi, Mic, it's Eric. I was wondering—"

"We're good," Mic says. "The mold dried overnight. I pulled it out. Held together tight."

"So, wait, it's all right?"

"Yep. The hole's a mud pit, though."

"What does that mean?"

"Means you can try to bail out the water and mud. If you can't, you gotta dig another hole."

"I don't mind, as long as the mold—"

"Hard as a rock," Mic says.

Two hours later, the sun out, Eric and Jayson stand over the pit they dug the day before. They stare at the bottom, no longer a dirt floor but a small lake of brown water. The sides, slippery and muddy, quiver as if they're about to collapse.

"I'm going in," Eric says.

He steps into the hole, sinks, takes the sides with him.

"Damn," Jayson says.

"Shit," Eric says, up to his thighs in mud, muck, and water.

Jayson sits on the edge of the hole, tucks his knees to his chest, and slides into the pit.

"This is disgusting," Eric says.

"Define disgusting," Jayson says, sloshing in the mud. For the first time in two days, Eric allows himself a laugh.

"Let's bail this crap out," Eric says.

For two hours, they scoop out water and mud. They try, anyway. Every time they scoop some mud out, more seeps in. The walls, on the verge of bursting, finally give way, surging into the bottom, replacing all the mud they've bailed out.

"Forget this," Eric says.

"Really?" Jayson says. He's covered head to toe with mud, most from working in the pit, some from handfuls he's slapped onto his body.

Eric grunts, climbs out of the hole, sits on the side. He packs a fist full of mud and flings it into the dirt at his feet. "We were so close!"

"Hey," Mic says, standing behind Eric. "I got an idea. It's like . . . obvious. I think I can make a second mold from the first one."

"Really? Would that work?"

Mic shrugs. "It should. Then you'd have two exact halves."

"Wow. How long do you think it would take?"

"I got another job to finish. Give me a week. I'll call you."

"Terrific. Thanks." Eric clears his throat, throttles a rising lump of disappointment. He's been through this before. "Mic, are you sure?"

Mic squeezes Eric's shoulder. "Don't worry."

*   *   *

A week later to the day, Eric gets a call.

Chris.

They talk about his time in London, but mostly they talk about the cave sequence reshoot and turning the large basement room into the Well of Souls. They arrange for Chris to come over in two days. Chris needs a couple of days to settle in, and Eric needs the time to take his driver's test. He hangs up. The phone rings immediately.

Mic.

"It's done," Mic says.

"Really?"

"Yep. Not a hitch. Made the second mold and fit it right into the first one. Like butter."

"*Really?*"

"I swear. So, come on over and pick up your boulder."

"I can't believe it. I mean, *wow*. Is it cool? How does it look?"

"I kinda like it," Mic says.

*   *   *

Before them looms a wondrous six-foot fiberglass boulder.

Jayson, squirmy, wants to rush it, throw his body at it. Eric stares, moon-eyed. The boulder, its surface grainy, pocked, and bumpy, looks indeed like a gorgeous mutant rock. Eric slowly steps toward it, reaches out his hand, and presses his palm onto its cool scaly surface.

"Amazing," he says. He rubs his hand in a circle, polishing, caressing. Then he raps on it. The boulder tings back, hollow and tinny.

"Let's roll it," he says to Jayson.

He and Jayson put their weight into it and shove. The boulder rolls like an actual pretend boulder.

"It's light," Eric calls to Mic, who watches, arms folded across his thick chest.

"I'd guess near a hundred pounds, most."

"I love it," Eric says, and Jayson nods and puts his arms around it as far as he can.

Then the boys lift the boulder and heave it into the back of a pickup truck they've borrowed, a friend of Mary's at the wheel. They climb up after it, pull up the pickup's metal flap, and sit on either side. Eric keeps both hands on it all the way, protecting it from deflating, crashing, smashing, or blowing away, thinking, *I've gone through four years of obsession, mental anguish, and failure for what will result in four seconds on film.*

Totally worth it.

* * *

Newly licensed by the state of Mississippi to operate a motor vehicle, Eric Zala makes his first legal drive from Manyoaks to the Riverhouse. Pulling into the driveway and tapping the horn, he flashes his driver's license as Chris bounds into the car.

"Dude," Chris shouts, slapping Eric's palm in congratulations. "We got wheels."

"Even better," Eric says. "We got boulder."

"Cannot *wait* to see it. To Manyoaks, James."

Eric grins, twists his head over his right shoulder, looks left, looks right, checks his mirrors, cautiously backs out of the short driveway, and pulls into the empty street. He eases the car forward, careful to keep a mile or two below the speed limit.

"You drive like my gramma," Chris says.

"Don't distract me."

Eyes riveted on the road, hands gripping the steering wheel at two o'clock and four o'clock, Eric crunches his forehead in concentration. Chris cracks up.

"I missed you, man."

* * *

Eric rolls the boulder the length of the garage. Chris, wearing his signature Indy *Holy shit!* scowl, runs from it.

"Awesome!" Chris shouts during his third or fourth run.

"Thank you, Mom, and the miracle of fiberglass," Eric says.

One more roll from the back wall of the garage through the open doorway—now in reverse—Chris pushing the boulder and Eric running, just for the hell of it. Laughing, leaning on each other, they spread a week's worth of newspapers onto the driveway, pull out their spray cans, and pelt the boulder gray.

*   *   *

The boulder, stained the color of smoke, sits safely imprisoned in the garage like a beached Buddha. As Eric circles the boulder, he thinks about *Raiders*, the original, and how that huge boulder appeared and barreled after Harrison Ford. He remembers reading how Spielberg shot the scene and realizes that even though they have their own boulder, they lack the means to roll it, to control it, to keep it on course, to allow it to pick up speed as it charges their Indiana Jones. On the flat floor of the garage, the boulder rolls at Chris like a big gray stumbling blob.

We're not quite there. We need—

Rails.

Two rails—logs, say—flanking the boulder, down which the rock can ride.

He turns off the light in the garage, swings the doors shut, and heads inside. He grabs the Yellow Pages, finds "logs" and "loggers," and jabs his finger at the largest ad. He'll call in the morning.

When he wakes up, he measures the length of the garage. He stretches the tape measure four times, calculates and recalculates: He needs two forty-foot logs. He goes inside and dials the number he's written down from the phone book. The address under the phone number tells him he's calling a logging camp deep in the woods beyond Mic's place. Middle of Nowhere, Mississippi.

A man answers.

"I want to buy two logs. I need them to be forty feet long."

"What are you looking to do with them?" A gruff voice. Possibly hungover. Definitely impatient.

"It's complicated. I need to roll a six-foot fiberglass boulder. It has to go straight for forty feet."

Gruff Voice pauses. Eric hears the click of a cigarette lighter. Gruff Voice drags on a cigarette. *Should he be smoking at a logging camp?*

"I don't have much money," Eric says. He might as well mention that right up front.

"How about a couple of untreated telephone poles?"

Telephone poles? Sounds insane.

"I think so. One question. Do you deliver?"

* * *

"Raiders of the Lost Ark, huh?"

Gruff Voice, a stocky man named Darryl with a neck the size of a tree trunk and a face lined like a grill, stands with Eric at the edge of a logging camp in Wiggins, forty-five minutes inland from the Gulf and Manyoaks. Behind them, chainsaws whine and heavily muscled long-haired men haul logs onto a squadron of eighteen-wheelers. Darryl wears earplugs and shouts.

"Yes, sir!" Eric hollers back.

"I can sell you two untreated forty-foot poles. Cost you fifty cents a foot."

"I'm not good at math," Eric says.

"Forty dollars."

"Including delivery?"

"Delivery? No way. You got to take them yourself."

"Sorry? It's loud. Did you say no delivery?"

"No big thing. Just strap those honeys across your hood. Folks will get the hell out of your way, I promise."

Darryl waits, then lets loose a phlegm-soaked laugh. "I'm fucking with you. Had you going."

"Yes, sir, you did."

"Don't worry, son, we'll deliver 'em for you. Say, two o'clock?"

"Great. Thank you." Eric opens his wallet and removes two twenties, the last of the cash from their *Raiders* secret cigar box stash, officially bankrupting the production.

* * *

As the boys staple Spanish moss to the garage walls and hang fake spiderwebs from the ceiling, a roar sounding like a crash of thunder drives

them outside. An eighteen-wheeler comes into view, backing up the
driveway.

"Holy shit," Chris says.

"The rails," Eric says. He untangles a gooey spiderweb and waves. Darryl, at the wheel, his bulging biceps hanging out the window, his no-neck
head craned over his shoulder, nods as he steers the semi from the street toward the garage. The semi, kicking up gravel and grass, screams like a jet
engine until Darryl lands it five feet from the open garage door. He grinds
up the emergency brake and jumps out of the cab. Four other loggers ma-
terialize. They form a line behind Darryl like backup singers.

"Where do you want 'em?"

"Oh, my *goodness*," Mary says from the porch. Her mouth hangs open.
"Eric. What—?"

"Telephone poles, Mom. I thought I mentioned—"

"I think I would've remembered."

Darryl pokes his head into the garage. "That the boulder?"

Eric beams. "Yep. A hundred percent fiberglass."

"Looks like the real thing."

"Thanks. Hopefully it'll look good on film. We'll see."

"So, a pole on each side, right?"

"Yes, sir. We need to make a ramp."

Darryl herds the loggers to the back of the eighteen-wheeler. "Gonna
need some help. These honeys are heavy."

Chris, Eric, and Jayson squeeze in among Darryl and the loggers and,
on Darryl's count, lift the first pole off the back of the semi, carry it into
the garage, lay the front end next to the boulder, and rest the back end onto
a four-foot stack of bricks they've built in the back of the garage.

"One more time, boys," Darryl says.

They gather around the back of the truck, lift the second pole, lug it
into the garage, drop the front of the pole on the opposite side of the boulder and the back onto a second stack of bricks. With these two sloping
rails, they've created a ramp.

"That should do it," Darryl says, herding the loggers back inside the
eighteen-wheeler.

"Thank you, Darryl," Eric says.

"Not a problem." He squints up at the porch, spies Mary. "He your son?"

"Afraid so," Mary says, but she's smiling.

*   *   *

The boulder scene. Take five.

Eric lining up the shots, Jayson manning the camera, Chris acting his ass off, they shoot Indy running out of the cave from every possible angle, the huge boulder crashing right behind him. Taking a break, wandering the grounds, Eric finds an abandoned shopping cart behind one of the cottages. He wheels it into the garage.

"What's that?" Jayson says.

"A dolly."

"Dolly shot. I like it," Jayson says.

"Get in it."

Jayson hesitates for only a second. Eric holds the shopping cart steady as Jayson climbs in. Eric hands him the camera.

"I'll push you next to Chris. Then we'll do a shot from the front of Chris running into camera."

"Cool. We'll dolly back."

"Right."

It works—Chris running, Jayson in the shopping cart, Eric dragging him along. Then, with Jayson in the shopping cart facing him, Chris gets an idea.

"Wait." He puts both hands on the handle and pushes the shopping cart. "Can you see my hands?"

"Nope."

"How's this?"

Chris runs slowly, pushing the shopping cart with Jayson in it, Jayson shooting up at Chris.

"Good," Jayson says.

"Let's try it," Eric says from behind the boulder. "Okay, everybody! This is a take! Five, four, three, two, *action!*"

Chris runs into camera, his hands out of frame, gripping the shopping cart handle, his face streaked with fear, the huge boulder filling the frame above him . . . rolling, rolling, ROLLING—

"And . . . *cut!* That's a print!"

*   *   *

"Well, that was quite something," the deep-voiced blond-haired man in the sport coat says. He turns to a twenty-something kid wearing shorts and a headset and holding a camera. "Did you get all that?"

"I did, Dave, yeah."

"Neat." David Elliott, the new cultural correspondent for the WLOX-TV Channel 13 *Evening News*, steps into the garage and corners Chris. "Can I interview you boys now?"

"Of course," Eric says.

"I'm ready," Chris says.

Jayson shrugs.

"Not gonna lie," David says. "When I got this assignment, I wasn't that excited."

"I hear you," Chris says.

"Then I get word that the kid playing Indiana Jones is the boss's stepson and I'm suddenly interested. Then I see what I just saw here and I say, *yeah.* You guys know what you're doing. This is really cool. I think, wow, I have to do this story. It's a must."

"What kind of camera is that?" Jayson says to Dave's camera guy.

"Chris, let me start with you," David Elliott says, shoving the microphone in Chris's face. "Why?"

"Huh?"

"Why remake *Raiders of the Lost Ark?* It's been done before. And pretty well."

"That is true. Like a lot of kids, I fell in love with Indiana Jones. But I didn't want to be like him, I wanted to *be* him. Be that cool, that daring. So Eric and I decided to remake the whole movie with our friends, kids we knew. Then I really could be Indiana Jones. That was five years ago."

"So, how's it going?"

"Great," Chris says.

At Eric's suggestion, Dave moves the conversation to the porch. Eric brings out storyboards and, with Chris, Jayson, and the cameraman packed in tight, leads Dave into the basement and shows him the remains of the bar set. They emerge from the basement drenched in sweat. Mary greets them with a tray of tall plastic glasses filled with ice water.

A few nights later, improbably, on the WLOX *Evening News*, his blond hair sculpted into a wavy newsman's do, David Elliott introduces a full one-minute segment about these kids in Ocean Springs remaking *Raiders of the Lost Ark* in their basement and backyard. *It feels surreal*, Eric thinks, as he sits with his mom and Kurt and watches Chris running from the boulder in their garage. Then Chris comes on camera, so comfortable, so cool, answering David Elliott's questions like a seasoned pro, followed by another short clip of Chris running and a quick shot of Eric's storyboards.

"Wow," Mary says when the segment ends. "I never would've imagined you boys on TV. On the *news*."

"Our fifteen minutes of fame," Eric says.

*   *   *

They drive in search of the Sahara Desert. They tool up the coast, then turn into the woods looking for sand dunes. They find shrubs, forests, landfills, vacant lots. They see nothing that could pass for a desert. At one point, they drive by a junkyard overrun with mountains of crushed metal, bashed-in bumpers, and mangled cars.

"We could shoot there," Chris says.

"You're kidding, right?"

"Eric, we're not gonna find sand dunes in southern Mississippi. We have to think out of the box. Let's go *Mad Max*. Think about it. Artifacts left over from an ancient civilization. Or better. This is it. A futuristic desert. Filled with metal and auto parts from the fucking *future*."

"I'm not going to dignify this with a response."

"I know. It sucks," Chris says. "But where are we gonna find *sand*?"

"The beach," Eric says.

*   *   *

They park next to the Gulf and walk along the side of the highway.

"It doesn't look like the Sahara Desert or Tunisia, where Spielberg shot," Eric says after a while. "It looks like Mississippi."

"Flat. No dunes," Chris says.

"What do you think?"

"I like the futuristic junkyard better."

"Let's keep driving," Eric says.

They drive for five hours. They drive into the woods, they double back, they snake along the coast, they head into the woods past Chris's grandparents' place. Driving through pine tree forests, they talk about how they will shoot the scene, how they really need sand dunes, especially since the storyboards call for Indy to be digging atop a freaking *sand dune*.

"The beach here sucks," Chris says.

"At least it's sandy."

"Look, I don't want to be the voice of doom, but this is fucked. We're driving around like idiots. We're not gonna turn a corner and all of a sudden it goes pine trees, pine trees, pine trees—*whoosh*—desert."

"Oh, my," Eric says.

He slams on the brakes, catapults Chris forward.

"Fuck! Give me a warning!"

"Red clay," Eric says. "Red freaking *clay*. And dunes. I saw *dunes*." Eric swivels his head, shifts into reverse, and floors it.

"Gaaaa!" Chris says, gripping the dashboard.

Eric backs up to a sliver of a gravel road. Wheels squealing, he pulls the car forward and bombs down the road, deeper into the woods. Within seconds, like a mirage, a plateau of red earth at least two acres wide appears— with several sand dunes carved into the earth. A quartet of bulldozers idles in the sand nearly blocking a sign reading FLEMING CONSTRUCTION. In a corner by a lone bare tree, a trailer teeters on cinder blocks.

"Welcome to Tunisia," Eric says.

*   *   *

Chris knocks on the door. His fist sags into what feels like tin. They hear a grunt and the clop of footsteps. The door creaks open on hinges in need of oil. A large man, a blur of muscle, a face smelling of aftershave, his fore-head creased in annoyance, stares at them.

"Hello, sir," Eric says. "My name is Eric Zala, and this is Chris Strompolos."

"Bo Jo Fleming. Pleased to meet you. Good-bye."

Chris steps forward, bathes Bo Jo Fleming in his high-beam smile. "We actually wanted to ask you a favor. I think you'll find it interesting."

He waits a nanosecond for Bo Jo Fleming to respond. Nothing. A shift of weight. A snort. A flick of his hand swatting a nonexistent flying insect.

"This is going to sound crazy, but Eric and I are remaking *Raiders of the Lost Ark*. I don't know if you're familiar—"

"Saw it."

"Great. Terrific. You may remember there's a sequence set in the Sahara Desert. We were wondering if you would give us the opportunity to shoot that sequence here."

Bo Jo Fleming's nose twitches as if he's gotten a whiff of spoiled milk.

"We would only need to shoot for a day or two, three at most. And in case someone happens to come by—so there won't be any surprises—they would see a bunch of kids our age dressed in traditional Arab costumes and others dressed as Nazi soldiers. We're very responsible. We'll clean up after ourselves. We'll follow any rules you set. So, what do you think?"

Bo Jo Fleming purses his lips as if he's about to hawk out a line of spit. "You boys are just dreamin'," he says.

He steps into his trailer and closes the door.

*   *   *

"We must shoot at that dirt farm," Eric says, steering the car out of the woods. "We can't do the movie without the Tanis Digs sequence."

"No doubt," Chris says.

"That's where Indy discovers the Ark," Eric says.

"I'm well aware."

"What are we going to do?"

"You think I'm done with that guy? We're coming back. Not tomorrow, not the next day, but soon. I'll offer him money, liquor, drugs, women, boys, barnyard animals, whatever he's into. I will wear him down. We *will* film in Bo Jo's dirt farm."

"I mean, what would Steven Spielberg think if he ever saw our movie without the Tanis Digs sequence?"

"He would think we were a joke," Chris says.

"Exactly."

Eric finds the highway that hugs the Gulf, eases the car into the right lane. "Can you imagine? It's ridiculous to think about it, but what if—?"

"Steven Spielberg ever saw our movie?"

"Yeah," Eric says.

"Oh, he *will* see it."

Eric glances at Chris.

"I'm serious. He will. That's a given. I'm going to take the movie to my dad in California. He knows people who are close with Spielberg. They'll put it right into his hands. Done deal."

"What do you think he'll say?"

"He'll love it. He'll congratulate us. Tell us we're amazing. Or—"

Eric waits. "Or?"

"He'll sue us."

* * *

They decide to shoot out of order and film the Well of Souls sequence next. In this scene, Belloq forces Indiana Jones and Marion into a pit filled with seven thousand snakes. Arguing and complaining nonstop, Indy and Marion fight off the snakes with lit torches, their bickering loaded with sexual tension. Finally, Indy sees a way out. He shimmies up a giant statue of a jackal and, clinging to it, pulls it over and crashes through a brick wall into an adjacent room where he finds a series of rotted-out, mummy-strewn catacombs. Eric figures they can shoot the entire sequence in two or three days—once they build the Ark, construct the jackal statue, create a sky-light, paint the basement walls with hieroglyphics and cave drawings, build a breakaway brick wall, and find seven thousand cooperative snakes.

We are going to do this, Eric thinks, wide awake, staring at the peeling ceiling of his bedroom. Sweating, he kicks off his covers and wanders out of the bedroom into the hall. *Steven Spielberg is going to see our movie. I'm so sure.* He rakes his fingers through his hair, paces, whispers, "Steven? If you can hear me? *Help.*"

*   *   *

Back in bed, still unable to sleep, his eyes fluttering, he pictures a hole in the basement ceiling. He realizes that the large basement room where they intend to create the Well of Souls lies directly below the main hall in the house. He flies out of bed a second time and charges down the staircase. In the hall sits a semicorroded long-defunct floor furnace. If he could pull that out, he should find an open space leading into the basement—the skylight for the Well of Souls.

"You can take out that old furnace," his mom says at breakfast. "As long as you don't leave a hole in the floor. My luck, I'll fall through it."

"I'll be careful. The furnace is kind of heavy. Not sure if I—"

"Oh, you can't carry it out yourself. You need to call someone. It's going to cost money, too."

"Forty dollars," Eric says, poking through his cereal. "They'll be here in an hour."

*   *   *

Momentum.

Eric feels it.

A slight wind at his back.

He feels it first when two burly men in wrinkled blue shirts, the names of two of the Three Stooges, Larry and Curly, stitched over their pockets, carry the old furnace outside and into their pickup truck without bashing into anything. Overlooking the space vacated by the furnace, Eric finds a removable metal lid, perfect for the skylight for Indy to be dropped down and for Jayson to shoot up, as well as protection for anyone traveling near the hole in the hallway.

So . . . *skylight*. Check.

Next, hieroglyphics.

Eric sets up on the back porch with a sheet of cardboard and a coffee table book his parents bought years ago at the King Tut exhibit in New Orleans. He opens to a page of hieroglyphics and copies the shapes and swirls onto the cardboard. He then cuts out the shapes with an X-Acto knife, making stencils. He's almost finished one entire row when Chris arrives, decked out in a dark suit with a blue tie, his hair spiked generously with gel.

"Saw the hole, man," Chris says. "Awesome."

"Cool, right? Where you going?"

Chris absently fumbles with his tie. "Mobile Bay, Alabama. Going to talk to"—he reaches into his suit jacket pocket and pulls out a letter— "Captain Deffley. He runs tours aboard these two dry-docked ships, the battleship USS *Alabama* and the USS *Drum*, a submarine. My mom gave me the idea. I wrote him and asked if we could shoot on his ships."

"What did he say?"

"Nothing. He didn't write back. Which is why I'm going there in person."

"Yeah. Talking to him one-on-one might be better."

"Definitely. By the way, I've been thinking about the Bo Jo Fleming situation."

"Good. When should we go back there?"

"I got a better idea. I have relatives in Florida. Couple hours from here. They got sand dunes up the ass. We can just drive there. Fuck Bo Jo."

"I don't know. We got a lot of stuff to cart. Plus about twenty cast members."

"Caravan, baby. Road trip. *Raiders* on location."

"Where's everybody gonna sleep?"

"My mom's minivan. Most of those kids are small, dude."

*   *   *

Eric finishes the stencils, paints the cinder-block walls of the Well of Souls with quick-drying umber, and, when the walls dry, tapes up the stencils. Takes him all day.

At day's end, Chris returns with hope but no promise.

Standing in Captain Deffley's office—the captain at lunch or at sea—Chris explains *Raiders* to the captain's second in command, a toothpick of a kid not much older than Chris. Chris waits while the kid shifts some papers and tries to appear important.

"So, do you think Captain Deffley will let us shoot here?" Chris asks.

"I don't know. He might. You have to get his permission."

"How do I do that?"

"Write him a letter."

The next morning, back in Mississippi, his suit retired to its hanger in the closet, Chris returns to the damp safety of the basement.

"It's not over with Deffley," Chris says. "I'm writing him tonight. And think about Florida."

"Oh, I will, definitely," Eric says, handing Chris a spray can.

They attack the stencils, slash the walls with black spray paint, feeling high off the fumes. Light-headed, they peel off the stencils, step back, and gawk at their wall of hieroglyphics.

*   *   *

Next, they gather spare bricks and build the breakaway wall. They pile the bricks carefully, staggering them, meticulously creating a self-standing wall. It takes hours. They endure several false starts, the fake wall approaching the ceiling, almost there, so close, and then a brick teeters, a row wobbles, and Chris or Eric supports the wall while the other catches the hurtling brick, then tries to dodge the ones that follow and prevent them from clunking the wall holder on the head. Finally, success. The breakaway wall stands on its own.

The boys tiptoe backward. Eric speaks in a hush. "We did it."

"We *rock*," Chris says. "Get it?"

"Shh. Not so loud."

"If talking makes the thing fall, we're fucked."

"You're right," Eric says, raising his voice, but only slightly.

"Boys?" Elaine, head low, wearing a sundress, sweeps into the basement. "Well, hello. How's it going in here?"

"Good," Eric says. "We just finished making the breakaway wall."

"Oh, wow. It looks so—"

She taps the false wall with one finger.

The entire wall collapses, crashes onto the floor in a deafening torrent of brick, rubble, and dust.

"—realistic," Elaine whispers.

"You don't really have to whisper now," Eric mutters.

"Ma," Chris says, his whole body trembling. "Go. Now."

"Yeah. You're right. Probably better if I take off. I just wanted to check in—"

"LEAVVVVE!!!"

Before Elaine can move, Chris, his face hemorrhaging red, blows by her and bursts out of the basement. He winds up and slams the door behind him. After a beat, the glass in the door's pane shatters.

"I can see my own way out," Elaine says to Eric, backing out of the Well of Souls.

*   *   *

They rebuild the breakaway wall, then test it by talking at normal volume and breezing by it trying to shake it down. It stands strong. They prepare now to take on the giant jackal statue. For that, Eric has a vision. Huddled in the corner of the next room sits a dead, rusted water heater, or, as Eric sees it, the body of the jackal. He and Chris drag the hunk of black metal into the Well of Souls set. Since Chris stands a head taller than the top of the water heater, they lift the water heater onto a barrel. They cover the barrel and the bottom of the water heater with a sheet of Visqueen plastic, which they form into a skirt and spray-paint gold. They create the jackal's head from an overturned flowerpot. Eric then covers two planks of wood with foam and black fabric, which he stretches and molds into the shape of the jackal's jaws. He rims the jaws with small finishing nails and cuts out tiny Vs from pieces of Styrofoam to make the jackal's teeth, seventy-eight, to be exact (Eric counted). He draws in eyes, then nails the completed jaw to the flowerpot head. The final touch: wide-outstretched jackal arms. Scrounging in the bowels of the basement, Eric finds two black poles—the arms. He and Chris suspend the poles from the ceiling using thin parachute-style cord they find in a pile next to a stack of broken toys and crumbling magazines.

On film, Eric assures Chris, the jackal will scare the crap out of you.

Next, they cover the floor of the Well of Souls with sand.

"All we have to do is cross the road, go down to the beach, fill up a few buckets with sand, carry them back here, and dump the sand on the floor."

"That's *all* we have to do?" Chris says.

"It's not complicated."

Not complicated, true. Just backbreaking.

They calculate that from the basement to the beach and back covers more than two and a half football fields. Filling the entire floor with sand takes dozens of trips. And a bucket of sand weighs a *ton*, especially uphill.

"I'm gonna kill you, man," Chris says, his back muscles burning, his arms straining, his lungs about to burst. Eric, behind him, lugging his own bucket of sand, grits his teeth and drives up the hill. Hours later, light-headed, panting, speechless—finished!—they sit in inches of sand, having turned the Well of Souls floor into their own tiny private beach.

"Do not," Chris says, "I repeat, do *not* call me if you think we're bringing this sand back."

Finally, snakes.

According to his *Raiders* research, Eric figures they need seven thousand snakes.

They come up with three.

They know a kid whose cousin works at Man's Best Friend, a pet store. The cousin arranges for the boys to borrow three harmless garden snakes for a day. The pet-store boy arrives in a minivan and comes out carrying a pillowcase inside which the three live snakes slither.

"Not that fond of snakes," Eric admits.

"Oh, I love 'em," Chris says.

"I'm so sure," Eric says, stepping away as the cousin coaxes the snakes out of the pillowcase.

That leaves them 6,997 snakes short.

"Movie magic," Chris says as he and Eric pool their cash and drive to

Toys "R" Us in Edgewater Mall. They purchase as many rubber snakes as their money will buy, leaving them 6,990 short.

They make the rest of the snakes out of a grungy garden hose, cutting off two-foot lengths and spray-painting them black.

"This is gonna work," Eric says.

"I hate snakes," Chris says, channeling Indy. "I hate 'em!"

*   *   *

The day they shoot the scene, Eric arrives on the set with an accessory he purchased months ago but has decided only now to introduce.

A megaphone.

Every director uses a megaphone. Eric's seen Spielberg himself speaking through his megaphone in several photos. Eric's sick of shouting at Kurt to pay attention or at extras to stop screwing around. The megaphone will amplify his voice and get everyone's attention.

What Eric doesn't know is that the megaphone pisses everybody off.

"Why does he need a megaphone?" Jayson asks Chris. "We're like five feet away."

"I don't know," Chris says, body-checking his hip into Angela's.

"I think it makes him feel like a director," Angela says, returning Chris's hip move.

"Okay," Eric says through the megaphone. "Places, everybody!"

"We're right here," Jayson says.

They shoot the sequence with Indy and Marion walking gingerly through the Well of Souls, fanning their torches in front of them, maneuvering around the floor filled with thousands of undulating snakes. Over the past year, Chris and Angela have stayed in touch, writing letters, occasionally speaking on the phone. Clearly, on camera, the sexual heat between them runs white hot, although Chris admits they've still never so much as kissed outside of the movie. Chris shows no signs of tiring of the relationship, although he seems to be hanging out with her less and sleeping over at Eric's even more.

"Cut!" Eric calls through his megaphone. "How was that, Jayson?"

"Let's take it again. I was off."

Chris says something to Angela. She laughs. They step around the dozens of toy snakes and pieces of garden hose.

"Get that green hose out of the way," Jayson says. "It's really clashing."

Chris mouths the word "clashing," picks up the green hose, and tosses it aside.

"One more time," Eric says through the megaphone. "And . . . *action!*"

*   *   *

The money shot—Indiana Jones climbing up the hideous jackal and rocking it back and forth until the statue tears off its foundation and falls forward, crashing through the brick wall in front of them.

Of all the stunts so far, casting his body into the breakaway brick wall worries Chris the most.

"What if the wall doesn't break?" he says to Jayson, who's lining up the shot.

"I don't know," Jayson says. "You might be maimed."

"I'll be dead," Chris says. "Falling headfirst into a brick wall? I will be *dead.*"

"It's possible," Jayson says.

"Thanks," Chris says.

"Okay, places," Eric says through the megaphone.

"Somebody's gonna wrap that thing around his neck," Chris says, low.

He slowly climbs up the jackal statue.

"And . . . *action!*" Eric calls through the megaphone.

"Here we go!" Chris shouts. He puts his weight into the statue and rocks it, thrusting his midsection into the old water heater, swaying back and forth.

"And . . . cut!" Eric says. "Jayson, how did that look?"

"Good. But, Chris, I'm telling you right now, it looks like you're humping the statue."

"Whatever," Eric says.

"Let's do the stunt," Chris says.

"Okay, you ready, Chris?"

"I'm ready. Let's do it."

"You guys ready?" Eric calls through the megaphone. "Kurt, I'm depending on you. Peter?"

"We're ready," Kurt says from somewhere off the set. Eric has assigned Kurt and Peter the crucial job of pulling down the wall precisely as Chris and the statue smash into it.

Chris clings to the old water-heater-turned-jackal. He grins into the camera. "Hi, my name is Chris. Five years ago, I started this movie. I think I'm actually crazy. So, here I am, about to die. This is my last will and testament. To all my friends, just go up to my room and take anything you want."

"Can I have your camera?" Jayson says.

"Yes. Eric, take anything. All yours. Angela, take anything you want. Because if I die—"

"You'll die a virgin," Jayson says.

"Yes," Chris says, trying to catch Angela's eye. "I will die a virgin."

"Okay, this is a take!" Eric shouts into the megaphone. "Are you ready, Chris?"

"I am ready."

Chris has a plan based on physics. Before he throws himself into the wall, he will lurch back, just a little, to make sure he has enough momentum to propel himself and the jackal forward.

"Four—three—two . . . *action!*"

Chris shoves himself backward a tad.

Unfortunately, he hasn't considered the physics of his own weight.

He falls completely over backward—out of frame—just as Kurt and Peter kick down the wall, which explodes with a crash without anything touching it, the jackal statue disappearing the other way.

Chris rolls out from under the water heater, alive. He raises his arms. "It's Miller time!"

Eric, on the verge of hysteria, lowers the megaphone and shoves his face into camera. "Jayson, tell me we can somehow make that work in editing. Or. *Something.*"

Chris does a jig through the set, his arms still raised in triumph. Jayson says nothing. Eric shakes his head as Kurt and Peter climb over the remains of the brick wall, *what the hell?* written on their faces.

Incredibly, years later, no one—film critic, filmmaker, film historian, or viewer—ever publicly questions the phenomenon of Indiana Jones and the jackal statue falling the wrong way out of frame and the brick wall collapsing for no apparent reason.

*   *   *

Barbara Salloum, venerable Southern lady and local institution, the longtime host of *Good Morning, South Mississippi*, phones Chris at the Riverhouse one morning and invites him and Eric to be guests on her show. She knows Elaine and she saw David Elliott's segment on the local news and she's fascinated. Two local boys, teenagers, remaking *Raiders of the Lost Ark* in their backyard and basement? What a hoot!

"This could be our break," Chris says to Eric.

"Seriously? *Good Morning, South Mississippi?* Barbara Salloum seems nice and all, but her shows are like, 'They just got a new line of blouses at the Edgewater Mall.'"

"She has a huge audience. Everybody watches her show."

"I guess so," Eric says.

"I'm telling you, man. This is gonna open some doors."

*   *   *

Theme music up. Close on Barbara *and*—

"Good Morning, South Mississippi!"

Barbara Salloum, put together in shades of blue, half-smiling into camera, half-stumbling through her opening, her hair rivulets of gold woven into a beehive, introduces the two young filmmakers sitting across from her: "Chris Strompolos and *Zaric* Zala."

She asks Chris, wearing his suit, his hair teased up, exploding all Flock of Seagulls down his forehead and covering his left eye, how "it all started."

As Chris explains the origins of *Raiders of the Lost Ark: The Adaptation*, we glimpse Eric beside him, dressed casually in a striped button-down shirt, khaki pants, and Top-Siders, recovering from being called "Zaric," his clothes choice on television a surprise since he's been known to wear a sport coat and tie to school.

Barbara swings the conversation over to Eric, whose name she gets right this time, and asks how he enjoys working on the movie. Eric says he's "intrigued by the challenge of it" and admits that he prefers directing to acting, even though there can be "a lot of stress and frustration."

"How far from finished are you?" Barbara asks Chris.

"We're about one-third finished," Chris says. "Another two months should do it."

"And then what?"

"Then we plan to show the film to Steven Spielberg," Chris says. "My dad knows some people who are close with him, so hopefully we'll show him the film and start our careers."

The show cuts to a clip of Chris running through the backyard woods, the neighborhood kids dressed as Hovito Indians in pursuit. Eric narrates. A second clip comes up, this one in the basement, featuring Chris as Indy punching a bad guy, flames shooting up on the bar behind him.

"How did you start that fire?" Barbara asks, back in the studio, real worry in her voice. "I want to know about that."

"We used rubbing alcohol," Eric says. "Very cheap, about thirty cents a bottle, and perfectly safe."

"Did your mother know you were setting the house on fire? You didn't burn anything down, did you?"

"Oh, no, no, yes, my mother knew. Everything was fine. Perfectly safe."

"What a wonderful project," Barbara says.

*   *   *

For the next six weeks, they film steadily. They complete the Well of Souls sequence, shooting Chris being lowered through the skylight, the opening left by the removal of the old furnace in the Zala hallway. They film Indy and Sallah lifting the Ark—constructed from plywood, overlaid with plaster, carved Styrofoam cherubim on the "Mercy Seat," and doused with tons of gold spray paint—to the Idol Room. They shoot a real live snake coiled in Chris's lap over a background of sophomoric penis jokes. They borrow Ted Ross's stepdad's Bentley to shoot a ten-second sequence with the character of Marcus Brody driving up to visit Indy at his house, a random residence in Biloxi that resembles the exterior of the house used in the original *Raiders*.

But at night, although he's managed to check off dozens of storyboards, Eric still can't sleep. He obsesses over how much they have left to shoot, how far away the end seems. He forces himself to smile at Chris telling Barbara Salloum that "another two months should do it."

When sleep doesn't come, he prays.

"Lord, if I ever had an opportunity to ask you one question, it would not be: Why did you create us? Or what is my purpose in life? Or what is humankind's destiny? No. It would be: Are we ever gonna finish this movie?"

At the end of July, the Tanis Digs sequence facing them and, with no place to shoot the Sahara Desert, the boys take another drive to the beach. Looking out at the Gulf, squinting as the noon sun blinds them, Eric says, miserably, "There is no way this looks like the Sahara Desert. We need dunes."

"I'm not sure the Florida trip is gonna happen," Chris says.

"Honestly, I haven't been counting on that."

"We should just go back to Bo Jo Fleming. Try again."

"Maybe if we took a different approach," Eric says.

"Like what?"

"I have no idea."

At dinner, the boys explain their sand dune problem to Mary.

"Well," she says, "you might offer him a waiver."

"Let's do it," Chris says. "One question. What's a waiver?"

"If I were him, I'd be concerned about a bunch of kids running around on my property, getting hurt, and then suing me. You need to have a lawyer draw up a paper saying that if anything goes wrong, Bo Jo's not responsible. Something simple. One page."

"We can't afford a lawyer," Eric says. "Unless."

Mary heaves a sigh. "I'll ask him."

A few days later, dressed in sport coats and ties, Mary along as backup, a one-page typewritten waiver drawn up by Eric's dad in hand, the boys return to Bo Jo Fleming's dirt farm. They knock on the door of his trailer and wait. Bo Jo pushes open the screen door.

"We brought my mom this time," Eric says.

"I can see that. Hello, ma'am."

"Hello. Mary."

"Bo Jo. You dressed up this time, too."

"We brought a waiver, too," Eric says.

"Waiver?"

"Means you're not responsible if anybody gets hurt," Chris says.

Bo Jo frowns.

"They had to explain it to me, too," Chris says.

Bo Jo takes the waiver Eric offers and scans it. "You know, this here is a high-capacity operation."

Eric, Chris, and Mary wait for Bo Jo to translate.

"If I was to let you shoot here, I'd have to shut down my operation at the cost of five thousand dollars *a day*." Bo Jo scratches his cheek, his eyes never leaving the waiver. "You boys prepared to pay me five thousand dollars a day?"

"We don't have that kind of money," Eric says softly.

Bo Jo slaps the waiver and wheezes. It takes the boys and Mary a moment to realize that he's laughing. He catches his breath, squints at them. "My wife saw you on TV with Barbara Salloum. She said, 'You better let those boys make their movie here, not Florida.' So, when do you want to start?"

"Wow," Eric says. "Thank you, sir. How's August eighth?"

"That'll work."

"Terrific. Oh, we probably need three days. Four to be safe."

Bo Jo Fleming folds the waiver. "You got two."

*   *   *

"Here we are in the Tanis Digs site," Jayson says, slowly panning the camera over Bo Jo Fleming's dirt farm. "Or Country Hickville."

Amusing himself, he flips the camera upside down, shoots the sky, the air, the ground, and then rights the camera and zooms in on the single line of Nazis marching toward him holding the Ark. Eric as Belloq, wearing his white suit and Panama hat, his stride erect, his expression serious, the guy in charge, heads the line. He stops abruptly, holds up his hand, drops his Belloq stance. "Nobody look at the camera!" he shouts. "Let's do it again."

The ten or so extras, fourteen-year-olds dressed as Nazis, grumble and slouch back to their spots.

After several more takes and Jayson shooting angles from behind the line of marching Nazis, then high above them in a very wide shot, Eric calls *print* and moves on to the next scene, a confrontation between Belloq and Indiana Jones, who vie over trading the Ark for Marion's release. Indy threatens to blow up the Ark with a bazooka resting on his shoulder if Belloq refuses to release her.

Standing in the center of a cluster of Nazis, including his evil henchman Toht, Belloq considers his choice.

"Okay, Jones, you win," Eric says in his starchy French accent. "Blow it up. Just blow it up! Blow it back to God!"

And then it starts to rain.

*　　*　　*

A dozen kids, their costumes sopped with rain and sweat, huddle under a canvas tarp as the rain pelts Bo Jo Fleming's dirt farm, washing away the day's footage. Jayson keeps the camera on, moves among them, filming reactions—obscene gestures of finger and tongue, kids' clumsy attempts at comedy, goofy facial expressions, out-of-context laughter. Some simply ignore him, stare at the rain. Eric says something, but the rain and another kid's voice drown him out. Chris, his mass of black hair awash over his forehead and covering his eyes, plants his face in front of the camera. "This has to be the worst fucking nightmare in the world. Life sucks."

Chris turns away, gazes into a lake of mud rapidly pooling up in the pounding rain. He shoves his face back into camera.

"Look at this. Four hours of work destroyed in minutes by the fucking rain."

Jayson pulls off him, goes back to the restless kids under the tarp, giggling, shoving each other, the brutal rain coming down.

Fade out.

*   *   *

Fade in.

The rain has stopped. Kurt works the camera. He pans the muck and finds a kid wading up to his chest in a gully full of mud.

Jayson.

Kurt keeps the camera on him. Jayson splashes around, then lies on his back and floats. A couple of other kids roll into the slop next to him. They stay for a moment, then drag themselves out, the mud dripping off their clothes. Jayson stays in the middle of the sludge, literally wallowing in the mud. Jayson may be showing off or simply enjoying himself. Perhaps both. Impossible to tell. Kurt trains the camera on him, watches him. Jayson finally stands up, the mud clinging to him like a rippling brown coat. For a second, you feel as if you're watching an outtake from *Lord of the Flies*. Something seems off, not exactly dangerous, but just a little north of strange. Then Jayson takes off his clothes, his bare butt to the camera. Off camera, kids holler, chant. Someone screams for him to turn around. He shrugs and faces front. He looks giddy, free, a nudist in training.

From then on, the day takes a sharp left turn. The temperature rises; the heat bakes the dunes. The kids in their white Arab robes, all sewn by Eric on Mary's temperamental machine, complain about burning up inside their costumes. When it comes time to shoot their scenes, they seem more inclined to screw around. It doesn't help that Eric impatiently shouts directions through his megaphone, which now seems like an extension of his arm, or that Jayson decides to operate the camera in the nude. Between scenes, the kids flop around in the muddy dunes, soiling the backsides of their white robes with blotches of wet red dirt.

By sunset, Eric, normally a model of Southern calm and patience, has become one frayed nerve ending. At one point, he screams, "Do it right!" into his megaphone. The last shots of the day have Arabs digging in silhouette as the light fades. Given the rain, the mud, Jayson's nudity, and kids screwing around, Eric feels fortunate to have completed even a few storyboards.

To save time, all twenty or so kids spend the night at Manyoaks, crashing in sleeping bags on the floor of Eric's and Kurt's rooms, the spare bedrooms, the living room. While most kids sleep, Eric washes the muddy Arab costumes and goes over the storyboards for the next day. He doesn't regret shouting at the kids, even though they're doing him a favor. Or he doesn't remember shouting at them. Or maybe he doesn't care.

Day two of the Tanis Digs sequence goes more smoothly. Eric announces first thing that they need to finish filming by the end of the day. The kids dig in. Jayson, with a prior commitment, arrives in the afternoon. Until then, Kurt and Chris operate the camera when they're not appearing in a scene. The rains never come, everyone cooperates, and the day goes quickly. In late afternoon, the skies threatening, Eric's voice echoes through his megaphone, "That's a wrap!" For a final good-bye shot, the kids once again huddle under the tarp as rain begins to fall.

But this time they flash victory signs instead of the finger.

YEAR SIX

"Where did you get this? From him?"   —Indiana Jones

1987.

Eric, seventeen, cast as Michael Saunders, the intellectual thirty-four-year-old *older man* in *Jenny Kissed Me* by Jean Kerr, Ocean Springs High School's spring production, stands in a corner backstage and studies his lines silently. He feels a rush of nerves, not because dress rehearsals start next week or he's afraid of going up on his dialogue, but because of the Kiss. So far in every rehearsal, he and "Jenny," played by cute Kathy Underwood, have only hugged. He wonders when they'll go for broke, when they'll kiss for real as stated in the stage directions. Of course, he knows all about Kathy's strong religious beliefs, her Baptist upbringing and being "born again." She even carries a Bible with her to school, which she sometimes reads during lunch. He respects that she's passionate about her beliefs and isn't afraid to show it. Some kids think she's weird and extreme. He doesn't see her that way. In fact, he can sort of relate. After all, he wears a tie and jacket to school, carries a briefcase, and has been directing the same movie in his basement for the last five years.

He also knows that high school kids can be immature. Two classmates kissing onstage always brings forth nervous giggles and a chorus of *woos* from the dumbasses in the back row. But you can't avoid the Kiss in Act Three, the pivotal moment in the play. The Kiss demonstrates Michael and Jenny's secret passion and defines their relationship. Without a convincing kiss, the play will not work. Eric decides that if Kathy backs off during their scene today and goes into that droopy hug again, he'll talk to her after rehearsal.

Wow, Eric thinks, *even when I'm not directing, I'm directing.*

* * *

Except for Kathy, the rehearsal sucks. Actors mess up blocking, blank on lines, enter scenes forgetting props; the crew screws up lighting and sound cues. Kathy, though, seems energized. The rehearsal picks up in Act Three. Eric speaks his dialogue, Kathy snaps back with hers, the give-and-take crackles, and then they come to the Kiss. Eric brings his lips close to Kathy's, expecting her to veer away at the last second, as usual. Not this time. This time she opens her mouth. And when Eric's mouth glances against her lips, she slips him her tongue.

His eyes glaze over. Then he slams them shut and greets her tongue with his own. A charge shoots through his whole body. He has no idea how long they French onstage because time stops. He does know that when they break the Kiss, Kathy flushes, sinks her eyes to the floor, and his face burns hot as an oven.

At school the next day in the scrum between classes, Kathy, toting her Bible, finds Eric at his locker.

"Oh, hi," he says. "Good rehearsal yesterday."

"Yeah, listen," she says. "Can I talk to you after rehearsal today?"

"Oh, sure, absolutely."

She swoops away, sliding into a herd of students thundering toward homeroom. He stretches to find her, sees her head bobbing above a pack of freshmen, her curly brown hair tossing this way and that, as if in slow motion.

He feels it again, the charge that swept through him when they kissed. He can't explain how, but he knows she feels it, too.

* * *

"We can't ever kiss like that again."

They stand in the hallway outside the auditorium. Eric, his eyes scanning her face, his mouth stuck in an **O**, forces himself to speak. "I agree," he says.

"I never . . . ," she says, fumbling to finish the sentence.

"You don't have to," Eric says, fumbling to find his own words. "It's fine." He nods stupidly at the binding of the Bible tucked into the crook of her arm.

"I'm really glad you understand, Eric."

"Oh, I do, sure, not a problem, really," Eric says, not understanding at all.

"Wow. Okay. Well, that's a relief."

"I totally get it. Totally. Moving on. So, I was wondering if you'd go to the prom with me."

"You are so sweet." Kathy fixes him with a look combining affection with pity. She sandwiches his hands between hers and squeezes. "No. I'm sorry."

"Ah. Okay. That's cool."

"But thank you."

"Sure. Don't mention it. Some other time."

Shock of shocks, Chantel Foretich asks *him* to the prom. Chantel is not only a senior, she is beyond hot. Chantel has a boyfriend who can't make it, an older guy from out of town who goes to college somewhere. Chantel considers Eric interesting and safe. Whatever. After being shot down by Kathy, his ego could use a boost. Kathy passes up the dance, probably so she can stay home and study her Bible. Not far from the truth, Eric soon learns. At the dance, Eric fields the usual barrage of questions, inevitable now since he and Chris have appeared on *Good Morning, South Mississippi* and twice with David Elliott on the WLOX Channel 13 news.

"Did you finish that *Raiders* thing yet?"

"Not quite. We should wrap it up this summer."

"You said that last summer. And the summer before that."

"No, I know. But this summer, definitely. For real. Chantel, would you care to dance?"

Feeling five hundred eyes on them, Eric steers the hottest girl in the room to the center of the dance floor. He places his chilly palm on Chantel Foretich's size zero waist and assumes the waltz position with the efficiency of a dance instructor. The music starts and Eric slides into his well-practiced box step, the image of Kathy, that kiss, her tongue, suddenly blinding him like a strobe light.

*   *   *

Eric's friend Mike, who attends the same Baptist church as Kathy and whose religious fervor matches hers, badgers Eric into attending a revival meeting in a stadium in Pascagoula. An evening to remember, Mike promises, because the fundamentalist evangelist preacher, the headliner, routinely blows the roof off.

They meet at the First Baptist Church parking lot to board a chartered bus, and as Eric and Mike find seats, they pass Kathy hugging a window, her Bible open on her lap. Eric waves. Kathy smiles, dips her head, her brown curly hair dances, and the electrical charge he felt up and down his spine during the Kiss returns with a sizzle and worms its way into the general vicinity of his heart.

I had no idea she would be going on this trip.

Which, of course, is a lie.

*   *   *

He stands among thousands of strangers, who don't seem like strangers, they seem connected somehow by blood, all caught up in the same feeling, their minds and hearts soaring and then taken over by a spirit they believe in, by a *goodness*, and the evangelist preacher shouts, wails, promises, cajoles, and convinces Eric that he should, right then, be saved.

"Will you let Jesus into your heart?"

Eric deeply feels . . . something. Before he can identify exactly what, his feet propel him off his spot, out of his row, down the concrete steps, into a mass of people, facing the preacher, waiting to be reborn.

About to board the bus afterward, he sees Kathy. He needs to tell her that he acted on his own, that becoming born again has nothing to do with her, nothing at all. He really felt moved, felt saved, felt *It*. He hopes that she doesn't think his feelings for her—his hots for her—played any part in it. He starts to explain. "Kathy, I—"

She throws her arms around him, holds him. "Shh, Eric. It's okay." She holds him, rubs his back in a circle, pulls away, and places her index finger over his lips. "I know."

"May I sit with you?"

"Of course."

They ride back to the First Baptist Church talking nonstop—religion, school, the play, and themselves. As the bus jerks to a stop, Eric tries again.

"Do you like movies? I mean, you know, going to movies?"

"I love movies."

"Would you like to see a movie sometime? I was thinking Saturday night—"

"I'd love to."

By the time the school year ends, they're dating steadily. When Chris returns from Long Island to resume *Raiders*, Eric introduces Kathy as his girlfriend. By July 4, they're deeply in love. By summer's end, they're planning their future together.

*   *   *

Closing out the previous summer with the Sahara Desert sequence, Eric felt energized. He longed to start year six and take on the most complicated and dangerous sequence in the movie—the seventy-six-shot truck scene. In the scene, Indy hijacks a Nazi truck that hauls the Ark away from the Tanis Digs. As he drives, he fights off Nazi soldiers—punches them, kicks them, and throws one through the windshield. At a climactic point, a Nazi soldier returns the favor and throws Indy through the windshield and over the truck's hood. To prevent being crushed beneath the truck's wheels, Indy reaches up and grabs the Mercedes-Benz hood ornament, which he accidentally pulls off. In desperation, he clings onto the truck's grill. He slides under the moving truck, comes out the back, lashes his bullwhip onto the rear bumper, and allows the truck to drag him along the ground until he pulls himself into the truck. He sidesteps his way along the running board, reaches inside, dispatches the Nazi driver, and resumes driving the truck.

Preparation. Rehearsal. Cooperation. Luck.

What they need to pull off this sequence.

First, they need a truck.

*   *   *

The boys don't find the truck. The truck finds them.

June 1987.

Chris, Jayson, and Eric sit on the ground beneath a tree in Eric's backyard, planning the truck scene. They need to find, for cheap, a junked truck that they can gut, paint, and push, either with another vehicle or by themselves. Jayson, looking for a comfortable spot, moves a few feet away, plops down on a soft spot in the grass. Something catches his eye.

"Hey. Whose is that?"

Eric and Chris scramble next to Jayson and see what he's looking at—the carcass of a 1964 Ford truck, two-toned, formerly gunmetal gray and forest green, slumped against the side of one of the cottages like a passed-out drunk.

"It's beautiful," Chris says.

"Belongs to Wayne," Eric says. "Cottage number four."

"Talk to him," Chris says.

"Not alone," Eric says.

They knock on cottage number four. Wayne, shirtless, long scraggly hair dusting a tattoo on his biceps that reads BORN FREE, opens the door, a hand scratching his belly. "What?"

"That your truck?" Chris says.

"Yeah. Rotted-out useless piece of shit."

"May we have it?"

*   *   *

First, they attack the engine. They get rid of it. Takes weeks. They take it apart with lug wrenches, pliers, a hammer, anything they can find to loosen and unbolt the motor. Chris wriggles underneath the hood and wails on the engine with a crowbar. Flecks of rust powder his face like fistfuls of rice thrown at a wedding. Wayne and his collection of hippie pals and biker buddies sit in front of his cottage and watch the boys work, laughing, hooting, cheering, the dismantling of the engine their daily entertainment.

Finally, the boys detach the engine. On Eric's count, the three boys lift together. The engine doesn't budge. *Huge* hippie-biker laughter.

Eric's sister's boyfriend, Eddie, comes to their rescue. His head wrapped in a colorful bandanna, he pulls up one day in his pickup. Attached in the center of the truck's bed swings a contraption that resembles a metal noose. A winch, Eddie tells them. He nudges his truck's belly up to the boys' old Ford, attaches a hook to the engine, starts up the winch, and lifts the engine out of the old truck and into his flatbed. Eddie drives them to the junkyard near the Riverhouse, where they dump the dead engine.

Next, they remove the trailer hitch from the back bumper. Enter Dontrelle, a biker friend of Wayne's rumored to have spent time "upstate," who travels with his own personal blowtorch. Dontrelle needs to be paid, in beer, which the boys pay for and Wayne supplies. Dontrelle flips down his welder's mask, mostly for effect, and blasts away, allowing the boys a turn or two. While Dontrelle burns off the trailer hitch, Eric wanders near the cottages and discovers four balding tires piled near a tree. These four can replace the flat tires currently on the truck. He and Chris roll the tires down to the truck and explain what they need to Dontrelle. They have to make certain that the truck doesn't run away from them during the stunt. Offering him more beer, they convince Dontrelle, after he's burned off the trailer hitch, to help them change the tires and weld on two of them.

Referring to drawings of the truck in stills from the movie, Eric and the boys drive to Ocean Springs Lumber, where they buy eighteen cans of army-green spray paint and a bucket of army-green flat. They buy and custom-cut two-by-fours to build a frame in the flatbed. They order two official army canvases from a mail order catalog. When the canvases arrive, they wire them taut against the wooden frame. They buy a cheap luggage rack that they put on top of the truck's cab, matching photographs of the original. For the engine's front piece, Eric attaches a grill he rummages from an old outdoor barbecue. For the Mercedes-Benz hood ornament, Eric bends one end of a cheap chrome towel rack.

Army green and Nazi ready, the truck requires a test drive. Jayson at the wheel, Eric and Chris push the truck around the loop of Eric's driveway. As they pick up speed, Jayson watches with horror as the asphalt flies by through a gaping hole in the floor where the gearshift used to be. He realizes he has no way to stop.

"Hey, hey! Slow down! Stop this thing!"

Brakes.

You can't remember everything.

Enter Kurt.

It's always annoying to give your kid brother props, but test scores, grades, and teachers confirm (and Eric admits) that Kurt is a genius. Especially when it comes to mechanics. He recruits Kurt to fashion brakes for the truck. Kurt wires a pulley system that he attaches to the brake cable beneath the truck. He then ties a hammer to a rope and runs that through the pulley. To work the "brake," all you have to do is grab the hammer and pull. Hard. The truck stops every time. Eventually.

Final touch, almost. Eric builds a portable wooden cage with a foam seat that can be hooked onto either side of the truck, allowing the camera operator to shoot directly into the cab as the truck moves. The day before the truck scene, he hooks on the cage to show Jayson.

"I am not sitting on that thing," Jayson says.

"It's perfectly safe. Watch."

Eric climbs into the cage and jumps up and down. "See? I weigh a lot more than you do. Perfectly safe. Come in with me."

"Man," Jayson says. "What I do for my art."

Final, final touch.

A wooden scoop.

A people catcher.

They connect the scoop to the front of the truck atop two poles that jut underneath the truck. The idea is to catch Chris and the kid playing the Nazi sergeant as they're thrown through the windshield over the truck's hood just before they roll under the truck and get crushed to death.

"Appreciate that," Chris says.

*   *   *

All told, it takes almost a month to shoot the truck scene.

They nearly give up the first day.

The boys find a location across from the Riverhouse, a dirt road lined with trees. Perfect.

Except.

"How are we gonna get the truck over there?" Chris says to his mom.

Jimmy Love III comes through. He asks Louis, a guy who works for him, to do him a favor: tow his stepson's dead hollowed-out shell of a truck from Manyoaks to the Riverhouse. The next morning, they hitch the truck to Louis's van. By ten o'clock, they're loaded for the shoot, ready to roll to the Riverhouse. By ten fifteen, the temperature hits 100 degrees. Eric rides shotgun with Louis. Chris, perspiration beading up, adrenaline pumping, takes the wheel of the truck. Fishtailing behind Louis, the truck grinds down the driveway, bangs onto Washington Avenue, and heads out to I-10, never breaking ten miles an hour. On the freeway, Chris grits his teeth, tries to ignore the sweat spilling into his eyes and the sounds of horns wailing and metal scraping. About halfway to the Riverhouse, a tire blows. Chris slaps the steering wheel.

"Shit! Louis! *Louis!*"

Eric, on vigil, catches Chris waving frantically. Louis stops on the side of the freeway. The boys and Louis scramble out, the wind kicking up, the heat rising off the asphalt. Every step on the road burns, the asphalt baking their shoes. They fear the soles will melt. Louis scavenges in the back of his van and finds a salvageable spare. Grumbling something about there not being enough money in the world, he fiddles with the jack and changes the tire. Chris climbs back behind the wheel. He feels dizzy, the adrenaline rush pulsing, threatening to lay him out. Without even looking, Louis jerks the truck forward and barges blindly into traffic, barely going five miles an hour, cars swerving to avoid plowing into them.

Finally, miraculously, they arrive at the Riverhouse. The trip, normally fifteen minutes tops, has taken three hours.

But at last they're here and they can start.

Then the rains come, washing out any chance of a shoot.

Chris groans, flies out of the truck's cab, stomps in puddles, flips the bird to the skies.

"Don't do that, Chris," Eric shouts. "That's all we need. More bad luck."

Jayson turns on the camera and films the rain and Chris sloshing around, pissed. Chris throws on his best Indy scowl, glares into the lens. "This is fucked!"

"At least we got the truck," someone shouts off camera.

Years later, in the credits, the boys thank Louis and his spare tire.

*   *   *

The truck scene calls for an antique black Mercedes convertible carrying Belloq, Toht, Dietrich, and a driver to lead the convoy. Eric knows that finding an antique black Mercedes in Ocean Springs is a long shot. He phones likely suspects and comes up with an acceptable substitute—a white convertible Volkswagen Beetle owned by a girl named Rachel who agrees to participate but refuses to allow anyone else to drive the car. Eric fits her with a uniform, stuffs her short blond hair inside a soldier's cap, and casts her as the driver.

The next day, the rain stops. By noon, the temperature reaches a balmy 105.

Eric pulls out his megaphone. Chris and Jayson, observing what they rightly interpret as grumbling by the cast, corner Eric for a heart-to-heart before the morning's shoot. They suggest he lighten up. They've been hearing words like "dictator" floating through the air.

"So, you're saying everyone hates me?"

"Not everyone," Jayson says.

"We're saying dial it down. Don't scream so much," Chris says.

"Anything else?" Eric says, trying not to look upset.

"Yeah," Chris says. "Bury the fucking megaphone."

*   *   *

Over the next three weeks, dodging another onslaught of hurricane rains and wind, the boys complete the most challenging and thrilling sequence in the movie. Buoyed by Eric's constant encouragement, in take after take Chris allows himself to be dragged on his stomach by the engineless army truck, pushed by another pickup truck off camera commandeered for the day, his only protection a second layer of clothes under his Indy costume. The first time he tries the stunt, dust kicks up all around him like a windstorm, pelting his face, searing his eyes, punching his nose and mouth with stinging clumps of sand. His gloved hands gripping the bullwhip, Chris scissors his legs back and forth, copying Indy's moves from the original. After fifty yards and twenty seconds, gasping, exhausted, the whip slips out of his hands and flops behind the truck like a tail.

Chris lies on his stomach, dust swirling around him. He lifts his head and spits out a mouthful of dirt. "I can't do it, man."

"You did it," Jayson says.

"You were wonderful!" Eric says. "Keep going! Chris, can you keep going?"

Chris waves feebly at Eric and hoists himself to his feet.

"Let's go for it!" he shouts.

Again the truck drags him on his belly through a hail of dust. They shoot from a different angle. They shoot from beneath the truck. They shoot Chris's legs. They shoot Chris's shoes. Satisfied, Eric moves on to the next storyboard: Chris on his stomach behind the truck, gritting his teeth, whipping his legs from side to side, pulling himself forward, grabbing on to the bumper, and climbing into the rear of the truck next to the Ark.

At one point, taking a break, his leather jacket filthy and soaked through with perspiration, Chris faces the camera. "It is so fucking hot. Like *so* hot. You have no idea. I'm probably gonna die. I'm so exhausted. I'm in such pain. Why am I doing this? I ask myself every day."

In midafternoon, they give Chris a break. They go to the second stunt sequence, turning the truck into a kind of mobile monkey bars. Kids in soldiers' costumes climb along the side and over the top; kids fling themselves into bushes; Kurt hangs off the top, then falls into a pond; kids throw themselves through the windshield and roll over the hood; Chris punches bad guys in the face and tosses them onto the side of the road. Eric rehearses the stunts until the kids respond with conviction and precision.

"It's all about preparation," he says, constantly, and as he watches the stunts come off without a hitch, he feels a tremor of pride.

It doesn't all run smoothly. At one point four or five days into the shoot, both Chris and Eric lose their cool at the same time.

In the shot, Chris hangs on to the front bumper, the truck picking up speed. When they finally edit the shots together—someday in the distant hazy future—Indy will come crashing through the windshield, slide off the hood of the truck, grab on to the hood ornament, which he breaks off, then hang on to the bumper and grille before he shimmies under the truck on his back. Now, though, Chris, wasted from the day, holds on to the bumper. He starts to lose his grip.

"I can't do it, man! Stop!"

"Stop, guys!" Eric shouts. "Slow down! Jesus Fucking Christ! Slow *down!* You want to kill him?"

At the end of those three weeks, Eric's preparation and professionalism, Chris's doggedness and wacked-out sense of humor, and Jayson's technical prowess and personal quirkiness—he again goes skinny-dipping and shoots scenes naked—push them through the seventy-six-shot truck sequence. They complete the final shots in an inspired frenzy and immediately throw themselves into changing the Nazi truck into a white pickup, which at the end of the Cairo street scene sequence crashes into a tree and explodes, killing Marion, or so Indy thinks. While slapping paint on the truck, Chris gets an idea. He dashes across the road and disappears into the Riverhouse. He returns with a small tripod and a 35 mm camera.

"We need to record this, man. Let's take a picture in front of the truck."

Chris sets up the camera and timer and poses by the door of the truck, scowling in Indiana Jones bravado. Eric, wearing unfortunate-looking white short shorts, folds his arms, leans against the hood, trying to appear cool and directorial. Jayson gazes off, throwing us a contemplative look, or maybe something on the horizon catches his eye.

They no longer look like children. They have teenage stubble and zero percent baby fat, and an air of accomplishment and confidence pops off the screen.

These few photographs that snap automatically will be the only "production stills" they will take.

*   *   *

The martini shot.

While Eric and Jayson touch up the truck's new white exterior, Chris calls the volunteer fire brigade, the Explorers. For a donation of thirty-five dollars, he arranges for them to meet the filmmakers across from the Riverhouse with their fire truck. Within the hour, the boys set up for the runaway truck crash and ensuing horrifying explosion. The Explorers in place, on Eric's count, the boys shove the truck directly into a sturdy tree.

The truck misses the tree and rolls past. *Cut!*

Take two.

They push the truck back to go position and try again. They shove the truck. The truck rolls up to the tree, stops, and gently cuddles against the trunk, unharmed. *Cut!*

Take three.

Back to go position. They shove the stupid truck and this time—*wham*—it slams into the damn tree, hard. *That's a print!*

The boys splash gasoline over every inch of the truck and torch it. Blue flames shoot up and engulf the truck from top to tire. The boys stand back and watch the truck crackle and burn and . . . *Cut and print!* The Explorers unspool hoses from their fire truck and drown the flaming truck. Chris hands the head Explorer thirty-five in cash, and the volunteer fire brigade heads home.

Eric and Chris consider the smoldering wreck, silently watch it smoke.

"That stupid truck," Eric says. "It was like a cast member."

"Are you going to cry?"

"I might."

"Do you want me to leave the two of you alone?"

"I'm over it. Let's junk it."

Chris borrows his mom's car, and they tow the charred and smoking hulk to the junkyard around the corner. They pull into the yard and, finding nobody around, dump the truck next to a wall of other corroded and unrecognizable crap—possibly its own discarded engine—and leave it there, its destiny, they imagine, to be crushed one day into the size of a toaster.

"I see a light at the end of the tunnel, Chris," Eric says as they drive back to the Riverhouse.

*   *   *

July 17, 1987.

The morning WLOX weather dude, the wacky one who shouts so loud his golden pompadour threatens to fly off, predicts the heat will be coming fast and sticky all day, smoking Ocean Springs like a barbecue. Typical. You wake up hot, and by midafternoon you're up to your neck in *swamp*. But today dawns anything but typical. Today the boys will blow up Belloq's face.

Jayson has the effect down. Weeks ago, he borrowed a new book on special effects from Chris. Jayson spends hours studying the pages that describe the effect, folding back the chapter so often that the binding breaks. The instructions committed to memory, he calls Eric and lists the materials he needs: a metal mixing bowl, a large spoon, a box of straws, a box of gelatin, a jar of dental plaster, and a shotgun.

The morning of the effect, Eric glances at himself in the downstairs bathroom mirror. Reddish stubble sprouting, long eyelashes, rust-colored eyebrows, thick brown hair. Dashing. He pictures himself a young Paul Freeman, Belloq in the original.

"Let's do zis," he says in Belloq's French accent.

He grabs a shower cap and stretches it over his head.

*   *   *

Consulting with Jayson, Eric envisions the exploding face effect in fifteen steps and jots them down in his notebook:

> 1-*Make plaster mold of my face. Remove.*
>
> 2-*Mix red gelatin. Pour into impression of Eric's face in "plaster bowl."*
>
> 3-*Take plastic skull bought from hobby store, pack cranium with Jayson's secret recipe of fake brains and gore.*
>
> 4-*Place plastic skull facedown in gelatin-filled bowl, lining up skull eye sockets with the plaster mold's eyes.*
>
> 5-*Put "plaster bowl" filled with red gelatin and facedown plastic skull into Mom's fridge to chill and harden. Chris, do not eat!*
>
> 6-*When gelatin hardens, remove "plaster bowl" from fridge.*
>
> 7-*Flip skull onto counter. Lie on nest of old towels.*
>
> 8-*GENTLY lift plaster mold off, revealing plastic skull encased within an outer layer of hardened red gelatin.*
>
> 9-*Paint surface—over the blood and gore layer—with flesh-colored paint. Paint in Eric's eyes, nose, lips, and screaming mouth. Face should look like me!*
>
> 10-*Once dry, stick fake head-skull onto a pike.*
>
> 11-*Slide pike with fake head into torso stand. Drape on Belloq*

costume—Hebrew High Priest robes and headdress that I wear
in melting scene.
12-*Film shot of fake screaming head wearing my costume.*
13-*With camera running, fire shotgun at head and blow it up. Be*
sure to blow up fake head, not mine!
14-*Put on costume. Film shot of me really screaming.*
15-*In editing, cut from shot of me screaming—to shot of ghosts—*
then back to fake head exploding. Seamless!

Eric pulls out two separate storyboards, one of a face melting, one of a face exploding. Beneath each drawing, he writes specific instructions. He's got every angle covered.

*   *   *

In *Raiders*, when the bad guys open the Ark, spirits shoot out and flitter here and there, circling, serene and mesmerizing. Then they turn horrific and attack the Nazis, going right for their faces. As the spirit dives into Belloq's face, he screams and his head explodes.

Eric's problem?

How to capture Belloq's scream inside the mold.

The dental plaster Jayson bought takes thirty minutes to dry. No way Eric can keep his mouth open in a scream for thirty minutes straight. He needs to wedge something into his mouth that will keep his face contorted in scream position while the plaster dries.

He rummages through the fridge and finds a pear.

He carves a section away with a knife and stuffs the pear slice into his mouth. He checks his expression in the mirror. He blinks in amazement. His expression nearly duplicates Paul Freeman's screaming face in the original.

*   *   *

Eric, the pear cupped in his hand, shower cap yanked over his hair like a cafeteria worker, pushes through the screen door onto the back porch and finds Chris and Jayson at work. His mom, arms folded, stands to the side. Since they almost burned down the house and nearly incinerated her son, Mary has kept close tabs on the production. Chris, on hands and knees, covers the final square of the floor with newspaper, then picks up a faded lime-green deck chair and places it down in the center of the porch.

Chris stands and grins at Eric's shower cap. "Jayson, your date's here."

Jayson grunts, doesn't look up. He's too preoccupied stirring a white pasty concoction in a metal mixing bowl.

"Well, it looks like you boys have everything under control," Mary says.

"Looks can be deceiving," Eric says.

"That I know. If you need anything, holler. I'll be working in the office."

"We will, thanks, Mom," Eric says.

"Hard to take you seriously, Eric, with that on your head," Mary says, heading inside, Chris's laughter trailing behind her.

"This is exactly how Chris Walas did the original effect," Jayson says, eyes fixated by his deliberate stirring motion. "It's like we're re-creating history."

Chris and Eric grunt in agreement.

"That should do it," Jayson says. He halts the stirring, pats his palms dry on the bottom of his fraying tee. He looks at Eric for the first time, snickers at the shower cap.

"What?" Eric says. "I don't want to get a bunch of plaster in my hair."

"Wuss," Chris says.

"I'm ready," Jayson says.

"Chris." Eric's eyes cloud. Chris reads something in them. Concern.

"I'm with you all the way," Chris says. "I'll give you the blow-by-blow."

"Good. That's what I want. Thanks."

Eric lowers himself into the deck chair. He adjusts the shower cap, flattens the top, shows the guys the browning slice of pear, and sticks it in his mouth.

"Did you forget this part?" Jayson says. "You won't be able to breathe."

"Umph?" Eric says.

Jayson produces a box of straws, eases one out, and, with scissors he pulls from his back pocket, snips the straw in half. He inserts a half into each of Eric's nostrils.

"Breathing tubes," Jayson says.

Chris steps back and studies Eric—shower cap stretched over his head, mouth in scream position propped open by a piece of brown pear, straws stuck up his nose. "Damn, you look sexy."

"Hold your head back," Jayson says.

Eric closes his eyes and leans back. Jayson spoons out a heaping portion of gooey plaster and slathers it onto Eric's cheek. Eric flinches. Jayson holds until Eric relaxes, then spreads the plaster carefully as if frosting a cake. He ladles out a second spoonful and deposits the glop onto Eric's other cheek. Chris closes in, watching Jayson work, smoothing the plaster, forming Eric's face into the mold that they make into a fake head and blow apart with a shotgun.

*   *   *

I can't see a thing. Everything's black. I feel like I'm walled up in a tomb. Sound is muffled, too. I can hear people talking, but I can't make out any words. It's all glub, glub, glub, as if I'm underwater.

I need to tell Chris something. Shit! This damn pear. I can't open my mouth. My jaw muscles ache like hell. This was a bad idea. Who shoves a pear in his mouth for thirty minutes? Maybe I should just eat it. No. That would kill the effect. We've come this far. What I do for this movie. Remember—pain is temporary, film is forever. I have to keep telling myself that.

Damn, my mouth hurts.

Relax. Breathe. Out. In. SHIT. Plaster just went up my nose! Fuck! Okay, okay, okay. Got air coming in one nostril. That's fine. One nostril is all you need. Gives you enough air to sustain life. More than enough. I'm pretty sure. Did Paul Freeman go through this? Easy, Eric. Slow down. Slow . . . yourself . . . down.

There. Better.

See? It's just a little dark and your face is slightly uncomfortable. That's all. A little sore. A little tight. And—

Warm.

Tiny bit warm.

Getting warmer.

Think cool thoughts. Dipping my feet into a pool. Sucking on an ice cube.
Rolling around in snow. Sticking my head in the freezer—
THIS PLASTER IS SERIOUSLY HOT!!!
FUCKING HOT!!! I'M BURNING UP!!!!
Chris! Can you hear me?
CHRIS????
Glub. Glub. Glub.

* * *

Chris stares into Eric's eyes. Silver circles hard as nickels stare back. Chris leans farther in. "I think he's trying to tell us something."

"The mold looks good," Jayson says. "Beautiful."

"Eric? Can you hear me? The mold looks beautiful, man."

"It's just . . . ," Jayson says.

Chris narrows his eyes at Jayson. "What?"

Jayson points a finger at the mold that now encases Eric's entire face. He taps his fingertip on Eric's plaster cheek. The sound careens at him, a too loud echo. Jayson retreats, newspaper bunching at his feet on the porch floor. "Where's that jar?"

Chris slaps the jar of plaster into Jayson's palm. Jayson spins the jar, searches the label, stops, reads, his lips moving.

"Yeah," he says. "Shit."

"What?" Chris says, voice cracking.

"Okay, see, this is *industrial* plaster—"

"So?"

"It's fast drying. I got the wrong stuff. I meant to get *dental* plaster. There are way more kinds of plaster than you would think, and they're all in a row on the shelf. It's totally confusing. Bonding plaster, finishing plaster, browning plaster, undercoating, limestone, Venetian, gypsum—"

"Jay!"

"Yeah?"

"How fast?"

"It's already dry," Jayson whispers.

Chris whips around to Eric. He grips the mold with both hands.

Hard as granite.

Chris grunts and pulls.

*   *   *

Someone is pulling on my face!

Where's Chris? CHRIS!

Voices.

"Glub . . . grab him . . . glub . . . glub . . . one . . . two . . . three . . . pull . . .
PULL!"

OWWWW!

My eyebrows! They're stuck in the plaster like footprints in cement.

Stop pulling!

A tap on my shoulder.

CHRIS! CHRIS!!!

My voice bounces back at me.

*   *   *

Eric punches the air with both fists, then flaps his arms like a deranged bird. Jayson stares, stumped.

"What's he doing?"

"A pad!" Chris shouts. "Get him a pad and pen!"

Jayson scrambles into the house, the squeaky screen door whapping closed behind him. He's back in ten seconds holding out a pad and pen advertising Mary's insurance company. Chris gently places the pad into Eric's hands. Hands shaking, Eric scratches something onto the pad.

"He's writing," Jayson says.

"No shit."

Eric blindly thrusts the pad and pen in front of him. Chris snatches the pad, reads: "Help."

Silence.

Followed by the crackle and hum of teenage boys thinking.

After a long moment, Chris clears away the static, straightens up, speaks to the Gulf of Mexico.

"Get the toolbox," he says, Indy all the way.

Sneakers slap on the porch floor. The screen door bangs, hisses. Chris, all business now, moves his mouth near Eric's ear.

"Don't worry, brother. We're gonna break you out of there."

*   *   *

They begin with a hacksaw.

"This won't hurt!" Chris screams.

Jayson, miserable, the guilt washing over him, waves weakly at Chris to give it a go. Maybe Chris can slice through the plaster and form a ridge, a place they can grip so they can pull the mold off. Or maybe he can lop off small pieces, one at a time. He feels useless and full of blame.

Chris, his face reflexively folding into the Indy scowl, white-knuckles the hacksaw handle, aims the hacksaw above Eric's cheek, drops it down hard, and cuts.

The saw blade snaps in half.

"Shit," Chris says.

"This is all my fault," Jayson says.

A man possessed, Chris forages through the toolbox and, clanking through pliers, wrenches, files, and drill bits, pulls out a screwdriver and hammer.

"Back away," he says with a trace of menace.

He arrows the point of the screwdriver into Eric's plaster cheek and gently taps the handle with the hammer.

Nothing.

Which is a better result than before.

Chris taps the screwdriver harder. No give, but he feels the screwdriver creasing the plaster slightly, jabbing in, taking a mini divot. That's all the encouragement he needs. He goes for it. He cracks the hammer down, and—

Crrrunch.

A small shred of plaster pops out near Eric's nose.

"Yes!" Jayson shouts.

"Eric!" Chris shouts into the tiny hole.

"He's alive!" Jayson howls.

"Can you hear me?" Chris says.

"It's all my fault!" Jayson screams. He puckers his lips against the pin-sized opening in the plaster. "I'm so sorry, Eric. I'm so, *so* sorry."

With surprising calm, Eric raises his arms and mimes writing on his palm, as if he's in a restaurant, asking a waiter for the check.

"Get him the pad!" Chris says.

A flurry on the porch. Jayson, a handoff of the pad, Chris shoving the pad into Eric's hands. Jayson, fumbling with the pen, drops it, chases it as it skitters along the porch floor, picks it up, places it between Eric's thumb and forefinger like a chopstick. Chris, pacing, plowing a hand through his thick black hair, watching Eric as he slowly scratches out a line of letters. Eric finishes, nods his clunky plaster creature head. Chris and Jayson lean over the pad, read it together. Chris says the word aloud.

"Hospital."

*   *   *

Mary, in her office in the back of the house, works over a claim, fingers rubbing her temple, trying to block out the odd soundtrack pounding from the back porch: someone running, footsteps slapping, the screen door slamming, muffled, anxious voices. Mary doesn't like what she hears. Something's off. An earsplitting *clang*—tools knocking together?—and she's out of her chair.

*   *   *

A squad car pulls up from Front Beach, belching sour exhaust onto the porch. Eric hears the car door open and heavy footsteps climb the porch steps. A whoosh of someone's minty breath blows over Eric, and a deep male voice, thick and sure, whistles. "Damn, boy, what you got on your *head?*"

"Eric!" Mary swallows a scream. "What in the world is going on?"

"Mary," Jayson says, "we didn't want to worry you—"

"Jayson, I was right inside. I told you boys. Why didn't you get me?"

"Want me to drive him to the hospital?" The cop, going for *Magnum, P.I.* Failing. Because Eric's plaster head has him coughing to keep from laughing.

"No, thank you. I'll take him," Mary says, her mouth a slit.

"Why don't you just follow me, then?"

Hands help Eric off his chair. Arms lift him, guide him, Mary's occasional, controlled *I got you, Eric* sneaking through the nick in the plaster hive covering his head. Eric hears a car door open, a crank of a seatback lowered, and he's stuffed into the front seat. He falls almost all the way back as the door closes; then Mary lands on the plastic seat next to him, and the car jerks down the driveway.

"You're going to be fine, Eric," his mom says, and like a little boy, he believes her, trusts her. "I know you're in a lot of pain, but try to relax. Just tell yourself that it's only pain, that's all, and let it wash over you, and it'll go away for a little while."

He tries it. He lets the pain come, allows himself to feel it, to flow over him like water, and then, just as his mom says, it ebbs a bit, eases up.

As they drive, he pictures the hometown newspaper. The police report. His mom often turns to that page first, sometimes reads it aloud when an item leaps out that's ridiculous or bizarre, so small town it's funny.

"*Residents Spot Suspicious Squirrel on Holcomb Boulevard,*" she read aloud just that morning.

To distract himself, he imagines the headline in tomorrow's edition. "*Local Boy Gets Face Stuck in Plaster.*"

When the paper comes out the following morning, he's hit the headline word for word.

*   *   *

Shafts of light stab him. The smell of ammonia seeps through the plaster.

"Chris?"

The word bangs inside his head, an echo.

"I'm here, Eric. You're in the ER. You're gonna be fine. The docs are gonna saw that thing off your face. Gonna set you free, man."

Wait. My mouth works! Chris can hear me! But I still can't see.

He feels in a daze. He remembers now that the young orthopedic surgeon knocked off chunks of plaster with a sledgehammer, freeing his mouth and sections of his cheeks. The surgeon left to find a chainsaw and a posse.

"You look like something out of a movie," the doctor said when they wheeled in Eric.

If you only knew.

"You're not in any serious danger," the doctor said. "You're gonna live. But I don't see how we can get that off. You're gonna have to wear that over your face for the rest of your life."

But I can't see! What good is a blind director?

"I'm playing with you. We'll get that thing off in a few minutes. It'll be like sawing off a cast."

A hand presses his shoulder. Then footsteps. Then silence.

"Chris?" Eric says.

"I got you, man."

"I need you to do me a favor."

"Name it."

"Tell Kathy I always loved her."

Pause.

"You're not gonna die, man."

"Well, you know. In case."

"Okay, if you die, I'll tell her."

"Thank you. Means a lot."

"No problem." Chris waits. Eric can hear him clear his throat. "So, hey, quick question. How attached are you to your eyebrows?"

"My eyebrows? I love my eyebrows. I'm very attached to my eyebrows. Why are you asking me this?"

Chris swallows. "No reason."

"Eric, it's Jay."

"Hello, Jayson."

Eric feels a hand drop onto his arm.

"I want you to know that it's okay if you never forgive me. Because I will never, ever forgive myself."

"Jayson, I forgive you."

"You do?"

"I do. Now, please, shut the fuck up about it."

"Thanks, Eric."

"Don't mention it." Eric tilts his head up slightly, barely, searching for Chris's voice. "Chris?"

"Right here, man."

"What did they say about my eyebrows?"

"Nothing. Nothing about your eyebrows. Except, you know, they usually grow back."

Then the invisible medical team, flashing scalpels and firing up chainsaws, descends.

*   *   *

The orthopedic surgeon removes the rest of the plaster mask in front of an audience of interns and medical students gathered in a horseshoe around Eric. When the surgeon saws off the last piece, he hands a couple of chunks to Mary, as souvenirs. Hands shaking, she slips them into her purse. Then, instructed not to move, Eric lies completely still as the doctor runs water into his eyes to prevent dust from collecting. Eric keeps the fear at bay, following his mother's advice to allow the pain to flow, to accept it, then to let it pass, even as the water runs into his throat. Finally, Eric's vision temporarily impaired, lost in a blur the color of charcoal, an attendant wheels him out of the emergency room, the casualties his eyelashes, one whole eyebrow, and half of the other. He looks like the survivor of a strange lab experiment or nuclear accident. Until his eyebrows grow back, which they do, he uses his mom's eyebrow pencil to draw fake ones.

"They said you were unbelievably brave," Mary says, driving home, her calm long gone, her heart thumping.

"I'm scared, Mom," Eric says. "I'm afraid I'm going to go blind."

"It's only temporary, I promise." She reaches across the seat, presses Eric's hand. "You deserve something special. What'll it be?"

"Popeye's," Eric says, no hesitation.

With money so tight, Mary simply can't afford to treat herself and the boys to a meal out, even if it's only fast food.

"It is a special occasion," she says.

She turns off the highway in search of the nearest Popeye's Famous Fried Chicken.

*   *   *

Thinking through where he went wrong, Jayson arrives at an *aha* moment. He not only bought the wrong type of plaster, he left out a crucial step: He forgot to apply Vaseline to Eric's eyebrows and eyelashes.

"If I had to do it all over again—"

"You don't," Eric says, shading his eyebrow black, his sight returned. "You won't."

He does allow Jayson to take his picture, a close-up of him screaming, which Jayson will use for the blowing up of Belloq's face effect, Plan B.

Hesitant now when it comes to humans, Jayson builds a plaster mold from a mannequin's head. He fills the fake head with a concoction of his most disgusting blood and gore, his best stuff, and the boys return one night to the road by the Riverhouse where they shot the truck scene. Jayson sticks the blood-filled mannequin's head onto a pike attached to a wooden stand, and the boys place weights on the bottom to make sure the stand won't budge an inch. Next, Chris runs a series of extension cords, over a thousand feet total, from a slide projector by the mannequin, down the length of the dirt road, across the main road to the Riverhouse, to an electrical outlet inside. When Chris returns, Jayson turns on the projector, drops in a slide he had made of the photograph of Eric scream-ing, and projects that onto the expressionless blood-filled mannequin head. He then picks up a shotgun and aims. His wrists shake. He lowers the gun.

"I can't do it." He looks miserably at Eric. "I can't kill you, man."

"It's not me. It's my picture."

"It's your *face*. I see it in my mind all blasted up and blown to bits and gory and gross and it creeps me out."

"Just fucking shoot him," Chris says.

"It's all right," Eric says, a hand on Jayson's shoulder. "You're doing this for your art. When Steven Spielberg sees the movie, he will see this incredible effect and he will be dazzled and amazed. And it will be all yours."

"Right," Chris says.

"I do believe that Steven Spielberg will see this movie," Jayson says. "I always have."

"So pull the trigger."

Jayson takes a long look at Eric's face, the real Eric's face, nervously picks up the shotgun, and aims it at the mannequin. He pulls the trigger.

BOOM!

The shotgun blows a hole in the middle of the mannequin, clean. No blood, no brain juice, no gore.

"Fuck," Jayson says. "It didn't splat."

"It was pretty good," Eric says. "Maybe we can edit it."

"I'm doing it again," Jayson says.

He quickly patches up the mannequin, steps back, aims the shotgun, and shoots again.

BOOM.

SPLAT!

Perfect.

The boys shout.

Then for the third time, the police come.

A short wiry cop this time, younger, his face and fingers twitchy. He pulls his squad car onto the dirt road at a crawl, flashes his brights, idles fifty feet away, steps out, and waits. "Need to talk to you boys."

"Shit," Jayson says, the shotgun in his hands feeling heavy and hot.

"I'll handle this," Chris says. He slaps on his best grin, approaches the young cop like a drinking buddy. "How you doing this evening, officer?"

The cop's right cheek pulsates. "You got some ID?"

"Absolutely." Chris flips opens his wallet, slides out his recent driver's license. The cop pores over it with a penlight, hands it back. "Neighbor said he heard gunshots."

Chris laughs. "I can explain—"

"You find gunshots funny?"

"Oh, no, sir, not at all. They weren't actually gunshots. I mean, they were, but we're not shooting at anybody. We're making a movie. We were shooting at a dummy made out of plaster. I know. It sounds crazy. I'll show you." He jogs back to Jayson, lowers his voice. "Bring the pieces of the head over. I gotta get back to Dirty Harry."

"What? It's *dark*."

"Find them."

Chris, beaming, jogs back to the cop. "That's Jayson. Our special effects master. He'll be right over. This is all my fault, officer. I live right over there. I should've informed the neighbors. I just didn't think of it. Jayson! How you guys doing over there?"

Jayson and Eric, on their hands and knees, feeling for pieces of blown-apart plaster face, wave.

"Got some!" Jayson says. He sprints to Chris and the cop, who spreads his legs, cracks his knuckles.

"This would be part of the cranium that I shot away," Jayson says. "And this is blood and bits of brain—"

"Thanks, Jayson," Chris says, translated: *You're not helping. Go away.*

"Wait a second." The cop flashes his light into Chris's face, then shines the light toward Eric. "I've seen you guys before. Where was it?"

"Barbara Salloum maybe? Or with David Elliott on WLOX—"

"That's it. Channel 13 news. You're those *Raiders of the Lost Ark* kids."

"Yes, sir," Chris says.

"Damn. How do you like that? *Damn.*"

Chris grins.

The fucking cop's starstruck.

He runs with it.

"You remember Toht? The Nazi with the glasses? We're gonna melt his face off. Jayson made a mold, filled it with blood and goop and brain matter that he's gonna have pouring out. Just like in the movie. You're welcome to watch."

The cop laughs. "I would, but I probably should be off fighting actual crime. Oh. Here's your head back."

He hands Chris back the plaster chunks Jayson gave him.

"If you need anything, or if any other cops hassle you, just give me a call. Here's my card."

"Thank you, officer."

The cop waves over his shoulder, ducks in behind the wheel of his squad car, and starts it up, cracking his knuckles one more time for the road.

*　　*　　*

September 1987.

Eric and Kathy, hot and heavy, enter senior year a couple. *Not sure where we're going,* Eric thinks, *but wherever it is, we're going there fast.* He'd like to slow down but, well, he really wouldn't. He enjoys having a girlfriend, enjoys fantasizing about their future. They picture themselves married, living in a big house, raising kids, a proper churchgoing family.

First, though, college. Ever organized, Eric fills out his applications over the summer, targets NYU film school as his first choice, film directing his concentration. He likes his odds. He has the grades, the scores, the recommendations, the extracurriculars, and according to his college counselor, coming from small-town Ocean Springs, Mississippi, gives him an edge. Plus, he has a kicker, an ace in the hole: He's an actual movie director who's been directing for six years. Of course, he's been directing the *same* movie for six years, but . . .

The night before the start of Eric's senior year, he and Chris hang out at Manyoaks. Talk turns to Eric's blooming relationship with Kathy.

"We gotta hang out, man," Chris says. "I have to get to know this girl, scope her out, make sure she's good for you. Gotta give her the Chris seal of approval."

"I don't know," Eric says. "We start school tomorrow."

"I got another week before I go back to Long Island," Chris says. "And Mom and Jimmy are gone, man. As in, I got the whole place to myself."

"That sounds cool. Let me check out the homework situation—"

"Fuck homework. It's senior year. You're coasting, man. Give yourself a break. Bring her over tomorrow. I'll cook dinner. I've got killer wine. You have to do this. Because if I don't like her, she's history, man."

Not wanting to geek out, Eric relents. "The first week is kind of light. I guess we could come for dinner."

"Beautiful. I'll grill steaks. And tell her to bring a friend. It gets lonely in the hot tub."

*   *   *

They sit around the table in the white-walled dining room decorated with contemporary art, Eric and Kathy, Chris, and Kim Russell, Kathy's quiet, more than likely virginal friend. Chris has gone all out—tablecloth, candles, roses, steaks, salad, mashed potatoes, and infinite pours of full-bodied California red wine. Although only seventeen, Chris could pass for a raconteur in his twenties, a dazzling conversationalist, eager and appreciative listener, sophisticate, world traveler, and unabashed flirt. If Eric didn't know him, he, too, would be taken in by his charm and want him for his best friend. But *being* his best friend, seeing him operate through his own numbing wine haze, Eric feels something stir, a pang that's slowly starting to spread into an actual stomach cramp. He doesn't want to consider its origin—he tries to fend it off, tries to will it away—because he fears that this now acute pain has nothing to do with something he's eaten but with something that's eating him up.

Tipsy, in no condition to drive, Eric and Kathy stay the night.

"Chris is great," Kathy says, pulling a brush through her hair.

"Oh, yeah," Eric says, the pain in his stomach flaring. "I mean, I of all people know that. He's my best friend."

"You guys are different, though."

"Well, sure. Absolutely. Chris is . . . what do you mean?"

"I don't know. Just . . . different. He's funny."

"I can be funny. I admit, as a rule, I tend to be more serious."

"Plus he's been everywhere."

"Indeed. A world traveler."

"He's great," Kathy says again. She hits the lights, snuggles into Eric, the pain in his gut throbbing.

Chris invites them all back the next night, promises an even cozier evening featuring exotic music he's discovered from far-off lands and a home-cooked Greek meal this time, more wine, and a signature home-made dessert. This time, Eric identifies the pain that lacerates his stomach when Chris goes into a story about living in London, and Kathy—to Eric's vigilant eye—all goo-goo-eyed, guffaws at every damn word.

Jealousy.

Yes. That's what this is. White-hot jealousy. Burning through his gut. Laying him out.

"Hey, man," Chris says. "Eric."

"Huh?"

"You don't look so good."

"Yeah, I feel kind of funny."

"You're white, man. Like a ghost."

"I'm a little nauseous."

Chris stands up, arrives at Eric's side, his forehead creased in concern. "Why don't you lie down in the guest room?"

"I'll take you," Kathy says.

"I got him," Chris says. He lifts Eric by his elbow, steers him away from the table.

"Probably too much wine," Eric says.

"Could be. Or maybe you're coming down with something."

"Maybe. I feel sick to my stomach."

Chris opens the door to the guest room, maneuvers Eric toward the made up single bed. "Just crash right in here. You need anything, holler. We'll keep checking on you."

WE'LL keep checking on you? WE?

As in Chris and Kathy?

Wait. This is nuts. I'm losing my mind. I'm imagining the worst. I need to get a grip. I'll lie down for a few minutes, catch my second wind, then go back and join my best friend and my girlfriend. Nothing's going on.

"Thanks, Chris." Eric rolls onto the bed, tucks his knees into a fetal position.

"You okay?"

"I'll be fine. Thanks."

"Not a problem. And don't worry. I'll take good care of Kathy."

I may hurl.

*   *   *

Eric falls asleep in the guest room, black as a tomb. He wakes to high-octave laughing, the girls shrieking to the point of crying, begging Chris to stop, then applauding a punch line, a chorus of chairs pulling away from the table, scraping the floor, and the eager thump of footsteps climbing stairs. A door opens, some giggling, an electronic hum, then bizarre music, a mash-up of African beat, screechy sitar, and harmony in a foreign tongue blasts full throttle out of Chris's top-floor room. A pause. Then an ear-crunching banging above his head like hoofbeats, which Eric identifies as dancing—*Chris and Kathy?*—the thought enough to make him clutch his stomach and retch.

He jams the pillow over his head and somehow dozes again. When he wakes, Chris stands over him, his forehead again clawed in concern.

"How you doing?"

"Still queasy."

"Why don't you stay over? I'll take the girls home."

Eric shoots up to a sitting position. "No, I'll take them. I feel a lot better."

"You don't look so great."

"I'm just not used to such exotic foods."

"That must be it."

Eric swings his legs off the bed, searches for the floor, which spins beneath his feet.

"You better have Kathy drive," Chris says.

"No, no, yeah, I will."

"You sure you're all right?"

"Oh, yeah, much better." To prove it, Eric stands, waiting for his knees to stop buckling and for the floor to stop swaying.

"Lean on me," Chris says.

"No, thanks, I'm okay."

Lurching like a drunk, Eric swerves into the kitchen where Kathy and Kim wait, coats on.

"You look pale," Kathy says.

"I'm fine. Little shaky, that's all."

"Here. Take this," Chris says, pressing a Tupperware container into Eric's sweaty palms. "I made you some soup. I didn't *make* it, make it. I warmed it up. Clear broth. You gotta go easy."

"Aw," Kim says.

"What a good friend," Kathy says.

"Yeah," Eric says.

*   *   *

Eric summons the strength to drive. He drops Kim off first and then, swallowing the jealousy and rage sitting like a lump in his gut, shuts down and seethes in silence all the way to the curb in front of Kathy's house. Kathy breaks the ice.

"You feeling better?"

"Yes. Physically."

"What is that supposed to mean?"

"I think you know."

"Eric, I have no idea."

"Really."

Kathy reaches for the door handle. "Well, this was a fun evening. See you tomorrow."

"I know you have feelings for him," Eric says.

"For Chris? You're crazy."

"Am I? I know what I saw. I might as well have stayed home. You two probably would've preferred that."

Kathy rests her head against the passenger side window, stares at the dashboard. "You're very irrational right now. You really need to think about what you're saying."

"So I'm crazy? I didn't see what I saw? You and Chris acting as if you two were a couple and not us."

Kathy speaks slowly, her voice shaking. She seems close to exploding or crying. "Eric, I don't know what you think you saw, but whatever it was, you are insane. Yes. Insane. And wrong. Dead wrong. Chris is great. I like Chris. Why wouldn't I? He's your best friend. There is nothing going on with us. Period. You need to get a handle on this. Because you're accusing me of something that's *ludicrous*."

Kathy whams the door handle down and shoves her shoulder into the door. She pivots toward her house, halts and straightens up as if shot, turns back, and leans into the car. "Good night, Eric. I'll see you tomorrow. I love you."

Eric calls her the moment he gets home. He sits at his mom's desk, his late night refuge, and cups the phone as if imparting secret information. Although he doesn't feel remorseful, he apologizes. He blames his behavior on the stress of senior year, on college applications, on money woes, on the weight of not finishing the movie, on feeling under the weather, on anything that pops into his head.

"Are we okay?" he asks her after his litany of excuses.

"We're fine," Kathy says. "Better than fine. We're great."

Eric hangs up, the knot in his stomach tightening.

*   *   *

In two days Chris will leave at dawn for New Orleans and take the early morning flight to Kennedy. On the phone with Eric, Chris promises to stop at Manyoaks and say good-bye before he leaves. He talks of unrest in his mother's marriage and more vague travel plans to Europe. They speak of what's left for *Raiders*—the melting scene, Indy and Marion tied at the stake, forcing themselves to look away from evil spirits flying overhead, an effect created by Jayson using swirling silk puppets in a filled aquarium, a few odds and ends and pickups, and the submarine scene, a stumbling block since they don't have a submarine. Chris has written a second letter to Captain Deffley and received no reply.

The day before Chris leaves, Eric takes the bus home after school and waits for Chris to come by. They have not set a time. Eric doesn't mind keeping it loose and doesn't want to pressure Chris. He's sure he'll come over after packing and saying all his good-byes. He is, after all, heading to the East Coast for nearly a year.

Eric sets up in his mom's office and plows through his homework, which takes less than an hour. He checks his watch. Close to five. He calls Kathy to check in. Her dad answers. He says that Kathy hasn't come home from school yet. Eric hangs up, wonders if she forgot to tell him about an afterschool activity or meeting. He hasn't seen her all day. Not unusual. Easy to lose track of friends—or your girlfriend—in the vastness of Ocean

Springs High. Most days, Eric and Kathy see each other infrequently. They share none of the same classes and have been assigned different lunch periods.

Still—

He calls Chris. No answer. He tries Kathy a second time, and again her dad answers. Eric apologizes, wonders if she mentioned what time she'd be coming home. Her dad has no idea.

He waits forty-five minutes and tries Chris again.

No answer.

He calls Kathy a third time. Her mom answers. "She's not home, Eric. She went out. She didn't say where."

He thanks her, hangs up, his hand trembling. He gets up from Mary's desk and prowls through the room, feeling caged. The searing pain in his stomach feels like a hot spike. His head pulsates.

"I can't believe this," he says aloud. "I physically hurt."

He tries to think of a plan. His thoughts come in a jumble. Should he drive to Kathy's house and wait for her? Should he drive to the River-house and confront Chris? Because he knows they're together. He just knows.

He calls Kathy again. He decides that if her mom or dad answers, he'll hang up.

"Hello?"

Kathy.

"Hi." Eric lands hard in the desk chair, fights to find a voice level that doesn't quiver with hysteria. He forces out a monotone. "I tried to call you—"

"I know. My mom told me. Kim and I decided to go to the mall. Her mom dropped us off."

"Oh. I guess you forgot to tell me."

"It was a last-minute thing. We left from school."

"Ah," Eric says. He rests his forehead on his left palm. He squeezes his eyes shut, trying to wipe out the surge of jealousy that rages. He doesn't want to accuse her, doesn't want to ruin them. He bites his lip, searching for something, anything to say.

"Eric? You okay?"

The sound of a car crunching up the driveway jerks his eyes open. Through the window, he sees Elaine's minivan roll up and come to a stop. Chris hops down, heads into the house. He won't knock, Eric knows. He'll just bound in and find him. He feels more at home here than at the River-house. The screen door on the back porch whips open, sings shut.

"Yo, Eric! Where are you, man?"

"Chris is here," Eric says into the phone. "He's heading out in the morning. I'm going to say good-bye to him. I'll call you after."

"Oh, okay, say good-bye for me, too."

"Will do."

Eric hangs up, dropping the phone harder than he meant.

The timing. I know they've been together.

"In here," Eric says, his voice rising. He forces himself to stand as Chris crosses the hallway into the office. Chris stops, shakes his head. "Another summer shot to shit. Can you believe it? Where did it go, man?"

"I know. Time flies when you're having fun."

"Right on. Well. I'm leaving on a jet plane at the butt crack of dawn. See you . . . I'm not sure when."

"Just stay in touch, you know, as usual."

"No doubt," Chris says. "So, what's left? The submarine scene—"

"Yeah. And face melting, the stake scene—"

"One more summer should do it—"

"If we can get permission to shoot aboard that sub—" Eric realizes that he's been staring at the floor. He raises his head, looks straight into Chris's eyes. Chris turns away as if blinded.

Judas. Betrayed by my best friend. This can't be happening.

"Well." Chris whirls, walks to Eric, engulfs him in a bear hug. He bangs him on the back. Eric hesitates, throws his arms around Chris.

I'm wrong. I'm crazy.

They break apart.

"I better hit the road," Chris says. "I have to get up at like four A.M."

"So," Eric says.

"I'll stay in touch," Chris says.

"Yeah, me, too."

"All right, man. Hang in."

"I will. Safe travels."

And then he's gone.

*   *   *

I'm probably paranoid. That's all. But what if I'm not? What if my suspicions are correct? I'm driving myself nuts. I have to find out the truth so I can move on with my life.

He calls Kathy back and sets a trap.

"Hey," Eric says. "Chris just left."

"Oh, how was it? Was it sad?"

"No. It was upsetting."

"Upsetting? Why?"

Eric pauses. "Kathy, he told me."

Kathy pauses. "Told you what?"

Eric puts some hurt into his voice. "I asked him flat out. I asked him if you two had been together. He admitted it, Kathy. He told me."

She speaks so quietly Eric has to strain to hear her. "That is such a lie. I was at the mall with Kim."

I'm wrong. I've been such a jerk. One last shot and I'll back down. I'm going to call her bluff.

"Okay, fine. I'm going to hang up now and call Kim. Because that's not what Chris said. He said you were with him, Kathy."

She cracks. "Oh, Eric."

Eric feels his palms sweat. The phone slips. He grips the receiver with two hands.

"He picked us up after school," Kathy says. "We hung out for a while, then he brought Kim home and we went to dinner."

Eric's voice flutters. "Then what happened?"

"Nothing happened. We ate dinner, we talked, he brought me home. That's all."

Eric closes his eyes, needing to paint a picture, needing to see. "Where did you go?"

"Bombay Bicycle Club. In Biloxi."

"What did you have?"

"What difference does it make?"

"I want to know. I want to know everything."

Kathy whispers. "I had a salad. He had a burger. What else do you want to know?"

"What did you talk about? And don't lie to me any more."

"I won't. I'll tell you everything." Kathy holds a beat. "We talked about us. I told him how close we've gotten, but, you know, you can get crazy sometimes, jealous, and it makes me uncomfortable."

"And he said?"

"He just listened."

"Kathy—"

"He said, quote, 'Well, maybe you two aren't meant to be together and deep inside Eric knows it.'"

"He said that?"

"Yes."

"Sounds like a fun dinner."

"Are you through interrogating me? Because I've told you everything."

"What happened after dinner?"

"He took me home. He didn't kiss me, if that's what you want to know. He hugged me and then he left."

"You hugged?"

"Yes. What did you expect? A handshake?"

Eric's hands feel cold. He presses two fingers against his stomach. Weird. No pain. His head has stopped throbbing. He feels, shockingly, nothing. No sensation. No emotion. He feels dead.

"Are you mad?" Kathy's voice sounds tiny. She sounds like a little girl.

"I am mad," Eric says. "But it doesn't matter. You lied to me. You lied to me all week, over and over. When I tried to talk to you, you lied to me. When I suggested you had feelings for Chris, you said no. You lied."

"I don't have feelings for him. Not in the same way—"

"Stop it." The words echo back, jagged and hard. "It doesn't matter."

"What are you saying?"

Kathy starts to cry because she knows.

"It's over."

"Eric, no, don't. You can't."

She's sobbing now, her breaths coming in gasps, almost as if she's panting.

"I don't want to see you again, Kathy."

"Eric, please—"

He hangs up the phone gently, as if the receiver were fragile, breakable.

*   *   *

The breakup lasts four days.

To Eric, the four days feel like one endless day. He moves through each hour in a sort of zombie trance. He feels gutted, lost. Most of all—worst of all—he feels weak. He hates admitting that to himself, but it's the truth. He doesn't want to take Kathy back. He *needs* to take her back.

He calls her on the fifth day, asks if he can come over. Once he's sitting in her living room, he tries to play it cool, fails. His love surges back, along with his desire for stability. They once again declare themselves a couple, stronger and more committed because they have come through a crisis.

As for Chris, Eric cuts him enormous slack. True, he initially felt stabbed in the back, but now that he and Kathy have survived and are thriving, he sees no point in holding a grudge. He will admit that at certain times when he thinks about the night that Chris came over to say good-bye after having just left Kathy, he feels a rush of anger, outrage, and sadness all clumped together. Now, thankfully, he can keep those feelings buried, forever.

In January 1988, the Ocean Springs High drama club elects Eric president and names him director of the school play, *The Magenta Moth* by John Patrick. He casts Kathy as one of the leads. The play runs at the end of March, and Chris, back home for spring break, attends closing night with his mom. Afterward Chris hugs Eric, compliments him on his directing, praises Kathy's acting. Cool as he's able, Eric observes how the two of them interact. He feels a rush of relief when he sees that Kathy keeps her distance. Only the tiniest ember of jealousy burns through him, left over, he's sure, from the summer before.

*   *   *

A couple of weeks later, the play wrapped, senior prom and graduation upcoming, the arrival of college acceptance letters imminent, Eric stretches out on Kathy's bed while she sits at her dresser, applying makeup. They talk about weekend plans. Maybe they'll catch a movie, grab some food, go for a drive, or just hang out here, especially if Kathy's parents have an engagement and vacate the house. Suddenly Eric bolts off the bed, sneaks up behind Kathy. She shrieks.

"Eric! You made me streak my eyeliner."

"Sorry." He tightens his arms around her.

"You're an animal. I have to wash this off."

She twists out of his grasp, kisses him lightly, and disappears into the bathroom. Eric plops down on the stool facing the mirror and considers his reflection. He grins, wonders if he should surprise Kathy by drawing dark cartoon circles under his eyes. Go for some heavy metal or goth look. Shock the hell out of her. Why not? He's fumbling through her makeup pencils, looking for the right shade, when he sees it, wedged in a corner under the mirror, partially hidden by a tube of mascara.

Chris's calling card.

He edges the card out and looks at Chris's name and address engraved and embossed. Expensive card. Impressive. He flips the card over. On the back, Chris has written his New York phone number. Eric holds the card in front of him, stares at it, as if willing it to disappear.

"All right, let's start again," Kathy says. "And do me a favor, cowboy. Try not to grope me."

She stops halfway into the room, freezes.

"What's this?" Eric's voice sinks into the floor.

Kathy waits a millisecond. Her words tumble out in a hush. "It's what you think it is."

"Chris's card."

Kathy's shoulders crater between a nod and a shrug.

"Have you been calling him?"

"Sometimes. Mostly we write."

"You've been *writing* to him?"

Kathy makes her way to the bed, her arms extended as if she's sleep-walking. She sits at the tip of the mattress. Her legs begin to shake.

"How long have you been writing him? Kathy, for once, tell me the truth."

"Since he left. Since the summer."

Numb, Eric fixes his eyes on her.

"I'll never call him again," Kathy says. "I'll stop writing him. I swear."

Something whips down in front of Eric like a curtain. For a moment, he can see only white. He stands, jabs the card at Kathy.

"Tear up his card and flush it down the toilet," he says.

She looks up at him, her eyes wet, her nose running. "What?"

"You fucking heard me. Tear up his card and flush it down the toilet." He shoves the card an inch from her face.

The air in the room lies momentarily still, murderous. Kathy takes the card from Eric and drifts into the bathroom, Eric at her back. Trance-like, she lifts the toilet seat.

"Tear it up," Eric says.

Kathy looks at him. For one tick, Eric thinks she might throw the card at him and run past him. She holds his eyes, then breathes deeply. She rips the card in half, then in half again, then into tiny pieces. She opens her hands and the pieces of Chris's card flutter into the toilet like confetti. She reaches over and flushes the toilet. They stand over the bowl, watching the specks of Chris's calling card whirl faster and faster until the water swirls and the remains of the card, a hazy milky glob, disappear down the drain.

Without a word, Eric storms out.

As he's driving home, the anger hits him like a blow to his chest. He has no sense of the road, or speed, or traffic laws, or other cars, or other drivers. When he pulls into his driveway and parks next to the porte cochere, he has no memory of driving at all. He has spent the past fifteen minutes in a blind rage. He prays he will not see his mom or Kurt. He can't imagine how he looks or what he will say. He walks straight to his mom's office and dials Chris's number on Long Island, the same number Chris scrawled on the card he gave Kathy. Chris answers on the second ring.

"Chris. It's Eric."

"Whoa. This is weird, man. I was just gonna call you. I swear. What's going on?"

"You son of a bitch."

"What?"

"You motherfucking son of a bitch."

A scratchy sound through the phone. Chris shifting the phone to his other ear. A throat clearing.

"Eric. Man. Calm down. What—?"

"YOU MOTHERFUCKING BACKSTABBING SON OF A BITCH!"

Eric lets go. A nonstop torrent of bile unlike anything Eric has ever spoken, ever, gushes Tourette's-like, *motherfucking backstabbing son of a fucking bitch* the refrain, repeated, pummeling Chris.

He stops, or pauses, and Chris, his voice shivering, says, "What the fuck are you talking about, man?"

"Kathy, motherfucker. *Kathy.*"

"Jesus, Eric. She's got issues, man."

"Oh, yeah? *You* got issues."

"Listen—"

"No, you listen. You fucked me behind my back! You call yourself my friend? My best friend? You're a piece of shit! You're a fucking piece of shit! Forget it. We're done."

Now Chris heats up. "You asshole, you fuck, what are you doing? You're choosing her over me?"

"We're *done.* We're over. You are a sorry excuse for a friend."

"Oh, please."

"You know what, Chris? You go to hell. *Man.*"

A thousand miles apart, they simultaneously slam down their phones.

Eric slams his hand on Mary's desk. He wants to scream, throw something, bash his head into a wall. He paces—through the room, through the house—not knowing where to go, what to do, whom to hate.

"Fuck, fuck, *fuck,*" he shouts.

Then, for the first time since he discovered the card in Kathy's room and called Chris, he thinks of *Raiders.*

What now?

Six years of my life, gone.

We never got to finish.

He pictures boxes of videotapes caked with dust piled in a corner of some closet, mementos of—

Of what?

Of shit.

Of a shitload of wasted time.

Because I will never work with that guy again. Never. Ever.

*   *   *

As Eric fumes, Chris sits in the dark of his dorm room at the Knox School on Long Island and seethes, his chest heaving, too angry to think. The letter, crumpled, lies in a ball against the base of his desk lamp. Seconds before, he'd read the letter for a third time, then reached for the phone to dial Eric's number. He couldn't wait to read the letter aloud to him and hear him scream and jump through the roof.

After two years, finally, incredibly, he'd received the go-ahead in writing from Captain Deffley.

They got the submarine.

Ice

YEAR SEVEN

"Everybody's sorry for something."   —Marion

Late June 1988.
Two months after the phone call.

Eric, eighteen, soon to be a freshman film major at NYU, his relationship with Kathy solid, his relationship with Chris over, sits at the kitchen table and flips through storyboards he's drawn for *Raiders*, as he has so many times, for so many years. He taps the corner of each page as he turns it, stops at the shots they still have left to do and never will. Two sequences, really, the submarine scene and the final scene. He sips an iced tea, tucks an ice cube into his cheek. Sloshing the ice in his mouth, he becomes vaguely aware of a timid knock on the screen door.

"Can I come in?"

Chris.

Eric doesn't recall the last time Chris knocked. Maybe seven years ago when they first met. He's used to Chris barreling into the kitchen as if he lived here, on a beeline to the fridge, or taking the stairs two at a time charging up to Eric's room.

"Sure."

Eric stands stiffly as Chris pushes the creaky screen door.

"Hey," Chris says.

"Hey."

A pause you could park a semi in.

"You want something? Iced tea?"

Southern hospitality. Nothing like it. The last time they spoke, Eric called Chris a motherfucking son of a bitch. Now he's offering him tea.

"No, thanks." Chris fidgets, in constant motion. He talks on the move. Eric notices that he's put on weight.

"Heard you got into NYU. Congratulations."

"Thank you. I start in the fall. Who told you?"

"I don't remember. Jayson. Ted. Somebody. Word gets around."

"Right."

"Storyboards, huh?" Chris rams his hand through his thick black hair, cropped Indiana Jones short for the summer.

"I was just looking at stuff. I'll put those away." Eric doesn't move. He forces himself to stand perfectly straight. He seems to have gotten taller while Chris has gotten wider.

"I want to show you something," Chris says. He pulls a crumpled sheet of paper out of the back pocket of his jeans and hands it to Eric. Eric's eyes flit from Chris's face to the letterhead on the paper.

"I wanted to read it to you the night you called, but we sort of got sidetracked."

Eric stares at the letter, reads. "Is this for real?"

"Totally."

"You got the submarine?"

"Only took two years."

Eric, reading, says, "We can have it for a full day."

"Think we can shoot the scene in one day?"

"Yes. I do. Assuming we're well prepared, properly rehearsed, and don't screw around."

"Speaking for myself, I can promise the first two—"

Eric smothers a laugh.

"I shouldn't have done it," Chris says. "I was out of line." He pauses. "You still pissed?"

"Yes. I'm still pissed. Not as much as I was. But yes."

"You guys seemed to be fighting all the time. I kind of became her adviser or something. I thought I was acting in your best interest."

"That's not for you to decide."

Chris pats the pile of storyboards. "You're right."

"Thank you."

"Will you stop hating me if I tell you I'll never do anything like that again? Because I won't. I swear."

Eric wags his head. "I don't hate you."

Chris swallows, nods. "Thank you, man." A loud exhale. "So."

"So," Eric says.

"Here we are," Chris says. "Another summer."

*　　*　　*

A week later, they caravan to Mobile, Alabama, fifty miles away, to shoot aboard the submarine USS *Drum* and the battleship USS *Alabama*, both wading in dry dock, retired as museum ships, exhibits open to the public. Captain Deffley has agreed to allow the boys to film for the day but refuses to shut down the park. They'll just have to shoot around the tourists.

As they begin, everything looks familiar—Jayson setting up the camera and smearing blood on his face for his own amusement, Eric rehearsing actors, Chris goofing around with Angela, stealing a kiss on deck—but nothing feels the same. Once they start shooting, an unfamiliar air of formality takes over. They no longer appear to be a bunch of kids horsing around in front of a camera. This feels like an actual movie set. Eric directs with smooth authority. The actors, grown from precious eleven- and twelve-year-olds to full-bodied deep-voiced teenagers, respond by locking down their blocking, cues, and dialogue. And rather than having to smear on Vaseline and fireplace ash, seventeen-year-old Chris just takes a day off from shaving.

Years later, Eric and Chris admit to some tension between them, but on this day, they never show it. Eric transfers any tension he feels to his brother, Kurt, bickering with him over nothing every time he appears in a scene. Chris, while he never says anything, projects an unmistakable undercurrent of *let's get this over with* through every shot.

Tipped off by Elaine, David Elliott and a WLOX news crew show up in the afternoon to film a segment for the ten o'clock news, the third time he's done a feature on the film. With the arrival of Elliott, the boys lighten up. He interviews Chris, Eric, and Jayson and sets up next to Jayson's camera to shoot Chris swimming from shore to the submarine, where he will reach for metal rungs, pull himself up, and climb aboard. Before the shot, he catches Chris standing next to a sign reading WARNING: ALLIGATORS CAN BE DANGEROUS AND UNPREDICTABLE!

"They tell me this water is filled with alligators," Chris says, hitching his thumb toward the sign. "Not sure what I'm gonna do. I guess I'll just have to deal with it."

When Eric calls *action*, Chris, his stomach bulging against his Indy shirt and threatening to pop off the buttons, dives into the water and swims for his life. When he reaches the submarine, ten feet away, he hoists himself out of the water. Eric yells, "Cut!" and spontaneously everyone begins humming the *Raiders* theme, louder and louder, the anthem, their rallying cry, the period at the end of a long sentence.

*   *   *

They shoot at night. They dress the rear of Eric's house and the exterior of the basement for the opening of the Ark, the final scene in the film. Eric, wearing a priest's robe, incants some movie mumbo jumbo, the Ark opens, spirits fly out, swirl above, form a flock, and dive at the evildoers on the ground. Indy and Marion, lashed back-to-back to a stake, press their eyes shut, believing this will protect them from the wrath of the spirits. Employing easily obtainable items such as fans, tissue paper, baby powder, and dry ice, Jayson's special effects wizardry shines. Sadly, the people in the cast do not.

Perhaps knowing that they have come to the end, Eric seems impatient and cranky. Out of earshot, kids playing Nazis bitch and laugh sarcastically. Between takes, Angela abandons Chris and hangs out with some kid recruited to play a Nazi. They find a spot on the back porch, cozy up, and smoke. Chris, always confused by his relationship with her, knows he shouldn't care, but for some reason, he does. He wonders if he let it slip that he started seeing someone at school. Either way, Chris not flirting with Angela between takes signifies another part of the film coming to an end.

Unlike the submarine sequence, which they shot with focus and efficiency, the Ark sequence drags, each moment feeling like an hour. At last, Jayson ties Chris and Angela back-to-back to the stake. The final shot. There will be no dialogue. In the shot, Angela and Chris close their eyes and writhe as the spirits circle above them, their mouths open in silent screams. For the very last take, Jayson removes the lid of a cooler at their feet containing a slab of dry ice. Steam floats up, engulfing Chris and Angela in a mist. They roll camera.

"Cut!" Eric wants one more take. Just one more. The last, *last* one. Neither Chris nor Angela objects, but their lips curl in frustration. *We are so done*, Chris screams silently. *This is so fucking over.*

As Eric asks Jayson about the position of the camera, Angela reaches behind her and stretches her fingers in search of Chris's hand. He feels her fingers touch his. He reaches back and holds her hand until Eric yells, "Action."

"We never have to film anything ever again," Chris says, his voice laced with relief.

Angela squeezes his hand either in solidarity or because she misinterprets his statement of relief as one of sadness.

"Okay, this is a take," Eric calls, then adds, "The final take. Hopefully. And *action*."

Chris and Marion writhe, not very convincingly, but at this point Eric, too, has had enough.

"Cut and print," he says flatly.

Silence.

Seven years.

Seven years since four half-naked scrawny blond kids dressed as Hovito Indians holding shafts of bamboo ran across the backyard at Manyoaks, chasing twelve-year-old Chris.

Seven years.

They end with no celebration, no hugs, no tears, no whoops of joy or triumph, no toasts, no party.

Silence.

Angela walks off to find her new flame and light up another cig.

Eric collects the costumes, gathers props, mutters a low "Thanks" to the kids who played Nazis in the last scene and endured his crankiness. The kids drift off, most heading home.

By habit or instinct, Jayson keeps filming, sensing that sometimes the good stuff happens after the director calls *cut*.

"The movie's done, Chris," Jayson says. "How about that?"

Chris pushes his face an inch away from the lens and mumbles, "Who cares? Big fucking deal. Yippee. Hip hip hooray. Now we have to edit this fucking thing."

Jayson keeps rolling for a few more seconds, shuts off the camera. Chris finds Eric. Together, without a word, they put away the props and clean up the mess in the driveway. They don't even shake hands.

*   *   *

Six years of footage. Hours—maybe *days*—of videotape. Now to put it all together into something resembling a movie.

Chris's mom makes a call, arranges for an editing room to be available at WLOX every night. One catch. It's available only from 10:00 P.M. until 6:00 A.M. To edit the film, Eric, Chris, and Jayson, all of whom have summer day jobs, will by necessity become vampires.

They give themselves a few days to unwind. Finishing the film finally hits Eric. He feels a burst of energy, a sense of completion, then something approaching awe. *They did it!* Then he barricades himself in Mary's office and starts sifting through the boxes of videotapes. He freaks. *There is so much.* To fight feeling crushed and overwhelmed, he organizes. He writes down all the shots, creates a shot log, identifies the best takes and puts them in order on separate tapes. Eventually, over the course of years, he discovers that after they transfer his pre-edited tapes onto a three-quarter-inch master, which they will use to edit at WLOX, and when they transfer that onto a final three-quarters master after they finish editing, when they dub *that* onto a VHS version, the original film will have gone through five generations. Ultimately, they will digitize the film, the *sixth* generation.

"I don't have many regrets," Eric says years later, "but the picture quality makes me wince. If only we could have skipped a generation and found a more efficient way of editing. We lost so much picture quality. I regret that."

While Eric pre-edits the boxes of tapes, Chris crashes at the River-house. For the most part, he has the whole dark fortress to himself. His mom and Jimmy Love III never seem to be around, and when they do make an appearance, they're off in their own drama or, by the sound of their voices, at war. Obliterating himself on Jimmy's expensive Scotch, a bottle of which he's borrowed, Chris blocks everything out—the screaming battles beyond his walls, the battle fatigue that settles throughout the Riverhouse like a fog, and the prospect of editing *Raiders*.

He doesn't really want to think about the film, doesn't want to deal with it. He feels over it. To Chris, *Raiders* has become an unfortunate home movie, a crude chronicle of his childhood. He dreads looking at himself, his extreme fluctuations of weight, his operatic voice changes, his twelve-year-old chubby self swinging like an idiot from a vine, splashing into the river. He wouldn't admit this to anyone, especially Eric, but at times he feels ashamed of the whole thing.

*   *   *

Stuffed into the five-by-five editing room, Jayson sits at the control board, a long-haired WLOX techie on the wing, Eric and Chris crammed behind.

"Who am I talking to?"

"Jayson," Eric says. "He's our editor."

"Listen up. This deck here where you put your source tape, that's your master. The other one, that's your slave. You cue it up here. You got your in point, out point, preview button, pause, stop, fast forward, rewind, play, good luck."

He's gone.

"You got that?" Chris says.

"Yeah, no problem," Jayson says.

"He lost me at 'listen up,'" Eric says.

"We'll figure it out," Jayson says.

"If that guy can do it . . . ," Chris says.

"Exactly," Jayson says.

"Well, shall we?" Eric reaches into the cardboard box at his feet and hands Jayson the first tape.

Chris and Eric hunch over Jayson, their shoulders banging. They jockey for position, fight for space, realize there is none, give up.

"Good thing we like each other," Jayson says.

A closet, Eric thinks.

A coffin, thinks Chris.

*   *   *

They slog through the footage a frame at a time. Whenever Chris sees himself, he cringes. "I don't match. Listen to my voice. In one part of the school scene, I sound like myself. In the next part, my voice hasn't changed yet. I sound like Alvin and the Chipmunks." Jayson laughs. "It's not funny, man. It's painful."

As they plow forward, they debate quality versus continuity.

"Takes three and five are definitely the best. Let's go with those."

"But they're four years apart. In take three, Marion wears her hair short, clipped. In take five, she wears her hair long and wavy."

"Plus she has *boobs*."

"Go with the best take, man. Nobody will notice."

"*I'll* notice."

"Fine. Whatever. Let's just move on."

"Move on where? What did we decide?"

A week in, Jayson, bored with cutting the film to mirror the original *Raiders*, argues to shake things up. "Why do something that's already been done? I don't see the point."

"Because we're doing a *remake*. That's the point."

"Maybe we should push the envelope. Be creative. Think Cocteau."

"Chris? Help me out here."

"I have a fucking headache. And somebody farted."

Some nights, though, the three of them click.

The map scene.

The entire scene consists of a red line moving over a map of the world, showing Indy's trip from San Francisco to Nepal, across the Pacific. This begins as a Jayson solo project, his attempt at stop-motion animation. Eric provides the map, Jayson the red marker. They tack the map to a bulletin board in the garage and shower it with light from a row of clip-on lamps. Jayson draws the red line one inch at a time, moving the camera as he draws, filming for half a second. Then, repeat. Another inch, another half second of film. Beyond tedious. But in this way, jerky and uneven, the line moves. In the editing room, they smooth it out, speed it up. When they play the final version of the unbroken red line moving across the map of the world, the guys roar.

"We got it in editing," Chris says, allowing himself a rare 3:00 A.M. smile.

In editing, they also create the moment when a deadly dart shoots out of a wooden tiki mask and lands in a torch held by Indiana Jones.

At the time of the cave sequence, Chris and Eric found the mask lodged in the middle of a junk pile in Chris's grandfather's backyard. They then bought a blowgun at a psychedelic biker T-shirt shop in Edgewater Mall. Out of money, they went DIY on the darts, building them out of pieces of wire wrapped with masking tape around a small plastic ball. Eric stood behind the mouth of the mask, lifted the blowgun to his lips, and *pfft*. The dart shot across the room. Next, they built a torch out of a section of broom handle. They rested the torch in a corner of the basement and—*pfft*—shot the dart into the base of the broom. They briefly discussed shooting the dart for real into the torch while Chris held it.

"We'll get it in editing," Eric said.

"Thank you," Chris says.

"Too dangerous," Eric said, moving on to the bar scene in which he allowed himself to be set on fire.

They do get the dart shot effect to work in editing. They simply cut from the dart shooting out of the tiki mask to Indy holding the torch, the dart already embedded in it. On film, thanks to the magic of editing, the dart appears to fly out of the mouth of the tiki mask and stab into Indy's torch in one continuous shot.

The morning after they piece together the tiki mask-dart shot, Chris and Jayson stand outside the station as Eric hustles into his car. He's on his way to grab breakfast with Kathy before he begins work at Burger King in an hour.

"That was actually very cool," Chris says, feeling a rare moment of triumph.

"Way cool. You can do a lot in editing," Jayson says.

"You can even make me look good."

"We're talking about editing, not special effects."

Chris ignores him. "I could see being a film editor. You know, as a career."

"Oh, no doubt."

"I'm definitely going to give acting a try, or singing, but if that doesn't happen—"

"Wait. We're talking about you?"

"Yeah. Why not?"

"No reason."

They say nothing for a while, squinting as the sun rises behind the TV station, knifes their vision.

"You'd be a great editor," Chris says finally. "I don't know if I can sit in a phone booth staring at a screen sixteen hours a day."

"Yeah, well, you gotta be kind of a freak."

"Plus my ass would be the size of a Buick."

The summer drags on. In the editing room, sometimes stoked by watching the film come together, sometimes just plain antsy, Chris takes short, frequent mental health breaks. He bursts into the hall, paces, breathes, returns to his seat ready to focus. But by late July, he starts to lose it again regularly. He feels wasted, worn down by the endless nights, his head thrumming from the constant discussion of what he sees as minutiae.

"Which take do you like better, Chris? Two or seven? Or three? Three's not bad. Slightly different angle. Chris?"

Man. It's like a fucking eye test.

"Can I see them again?"

He wants to be responsible. He wants to care. He wants to maintain the same passion that he once had, that Eric still has. The truth is, he's lost. He's forgotten the purpose of the project. *Why did we even begin this?* He honestly can't remember. His whole body pulses as if it's about to short out. He pushes Eric to make decisions. He wants to get this over with. He hears himself say again and again, "That take's fine, it's *fine*. Let's move this along."

"After all these years, I don't want to settle," Eric says.

"I know. I agree. But we gotta keep rocking, man."

Now when they leave the station at 6:00 A.M., Chris feels drained. He drives home bleary-eyed, races up to his room, afraid he'll bump into Jimmy, who seems moodier than ever. Sometimes he puts off going to the River-house and stops for breakfast at Denny's, where Angela works.

"How's the editing going?" she asks, filling his coffee cup for the third or fourth time.

"Great. Hard work. You know, tedious. Taking forever. You look good on film."

"I bet."

"No, I'm serious. You look hot. That sex scene. *Man.*"

"Yeah, right, sex scene. It was a kiss. You were twelve."

"Still, you look good."

She puffs out a sigh, moves to another table. Now that the movie's over, they see each other rarely, and when they do, they strain to fill the long pauses that linger between them.

*   *   *

In contrast, Eric finds editing a rush. For years, images of the finished film have filled his daydreams. He's imagined how he would put the movie together, how the shots would fit, how he'd build performances, action sequences, special effects, the sound effects he'd choose, what the final film would look like, how it would play. Now, actually doing all this feels glorious. He loves comparing takes, loves plodding along but always moving forward, even a little, every hour. To him, it feels as if they're putting together a giant living jigsaw puzzle.

One night, at last, they complete their final cut and lock it down except for adding the credits.

"Wow," Eric says, his voice quiet. "I think we're there."

"I think so," Jayson says.

"Please tell me we're really done," Chris says. "I heard you say you *think* we're done. I need to hear we're *done* done."

"I'm ready to sign off. Jayson?"

"Yep."

"Chris?"

"Fucking *A*, man. Except."

Eric looks at him, blinks.

"I want to add something, one little thing." Eric tries not to gape. For weeks, Chris's mood has swung between squirmy and unbelievably impatient. Now he wants to add something?

"After the credits, can we end with a Jim Morrison quote? 'This is the end, my only friend, the end.'"

"I like it," Jayson says.

Eric doesn't love the idea, but what the hell. It's Chris's film as much as his. "Sure, why not?"

"And what about the credits?" Jayson says.

"I made a list," Eric says. "It's long. Basically I wrote down every kid I could think of and all the adults who helped."

"It doesn't matter how long," Chris says. "Just slap it on. But put the quote last. So, is this a wrap?"

"Well, yes, for the picture," Eric says. "We still have to add music and sound effects."

"That shouldn't take long, right?"

"What do you think, Jay? Another couple of weeks?"

"Couple of *weeks?*" Chris says. "Are you shitting me? I'll go insane. I'll kill somebody."

"But then we'll be done. We'll have our movie."

"Yeah, that's true," Chris sniffs. "We'll have our movie."

"You guys can start tomorrow night," Eric says. "I can't be here."

"Where you gonna be?" Chris says.

"I promised Kathy we'd go out when we locked picture. It's just one night."

Chris turns away, says nothing, shoulders heaving. Eric can see that he's pissed.

"Come on. I've never missed a night, ever. You guys will be fine. I'll jump right back in the night after."

Chris stands, stretches. "Yeah, we'll be fine."

*   *   *

The next day, after work, Eric calls Chris.

"How'd it go last night?"

"Great. We're done."

"What?"

"We finished."

"The whole thing? All the music, the sound—"

"Yep. The whole fucking thing."

"Are you sure? How did you do everything in one night?"

"I don't know. We did. It's all done. Totally finished."

Eric clears his throat. Chris huffs. For a moment, they listen to each other breathe.

"Wow," Eric says. "Great."

"Yeah."

"Exciting. Can't wait to see it. Hey, how about meeting me tonight as usual, you know, at ten, and we'll look at it together?"

"Cool."

"Okay. See you tonight."

"Right."

*   *   *

Ten o'clock.

Eric waits in the parking lot, his back arched against the outside of the TV station beneath the buzzing of the white WLOX sign. Even this late, the heat still hangs in the air, thick and sticky, but Eric feels chilled. He tilts his head toward the slate sky and waits. He closes his eyes, tries to find calm, hoping to feel Chris's headlights wash over him. After several minutes, he lowers his head and checks his watch in the light from the call letters. Ten fifteen. *Maybe Chris beat me here and he's waiting inside.* Eric pushes off from the wall and goes inside. Head down, he speed-walks to the far end of the building, dreading yet knowing that he will find the editing cubicle empty.

He finds the door closed, the lights off. He hits the overhead light and sees a note taped to the control board: *Eric, movie's done. Chris and Jay.* He stares at the note, balls it up, and lobs it into the wastebasket. He feeds in the master tape and sits at the edge of Jayson's swivel chair.

The film rolls. Chris and Jayson have popped in occasional snatches of music from the original John Williams score, much of which plays out of synch with the action on the screen. For the most part, scenes go by with no music at all. Chris and Jayson have thrown in a few scattered sound effects, miscuing the ones they bothered to slap in.

Eric watches, horrified. Chris hasn't finished the movie. Not even close. What he and Jayson have done is a joke. A disaster. He checks the time: 11:13 P.M. Hands trembling, he calls Chris. No answer. He hangs up, slumps in his chair. He lifts the phone, again dials Chris's number, hangs up before the phone connects. He doesn't feel right calling at this hour. He faces the control panel, hits REWIND, and views the movie a second time, noting on a pad all the sound and music cues they've missed or screwed up. As he watches, he feels physically sick. He can't believe that Chris really thinks he finished the film. They couldn't show this to anyone. It's a total embarrassment. He tries to get inside Chris's head. What made him do this? What made him quit? He knows Chris feels burned out. He's often said, "Guys, I'm fried." *Well, I'm exhausted, too.* But to come this close, to trash their movie now, after seven years? Makes no sense. For the rest of the night, for eight hours, Eric fiddles with the master, adds in a little more music, puts in a few proper sound effects, and lines up the sound to the video as closely as he can. Mostly, though, he presses RE-WIND, and then PLAY, and watches Chris's "finished" movie, feeling numb.

At 6:00 A.M., he packs all the videotapes into boxes, loads them into the trunk of the Honda Accord, and drives to the Riverhouse. As he approaches, he sees Chris's minivan idling in the driveway and Jayson climbing into the passenger side. Eric pulls over, hustles out of the Honda. The minivan starts to back out of the driveway. Eric circles to the driver's side. Chris sees him, jams on the brakes, rolls down the window. His face looks flushed, his eyes tiny red dots.

"What?"

"Where were you last night? You agreed to meet me in the editing room."

"Yeah, well, you saw my note. There's nothing left to do."

"Chris, come on. I watched it. It's not done. I was there all night." Eric feels a quiver in his voice. He waits for Chris to speak, expecting him to apologize for standing him up and to admit that they still have work to do. Instead, Chris raps his knuckles on the steering wheel.

"Chris," Eric says, a moan.

"*What?*"

"There's hardly any music. When there is music, it's not synched up. There are almost no sound effects. The ones you put in are messed up. Come *on*. We're almost done—"

"No, Eric. We are done."

"Chris, there are gaping holes throughout—"

"You didn't hear me. It's done, man. I'm done."

Eric feels his hands shaking. He pulls them away from his grip on the driver's side door and fastens them to his side. He looks at Chris, or tries to. Chris refuses to look at him. He stares straight ahead, his fingers ferociously tapping the steering wheel.

"Come on, Chris," Eric says softly, his voice cracking. "It's not finished. It's not."

"Stop whining," Chris says. "Just stop whining."

"But you know it's not done."

Chris whirls on Eric. "Fuck you, man. I'm *done*. *Fuck you!*"

He throws his elbow out the window, forcing Eric to back away. He hits reverse. The minivan jerks and screeches and peels out, buzzing by Eric. The van fishtails into the road across from the Riverhouse, the road where they shot the truck scene, stops, kicks up dirt, and tears down the street, past Eric's car, disappearing, leaving Eric standing in the driveway, weaving, lost in a cloud of dust.

THE LAST CRUSADE

"How odd that it should end this way for us." —Belloq

New York City, 1988.

They drive in the Honda Accord from Ocean Springs to Manhattan—
Eric stretched out in the backseat, Mary at the wheel, Kathy riding shotgun. Eric navigating, they follow the map and directions provided by the
Automobile Club of Southern Mississippi and somehow maneuver through
the confusing streets of Greenwich Village until they land curbside in
front of Eric's dorm at NYU.

"A little different from Ocean Springs," Mary says, allowing herself
to exhale for the first time since hitting the Henry Hudson Parkway. She
fishes in her purse for a couple of aspirin.

"Much different," Kathy says. "Overwhelming."

"The noise," Eric says. "That's what you notice most."

"So exciting, Eric," Kathy says.

"It is," Eric says. "I am. So excited."

Hard to be convincing when you're freaking out.

They help Eric move in, rolling gray plastic tubs filled with his suitcase, books, bedding—his life—down a sterile corridor, into an ancient
elevator, and up to his room, fourth floor, end of the hall. Kathy and Mary
unpack while Eric, methodically, meticulously, sets up his side of the room.
Then, facing hours in the car, his mother and future wife accompany him
back downstairs. He hugs his mom briefly, then holds on to Kathy, trying
not to lose it as she cries. He kisses her, promises to write, call, and be true,
then hugs Mary again and thanks her. He watches them—the two women
in his life—walk uncertainly down Broadway toward the parked Accord.
They get in, roll down the windows, wave, drive off, and fade away. He

turns around and begins his new life, holding off his tears until the elevator doors close.

An hour later, unpacked, he takes a walk across the street and explores
Washington Square Park, swerving in and out of a circus of street musicians,
sidewalk painters, food vendors, chess players, drug dealers, homeless poets,
underage hookers, and unfunny mimes. He returns to his room and discovers
his roommate moving in, hanging posters on the walls. Bruce. Flamboyantly
gay and chain-smoking. Eric's eyes begin watering. They introduce themselves.

"The smoking," Eric says, as gently as he can. "I have a problem. I'm
allergic."

"I'm so sorry. Sadly, nothing I can do about it. Why didn't you request
a nonsmoking roommate?"

"I did," Eric says.

By the end of the first week, Eric finds his way. He makes friends with
two guys on his floor and throws himself into his studies. For a directing
class, he buys a used Super 8 camera at a pawnshop and shoots roll after
roll of black-and-white film, developed for free at the school's film lab. He
carries a full load of courses and works part-time at the administration office. He devotes long hours to his studies, practically lives in the library.
He socializes rarely, as money permits, usually to see classic films at the
local art house. *I'm here to learn*, he reminds himself.

And to forget.

*   *   *

Chris, too, tries to forget.

A senior now, he applies to college, looking into schools that focus
on acting and music. He starts writing songs and begins to take his singing more seriously. His friends tell him he has a big clean voice. He
reminds them of Lou Gramm of Foreigner or Steve Perry of Journey.
He becomes obsessed with his music, and with Meg, his full-time girlfriend. He grows his hair long. He dresses in black.

He and Meg become inseparable. She's tall, blond, intoxicating, a living
fantasy. Arm in arm, they make a striking couple, a kind of rock star duo,
the Cobain and Courtney of the Knox School. Unlike in his relationship
with Angela, which excited him, frustrated him, and confused him, he

knows where he stands with Meg. Although he's only eighteen, he believes he could actually be in love. He tries not to think too much about it. He tries not to think about *Raiders* at all.

*   *   *

One gray evening in November, the sky the color of smoke, a light snow falling, Eric's wound opens.

Studying nonstop for an exam, he feels the urge to take a break, go for a walk, maybe grab a snack, and pick up some film stock at the film studies building. He strolls along Broadway, holding his face up into the frosty air. Then, for some reason, as if someone suddenly shoved a photo in front of him, he sees himself standing outside the Riverhouse, watching Chris drive away. *Seven years. Seven years wasted. My best friend, gone. What happened? What did I ever do?*

"Where do I go from here?" he says aloud.

The snow falls harder, starts to come down in lines. He pulls his coat collar up, rummages in his pocket for his gloves. He turns a corner and, with his head down, passes a guy walking the opposite way. They nod at each other. Eric walks a few feet and stops dead. It can't be.

Was that . . . *Chris?*

He whips around, starts to call his name, runs back to the corner. He's gone. He looks frantically right, left, retraces his steps. No sign of him. Chris has disappeared.

I'm snow-blind. Imagining things. Wishing things.

But it's possible. Chris goes to school on Long Island. He often comes into the city. It's *possible*.

"Chris!" he shouts into the graying sky. "Where are you?"

*   *   *

Ocean Springs.
June 1989.

The vision of Chris haunts him. But the eight months since the editing room mutiny have dulled his anger, softened his hurt. He misses Chris and mostly now feels loss. And because of his faith or his nature, despite the traces of hurt that linger, he forgives him.

As for *Raiders*, he feels robbed. What started as Chris's dream evolved into his vision. He needs to finish the film. Call it a personality trait or character flaw, Eric's drive and focus just will not let him quit.

But how to get Chris back into the editing room?

He finds the answer in the newspaper.

Indiana Jones and the Last Crusade arrives in Biloxi on Friday. Eric studies the theater listings and chooses a time. While he still has the nerve, he calls Chris.

"Hello?"

"Hey."

Pause.

"Hey."

"I know we're not speaking and all and this is awkward." Eric feels the heat rise in his cheeks. *Maybe this is a terrible idea.* "But I was thinking. Do you want to see *Last Crusade?* It's playing Friday at Edgewater. We could go to the two o'clock show."

No sound. Has the phone gone dead? For a moment, Eric thinks Chris has hung up.

"Okay," Chris says. "Sure. Why not?"

"Great. See you there."

Eric eases the phone down carefully. Chris may still hate him, but Eric knows he can't resist Indiana Jones.

*   *   *

No handshake when they see each other, no hug. Waiting for the film to start, they catch up. Eric speaks of freshman year at NYU, film classes, New York, his horrid pot-smoking slob of a roommate, making friends down the hall, the challenge of keeping the long distance romance with Kathy going. Chris talks about Meg, music, acting, starting the College of Wooster in Ohio in the fall, and dreams of exploring Europe on Jimmy Love's dime, which doesn't bother him because his mom can't really stand him anymore. A chill blankets them as they trade the events of the last year, two guys reading each other the news. As the lights dim and the previews roll, Eric second-guesses this whole afternoon.

Then the *Raiders* march comes up, swells, *The Last Crusade* begins, and they are ten again.

After the movie, they don't say much, but both feel the ice starting to thaw.

"That was pretty cool," Chris says. "I'm glad you called."

"Me, too."

"This was fun," Chris says. "So, okay, later."

The next day Chris calls Eric.

"Hey, man, I've been thinking. You were right. I think we should go back into the editing room and finish the film."

Eric feels his heart pump faster. "Cool," he says.

*   *   *

Elaine again arranges for the editing cubicle to be available from 10:00 P.M. until 6:00 A.M. at WLOX. Eric and Chris will proceed without Jayson, who has moved to Oakland, California, to pursue his dream of a career in special effects. They begin the next night. They settle in, grind from cue to cue. They work smoothly, without a trace of tension. They lay in the right amount of music and proper sound effects, bouncing suggestions off each other with ease. They work with focus and patience, and the time passes quickly. They actually have fun.

Putting in the sound takes most of the summer.

Then, finally, truly, they finish.

They dub copies for each of them and for Jayson.

This time, they hug.

And then—?

"You need to have a premiere," Elaine says. "Tuxedos, a limo, the whole deal."

"Where?" Chris says. "How?"

"You guys just make sure the movie is totally *done*. The way you want it. I'll produce the premiere."

*   *   *

They set a date. Elaine books an auditorium at a bottling plant in Gulfport. They send out invitations to everyone they can think of, from family
members to Chris's voice teacher to Eric's sixth-grade teacher and director,
Mr. Bienvenu, the mastermind behind "Survivors Have It Tough," to a
friend of Elaine's from *The Dick Cavett Show*. They rent tuxedos, and Elaine
hires a caterer and a white stretch limo. Jayson flies in from Oakland, Meg
from New York. They decorate the auditorium with potted plants and
props from the film, including the Ark and a Nazi banner. Eric and Chris
prepare speeches. Elaine rents spotlights that search the sky as the boys
arrive in the limo, her attempt to turn Gulfport into Hollywood for this
one night.

Local celebrities turn out. Barbara Salloum steps out of her car wearing a tomato-red gown and matching feather boa. David Elliott, in a tux,
arrives with a news crew. The boys emerge from their limo to the *pocketa-
pocketa-pocketa* of cameras flashing in their faces. Angela arrives solo and
seethes when she sees tall blond Meg on Chris's arm. Eric strides into the
auditorium with Kathy on one side and Jayson, wearing sunglasses and tails,
on the other. Eric's dad shows up, and Jimmy Love III in a white suit comes
in waving to the crowd, looking juiced and a little out of place. Elaine walks
in with her parents and escorts them to their seats. People jam the auditorium, fill every seat. The overflow stands against the back wall and along
both sides.

Eric briefly introduces the film. The lights dim, and the first-ever
and potentially only viewing of *Raiders of the Lost Ark: The Adaptation*
begins. For the next 100 minutes, the audience laughs, cheers, and applauds, and when the lights come up, everyone in the auditorium springs
to their feet. When they settle, Eric and Chris thank them for their gen-
erous response.

"I'm glad you liked the film," Eric says. "We could not have done it
without the unwavering support of two very special people—our moms."

To thunderous applause, Eric hands a bouquet of roses to Elaine and
Chris hands a bouquet of roses to Mary.

The rest of the night buzzes by, a high, with friends, family, and locals
gushing compliments, Dave Elliott conducting an interview, and even a
touch of awkwardness and melodrama when Angela bumps into Meg in
the restroom.

In the morning, Chris and Eric meet at the auditorium to clean up, collect the props, and carry off the Ark. As they leave the auditorium, still tripping from the night before, they hug and prepare to move on with their lives. They don't know then that—

Jayson will fly back to Oakland and stay there.

Kurt will enter MIT.

Peter Keefer, their "fire marshal" and former movie zombie, will disappear.

Angela will join the army.

Mary will marry Dave, a former air force man and gifted carpenter, who will renovate Manyoaks into a showplace.

Elaine and Jimmy Love III will divorce. Their marriage will sour so horribly that years later, after his death, Elaine says, "I did not kill him. I wanted to . . ."

* * *

Life without *Raiders*.

The thought sobers them both.

After the premiere, Eric returns to New York and Chris heads to Ohio, both intending to lose themselves in the next stage of their lives. Both approach college as preparation for their careers. At NYU, Eric immerses himself in directing, while at the College of Wooster, Chris commits himself to acting and writing and performing music. When they think of their time together on *Raiders*, they remember those days as fondly as others recall their best summers at camp or with family at the shore.

After a few months in college, Chris sticks his copy of *Raiders* in a drawer, relegating it to the back of his mind. He files it away as this crazy movie he and a bunch of friends put together summers when he was a bored kid in Mississippi. But at NYU, on slow nights in the dorm, Eric brings out his videotape and plays the film at the request of friends or curious film students, or just for the hell of it. As the months tick off and a new summer awaits—their first without *Raiders* since elementary school—Eric finds himself fielding a range of questions:

How did you do it? Who helped you? Were you really on fire? How much did the film cost? Why did you do it? What made you keep going?

And one question he continuously asks himself:

Does anybody care?

*   *   *

Summer 1990.

Back in Mississippi, Jimmy Love III comes through with a project for Chris and Eric, a paying gig that involves a car, a camcorder, and their moviemaking talents. They spend the summer on the road, driving all over the state making cheap TV commercials for small local businesses. In a typical spot, Eric directs and Chris reads voice-over copy. They film spots for Bypass Texaco, Gus's Auto Parts, Kimbrell Office Supply, Day Motors, Dr. Christy Graves, MD, and Rawls Saddle Shop, featuring Chris in a slick, convincing baritone, *"Because there's a little bit of west in all of us."*

They drive, they schlep, they film, they move on. Between stops, on long stretches and open roads, they talk. They talk as they never have before. They talk about *Raiders*, what the experience meant for each of them. Chris reveals that while the movie began as his idea, born from his need to *be* Indiana Jones, the project shifted into something that became more important to Eric. They talk about how they needed Chris's passion and vision to begin and Eric's drive, focus, and attention to detail to finish. Chris says that he once saw *Raiders* as a stepping-stone to a career in show business. He doesn't see it that way now. He's not sure what it is anymore, or even how he feels about it.

They talk about their moms, how they once shut down production but never withdrew their support. They talk about Mary's divorce and Elaine's remarriage, and how both events shook up their worlds. They put their conversation on hold to film a thirty-second commercial for Dutch Ann Pie Crust. *"Great to come home to,"* Chris reads, selling it. They pile camera, tripod, and sound equipment into the car, drive to their next stop, and continue talking.

Eric brings up Kathy. He tells Chris how deeply he hurt him and how angry he felt. Chris admits that he did try to steal Kathy. He doesn't really know why. A power play, perhaps. Maybe he saw that Eric had taken control of the movie, made it his, and he in turn wanted to take something away from Eric. They realize that they briefly became their roles—Indy and Belloq—living out their on-screen rivalry in real life. Chris apologizes, sincerely, takes full responsibility.

They film a spot for Concordia Bank, Chris punching the tagline, *"Rely on us,"* and head to their next appointment. As they talk, they feel closer than they have in years. Eric tells Chris about his senior thesis, a short film he's started outlining, *An Early Twilight*. He's writing a part for Chris. Chris says he'd love to be in it.

They set up for their last commercial of the summer, a spot for Bill Garrett Toyota. As Eric films, Chris reads the button: *"You're among friends."*

*   *   *

Spring 1991.

Kathy spends part of spring break with Eric. He shows her his haunts— Tower Records, Gray's Papaya, the NYU film department—and introduces her to his friends. They spend their last day in Washington Square Park, holding hands, horsing around, talking about their future, marriage, their life together. He puts her in a cab to the airport. He physically aches when the cab pulls away. A few nights later, he returns from the library to find Kathy's voice on his answering machine. She won't be home to receive his usual phone call. She's spending the night with her friend Mindy.

Eric decides to surprise Kathy with a phone call anyway. He digs up Mindy's number and gives her a call. When he asks to speak to Kathy, Mindy says she hasn't spoken to Kathy in months. *I must've misheard the name.* He calls Kathy's house, speaks to her mom. She tells him Kathy's spending the night with her friend Sheila. Eric calls Sheila. Sheila hasn't heard from Kathy and isn't expecting her. Eric calls Kathy's house again.

He reaches the answering machine. He leaves a message. He paces in his dorm room, his head pounding. He calls Kathy's house again, leaves another message. He calls five more times, apologizing for each frantic call. He gives up when he realizes it's after eleven.

He stays up all night. He tries to do homework, fails. He tries to read a magazine. He can't concentrate. He stares out the window. *Why has Kathy lied? What the hell is going on? What is Kathy doing?*

Of course, he knows. But he doesn't understand. He feels ambushed.

Bleary-eyed, sick to his stomach, his voice shaking, he calls her in the morning at the diner where she works. Her boss answers. He asks to speak to Kathy. After a pause, Kathy comes on the line.

"Hi," Eric says.

"Hi."

"I miss you."

"Me, too."

"How was Mindy?"

"Great. We had fun. We rented a couple of movies, had girl talk, then crashed pretty early."

Eric's mouth goes dry. "Kathy, I called Mindy. You weren't there."

Through the phone, Eric hears the sound of the breakfast rush—loud voices, laughter, the shouting of orders, the clatter of dishes, the ring of the cash register.

"Kathy," he says. "Where were you?"

"I can't talk now. I'm at work."

"Kathy, please."

"I have to go."

She hangs up. Eric grinds his teeth, counts to five, calls back. Kathy's boss answers. He asks to speak to Kathy again.

"You can't call in the middle of her shift. Call her at home."

She hangs up.

He spends the next seven hours in agony. His body feels like a scream. He wants to crawl into bed and sleep off the pain, but he can't get himself to stop moving, to stop shaking.

That evening, more than twenty-four hours after his initial call to Mindy, he calls Kathy at home.

"Kathy, you have to tell me what's going on. Please."

She explodes. "What are you doing? I find out you've been calling my friends, my parents? How dare you check up on me? And then you trick me. You've turned into this jealous monster."

Somewhere, from the depths of his exhaustion and pain, Eric finds surprising calm. "Kathy, I've been in this room for twenty-four hours trying to find out where you are. You lied to me. You won't talk to me. Just tell me the truth. Tell me his name."

A pause.

"It's not like that," Kathy says, her voice changing, dripping with chill. "I wanted to wait until you came home so we could talk about this face to face."

"Talk about *what?*" Eric loses it. "Put me out of my misery. WHAT IS HIS NAME?"

Kathy hesitates.

"Bill," she says. "Bill Seaver."

Eric swallows. "How long have you been cheating on me?"

"It's not what you think."

"Then what is it?"

"Bill asked me out. I didn't want to go, but I said yes. We've been—" She pauses again. "I've never met anybody like him. We're in love."

Her words slice into him. As he speaks, he feels as if he's hearing another voice, not his own, speaking from far away. "This isn't happening. You were just here. What was that? That was all a lie, too, huh?"

"I'm not going to sit here and listen to you turn on me, Eric. I'm hanging up."

"I'm turning on *you?* Fine. Good-bye, Kathy."

"Good-bye."

He doesn't slam the phone down. He hangs up slowly, heavily, his eyes blinking rapidly. Tears sliding down his cheeks, he thinks, *So that's it. I guess I was wrong. We weren't meant for each other.*

Followed by another even more surprising thought:

Chris was right.

*   *   *

The breakup hits Eric hard. He slogs through his days feeling alternately burned up with rage and hollowed out. He tries to salvage his spirit through writing. He fills notebooks with painful scribbling, vowing to turn them into a screenplay after he finishes his student film. In autumn 1991, he and Chris reunite in upstate New York for the shoot. Chris, wearing his long hair in a ponytail, plays the role of an orderly at a nursing home, a supporting role. His acting is understated, powerful; Eric's directing, confident, matured. Chris returns to Ohio for his junior year of college. Eric spends the rest of his senior year and into November working on the film.

After he graduates NYU and finishes the film, Eric returns to Mississippi to pay off the debt he took on while making his student film, around fifteen thousand dollars. He sells his car, an old Porsche 911 given to him by his dad, and takes a job as a host at a casino restaurant. He enters a period of "sport dating," going out with as many women as he can, most of them one-night stands. His goal? Make up for all the dating years he missed in college. "My Promiscuous Period," Eric calls it. Or as a friend refers to that time, "Eric's Man Whore Days."

Meanwhile, he decides to "push his baby as far as it will go" and submits *An Early Twilight* to as many contests as he can find and afford. Over the next year or so, the film racks up twenty-one awards, wins at least one first-place prize, and brings in over five thousand dollars in prize money.

While he hosts at the casino, pays off his loan, and watches his film clean up at festivals, he considers his future.

I'm a filmmaker. I want to make movies. I know I can do it.

He decides to move to Los Angeles and take his shot.

*   *   *

With graduation day approaching, Chris plans his escape. Everywhere he looks, he sees turmoil. His mom's marriage to Jimmy Love III seems about to capsize. She talks of splitting and moving west, perhaps to San Diego. Meg wants to settle down, but while he has no definite postcollege path in mind, that's the last thing he wants to do. He sees himself striking out as an actor or singer, but with Jimmy about to be kicked to the curb, he sees no way to finance this iffy amorphous career. He imagines himself returning to Europe, living the romantic life of a floating poet, writing songs and poems in cafés by day, hanging out in bars and picking up women at night. First, though, he needs cash.

After graduation, Chris avoids the firestorm that's raging in the Riverhouse and crashes in Florida in a crappy apartment his uncle sets up for him while working as a fry cook in his restaurant. He has no bed, no wheels. He finds a sleeping bag and buys a cheap bicycle. He doubles his hours at the restaurant, works as a busboy when he's not in the kitchen, and banks as much money as possible. But something about his uncle gives him the creeps, a feeling that's confirmed when one night his uncle fires him for no apparent reason and kicks him out of the apartment. Chris moves in with another relative and takes a housekeeping job at a nearby Marriott. He saves as much money as he can, tolerates the job longer than he would've thought possible—regularly smoking a bunch of dope helps—and finally takes off for Ireland.

He spends the next year hitchhiking across Europe, finally landing in Vienna. By now, he has become a professional partier, a dabbler in song lyrics and poetry, a sometime singer and full-time baroque myth, at least in his own mind. He wears his hair long, grows out his fingernails and paints them black, dresses like Dracula or Zorro, all in black, including an assortment of scarves and capes. Meg visits him, finds Chris out of control and deeply in love with the character he's created. She heads back to the States, their relationship shattered.

After a while, the money runs out. Having no choice, Chris heads back to Mississippi to plot his next move. He arrives in Gulfport, his vampire look retired. He finds an apartment and a roommate, grabs a job at Gold's Gym selling memberships to pay the rent. *It's about the music*, he vows. He starts playing the piano every day, writing songs and singing, his goal now to form a rock band and take his band—which he envisions as a cross between Styx and Queen—on the road and one day into the recording studio. He puts an ad in the paper for musicians. Donnie, a heavy-metal guitar player with a flock of long curly hair and a burned-out look, answers the ad and auditions for Chris in his apartment. Donnie goes *off*, to Chris's ear, playing like a white Hendrix.

"Fuck, man," Chris says. "You play the *shit* out of that thing."

"Yah. And you can *sing*, brah. Your voice is *lush*. Plus you're good-looking."

Chris grins. "Don't see how we can miss."

*   *   *

In 1994, they make their move. Eric hits L.A. first. He moves to the San Fernando Valley, sharing an apartment with Frank Reynolds, a classmate from NYU, a film editor. Frank, bespectacled, pudgy, good-natured, neat, geeky in a good way, has already lined up an editing gig. Eric intends to shop *An Early Twilight*, hoping to set up meetings, and work on his screenplay, a cathartic, fictionalized version of his breakup with Kathy. To support himself, he finds a job as a receptionist at the Columbia Charitable Foundation, over the hill in West Los Angeles, an irritating forty-five-minute stop-and-go drive.

Eric lives with Frank for six months. One night, having no plans, short on cash, they decide to stay in, maybe watch a movie. Movie buffs, they browse the aisles of their local Blockbuster, fail to find anything of interest that they haven't already seen. They return to their apartment empty-handed.

"I've got something you haven't seen," Eric says, and busts out his copy of *Raiders of the Lost Ark: The Adaptation*.

Eric hasn't seen it in over two years, and he's surprised by how well it holds up. Frank roars in all the appropriate places and compliments Eric when the credits roll.

"You like it?" Eric says. "You're not being polite?"

"No. I really like it."

Eric can't know how much. Because the next day, when Eric's at work, Frank makes a copy for himself. Years later, Frank says that he asked Eric's permission. Eric doesn't remember Frank asking him, and because of what eventually happens, he no longer cares.

*   *   *

A few months later, Chris calls Eric from Mississippi. He and Donnie have decided to move to L.A. to scope out the band scene.

"It's our time, man," Chris says.

Couple minor problems. First, they have no place to live. Second, they have no songs and, except for the two of them, no band. They've tried to write together, but their styles clash. Chris writes in the style of Billy Joel with a hint of Journey and Foreigner. Donnie writes with another band in mind, the one playing in his head. Still, Chris knows they're not going to break out playing seedy bars and strip clubs in Biloxi. They may as well play seedy bars and strip clubs in L.A.

"Unfortunately, I'm not going to be helpful when it comes to the L.A. band scene," Eric says, no shock there. "But as far as an apartment, I can set you up."

"Seriously?"

"Done deal. Frank moved back to New York, and I've just rented a new place on the other side of the hill, near my work. The commute was murderous. Our old apartment's paid off and sitting empty. You can have it for a solid month, gratis."

"*Sweet.* I owe you, man."

While Eric moves into his spacious Spanish-style apartment with someone else from NYU, Chris, Donnie, and Ramona, Chris's new girl-friend ("She's a total trip, man,") move into Eric's old apartment for a month. Within those four weeks, the band—well, Donnie and Chris—falls apart, Donnie disappears, Chris and Ramona move in together, and Chris decides to dump the band idea and try acting.

Armed with head shots, he pounds the pavement, looking for acting gigs and taking acting classes at night. He lands a role in a play called *Criminal* in a forty-five-seat theater in Hollywood attended by an average of ten brave souls a night, most of them related to or paid for by the direc-tor. Eric goes to a couple of performances, and after the play's run, on Chris's twenty-fourth birthday, Eric and Ramona kidnap him, blindfold him, and take him to a sleazy Hollywood bar, where Chris has more than one too many. They wind up at a tattoo and piercing parlor. Chris wakes up the next morning with a hammering headache and a pierced nipple.

To pay his bills, while he studies acting and auditions for plays, Chris takes a low-paying job at Activision, testing video games. The work calls for him to play games such as *Muppet Treasure Island* before they become available to the public, playing eight hours a day for months, searching for flaws and loopholes that might crash the game. He finds the work mind-numbing but not stressful, perfect for his current lifestyle. He gets to play video games all day, bring home a steady paycheck, and pursue acting at night. One night over drinks, Eric and Chris have a heart-to-heart.

"How's the screenplay coming?"

"It's not," Eric says. "I'm so wasted when I get home after my soul-sucking job that I don't feel like doing anything but vegging out in front of the tube. And, frankly, I don't know if I have the same passion for it I once had."

"I hear you," Chris says. "At least about the soul-sucking part."

"Chris, I have to find a new job," Eric says. "This one's killing me. At least emotionally. I'm angry and anxious all the time."

Chris polishes off his beer, orders another. "I can see if they need any game testers."

"Really? I'll take you up on that."

"We're talking long hours and shit money and you need a high threshold for monotony."

"Sounds perfect," Eric says.

Within the week, Dave, the quality assurance manager at Activision, phones Eric for an interview. The company is entering a period Dave calls "crunch time." They're about to debut the latest version of *MechWarrior 2*, a hot new game, and they need qualified, motivated testers who can work fast and put in long hours. Dave offers Eric a job on a trial basis, telling him they'll see how things go, then take it from there. Dave can't offer Eric anything more long term. He's seen too many testers burn out.

"You can take twenty-four hours to think about it," Dave says.

"I don't have to," Eric says. "I'm in."

When I'm in . . .

The first day, Eric works twelve hours and sleeps at the office. Sometime after midnight, he curls up on the carpet under Dave's desk, grabs a few hours, returns to his cubicle, and jumps back in. Driven partially by the extra money he makes by putting in overtime but mostly by his otherworldly work ethic, Eric powers through crunch time. *MechWarrior 2* ships on schedule, and Dave moves Eric to the next game. He finishes testing that before crunch time, and Dave assigns him to the next game. In September 1995, Dave calls Eric into his office and asks him to close the door.

*   *   *

They sit on vinyl armchairs in the lobby of the Activision building on Wilshire Boulevard. Eric, tucked in a corner, the leaves of a potted plant brushing his shoulder, studies his hands folded in front of him. Chris, unshaven, his thick black hair growing wildly, his eyes bloodshot and heavy lidded, sits across from Eric, his legs bouncing. He notices that Eric wears a crisp new button-down shirt.

"I've arrived at something of a crossroads," Eric says. "I need your advice."

"Talk to me."

"Dave offered me a promotion." Eric pauses. "The department's first-ever senior lead. A newly created position apparently."

"What does it mean?"

Eric turns his hands over. "Thirty-five thousand dollars a year. Two-year guarantee. Plus benefits."

"Fuck, man," Chris says.

"Exactly."

Eric nods gravely, waits for Chris to react. Chris claws at his beard stubble. "So what's the problem?"

"Well, simply, if I go down this path, I'll be starting a *career*. I would be abandoning the whole reason we came out here. The job will be so demanding, the hours potentially long, when will I have time to work on the screenplay?"

"You won't have time to do both?"

"I don't see how. Do you?"

Chris stretches. "Depends how seriously you take this." Eric groans. Chris smiles. "My bad. I forgot who I was talking to."

"It's a flaw," Eric says.

"Have you been sending out *Early Twilight?*"

"No," Eric admits. "Not really. I don't know why."

Chris just nods. "Well, look, it's a shitload of money."

"More than I could've imagined. Especially since I haven't been with the company very long."

"I've been there longer," Chris says. "But to me, it's just a job. I don't really give a shit."

"I'm only twenty-five," Eric says. "I could put some money in the bank, and then in a couple of years—"

"Right. Then you can go for it."

Eric shoves his hands under his thighs. "I wanted to tell you. I wanted to seek your council."

"I'm like Robert Duvall in *The Godfather.*"

"Yes. Tom. The consigliere. So, you think it's the right thing to do?"

"I do, man. Yes."

"I'll be this little upstart, moved to management, leapfrogging over others with more seniority."

"Who cares? Wait a minute. Will you be my boss?"

"No. Different department, different team."

"Cool," Chris says. "Go for it, man."

And with that, Eric leapfrogs over Chris.

*   *   *

A few weeks later, Chris comes into Eric's office to ask him a favor.

"I gotta move, man."

"What happened to your roommate?"

"Going to Thailand. I can't afford this place on my own. Not on my lowly tester's hourly wage."

Eric laughs, hopes Chris was going for a joke.

"You don't suppose—"

"What?"

"Nah. Never mind."

"Chris, what?"

"Well, it'd be really cool if we lived together."

"It would be very cool, except for the inconvenient fact that I have a roommate."

Chris taps his fingers on Eric's desk, waits for Eric to take the hint. Eric blinks, gets the point, swallows Chris's idea as if it's a dose of foul-tasting medicine.

"Technically, it's my apartment," Eric says. "I found it. I invited him in. I guess if I wanted to, I could ask him to leave, however awkward that conversation would be, but—"

"This is great! Dude, we're gonna have a blast. One nonstop party. Thanks, man. And don't worry. Your roommate will understand."

He doesn't understand. In a feverish state of silent anger, he gathers his belongings, refuses to acknowledge Eric as he packs. He moves out one day when Eric's at work, trashing the place for his parting gesture.

Chris and Eric clean up the mess. They put the apartment back together, and Chris moves in. They hang out most nights and every weekend, Ramona having moved into her own place on the other side of the city. Their relationship having cooled, she and Chris remain good friends, though she announces one night that she plans to enlist in the army.

"You seem to attract a certain type of woman," Eric says.

"Yeah. After you date me, you want to pick up a rifle."

Eric and Chris chill out regularly in the apartment, living with the ease of brothers, sharing meals, bottles of wine, and crashing in front of the TV devoted to their latest project—watching every episode of *The X-Files*. Chris is right. They do have a blast.

For six months.

*   *   *

February 1996.

Activision launches a new game, *Spycraft*, which means crunch time, this one overseen by Eric. Crunch time amounts to sixteen-hour days, sleeping in the office, stress, and no time for incompetence. At one point, Eric fires a temporary employee, a tester. The moment he gives the guy the bad news, he feels sick to his stomach. But then he thinks: *The guy was dead weight.*

He was holding us back. I had to do it. He fired the guy for the good of the company, which makes him, by definition, a company man.

A company man.

Is that what he has become?

Have I gone to the dark side?

The phone rings. He picks it up assuming his boss has called for his report.

"Eric?"

Mary.

"Mom. Hi. What—?"

"Eric, your father has died."

Behind him, the clack of computer keyboards. The whir of the copy machine. Laughter. Phones jangling.

"He'd been sick—"

The pen Eric holds drops onto his desk. His hand starts to shake. He watches his fingers twitching as if the hand belongs to someone else.

"Eric?"

"I'm here. I'm just—I'm sorry. I have to figure out when I can come. I'll call you later. Thanks, Mom."

A mist seems to roll in. He's only dimly aware that he hangs up the phone and dials Chris's extension.

A few minutes later, Chris pokes his head into Eric's office. Lately, when Eric has asked him to go to lunch, Chris has turned him down, saying he'd committed to a working lunch with members of his team—Randy, Paul, Bailey—guys Eric leapfrogged over. He's also noticed that he and Chris have started hanging out less at home. Chris often goes out for the evening and comes home well after Eric has gone to bed.

"What's up?" Chris drums his fingers on the doorframe. He seems vaguely annoyed, impatient.

"Come in," Eric says. He rests his hand on his lap to try to keep it from shaking. "Shut the door."

"I promised the team I'd meet them for lunch. Being lowly testers, we only get a half hour—"

Chris notices then that Eric has started to cry.

"My dad," Eric says. "He's dead."

"Oh, no," Chris says. "I'm so sorry, man."

He moves around the desk, kneels, and grips Eric's forearms. Eric dips his head, sobs silently.

"I got you, man," Chris says. "I got you."

Eric nods, sobs.

"You need to get out of here, man. You need to go back to the apartment. Take a hot bath. Soak in it. Light some candles. Take a long hot bath. Then go home. Be with Kurt, your mom."

"It's crunch time. I can't, Chris."

"You can. It's your dad. Go."

Chris tries to find Eric's eyes, but Eric keeps his head bowed, his sobs coming slower. He nods again, wipes his nose with the sleeve of his dry-cleaned oxford shirt.

"You gotta talk to Dave," Chris says. "Tell him you're going. I'll go with you."

"Your lunch," Eric says.

"Come on," Chris says. "Let's find Dave."

*   *   *

Dave sends him home. Eric makes travel arrangements and then takes Chris's advice. He soaks in a hot bath and sobs, trying to sweat out the surprisingly deep hurt he feels. Back in Ocean Springs a few days later, he and Kurt, down from Boston, attend the small funeral and then box up their dad's office, where he seemed to have slept most nights. In a kind of trance, Eric packs his dad's things. He remembers sitting at the receptionist's desk, playing games on the clunky old computer. He recalls the day his dad announced he was moving out. He remembers his drinking, the dozens of empty jug wine bottles in the basement used for props in the bar scene. He cringes as he remembers how his dad belittled him for working on *Raiders*. Mostly, he remembers how his dad disconnected himself from Eric's life. He replays the moment after his graduation from NYU, seeing his dad approach, hand extended, offering Eric a congratulatory handshake. Eric, shocked to see him, blurted, "What are you doing here?"

Yet, as he packs up his dad's office with Kurt, he feels a deep loss.

And he wonders:

Can you miss something you never had?

*   *   *

Eric returns from Mississippi and escapes into crunch time. Chris comes and goes, drifting on Eric's periphery, his hair grown long, wild, pulled back. Chris spends less and less time in the apartment, socializing more with the guys on his team than with Eric. When they do run into each other at home, their conversations are clipped, strained. Eric helps launch one video game, then another. His status at Activision grows. Dave gets him a raise.

As Eric's star rises at the company, Chris's falls. He may have cared about his job once, but now he shows up at work late and leaves early. One time, on a rare outing together, shopping at a mall, Chris tells Eric that Randy, Paul, and Bailey resent him.

"They don't think you deserved being made senior lead over them," Chris says. "They're better testers than you and they've been there longer. They're pissed."

"Is that right?"

"That is right."

"They haven't taken into consideration that there may be a *reason* why I was promoted over them?"

"Funny. They can't think of a good reason."

"And what do you think?"

Chris doesn't even hesitate. "I agree with them."

*   *   *

As Eric's bank account fattens and his responsibility and visibility at the job expand, he decides to overhaul his wardrobe. He buys several pairs of dress slacks, new shoes, and a week's supply of Hugo Boss button-down shirts. When Chris sees Eric dressed in his new duds, he shoots him a snide smile.

One night, Eric locks himself away in his bedroom and pulls out the screenplay he's been rewriting. He reads through his most recent revisions. As he turns the pages, he discovers that he feels nothing. He no longer experiences the wrenching pain and blinding anger he felt toward Kathy when they broke up. This screenplay, once so cathartic, his attempt at literary revenge, has become irrelevant. He has changed, he realizes. Matured, he hopes. As he thumbs through the pages, he hears Chris come in with a friend. They laugh, bump into something, put on some music, break out some beers, possibly pass a joint. They start talking, annoyingly loud, and then Chris, his voice rising, talks about his job being nothing more than a gig to finance his acting future.

"As opposed to Eric," Chris says, his voice leaking through the seams of Eric's closed door. "We came to L.A. on the same page. Not anymore. He changed. He's become this corporate sellout. I thought he was better than that. I don't recognize him anymore."

"Back at you, Chris," Eric mutters.

Eric closes the screenplay and shoves it into his desk drawer.

He will not pick it up again.

* * *

One day at work, a co-worker beckons Eric into her cubicle.

"People are talking about Chris," she says. "He's late all the time. Once he came in right before lunch, left right after."

"He's not in my department."

"No, but he's your friend."

"There's nothing I can say to him."

"Even if it means saving his job?"

Eric takes off his glasses, presses the bridge of his nose. "I'll talk to him."

They go to dinner. They order, then sit silently, the tension feeling like a wall between them.

"I wanted to talk to you about something," Eric says.

Chris shrugs, reaches for a breadstick.

"Gina spoke to me. Your habitual tardiness has not gone unnoticed."

Chris chuckles, rolls his eyes.

"Well, if you find it funny."

"So, is this a warning from my *boss?*"

"I'm not your boss."

"No. Fine. Whatever."

Eric looks longingly at the door. He turns to face Chris, finds him avoiding his eyes, looking away as if he wants to flee.

"I know you think I'm a sellout," Eric says.

Chris shrugs.

"I'm just doing my job. You know when I commit to something, I go all the way."

"And what about your screenplay and directing and all of that?"

Eric rustles in his chair, then straightens. "It's on hold. For now."

"Yeah. Okay. At least I'm still focused on my career, not on my *job.*"

The rest of the meal goes no better.

A few months later, Chris leaves Activision and takes a job at another video game company.

"I need a change," he tells Eric. "I'm under too much pressure."

* * *

Ocean Springs High School Reunion.
July 10, 1998.

He sees her from across the room.

She stands at the punch bowl, talking to someone. She tosses her head back and laughs, holding her smile.

It's that smile that gets him.

Cassie Grace.

Ten years ago, in high school, he wouldn't have dared speak to her. *Out of his league,* he would've said. *Unattainable.*

Now, promoted again, highly salaried, his pay scale recently bumped, newly confident, Eric crosses the room at the Yacht Club and introduces himself.

"I remember you," she says.

"You do?"

"I do."

That smile again.

"We only had one class together," he says, fighting the stammer that has crept into his voice.

"Eighth-grade enrichment. For *gifted* kids."

They laugh.

"How'd we turn out?" Eric says.

"Let's see," Cassie says, running a finger around the lip of her glass. "I just got divorced and I'm unemployed. Impressed?"

"Highly."

"And you?"

"I live in L.A. I work for a video game company. We just launched a hot new game, *Tenchu: Stealth Assassins*."

"I was wondering when that was coming out." They laugh again. "Did you ever make another movie after *Raiders?*"

"You knew about that?"

"Everybody did." She hands him her empty punch glass. "More, please."

He fills her glass and returns to her side.

The reunion ends an hour later.

They stay together for the next seven days.

*   *   *

A few weeks later, Cassie visits Eric in L.A.

"I met someone at my high school reunion," he tells Chris late one morning, on his way to pick her up at the airport.

"Yeah? Cool."

"Cassie Grace. Did you know her?"

"Doesn't ring a bell," Chris says, lying on the couch, channel surfing.

Aren't you supposed to be at work?

"I called in sick," Chris says. "I'm under the weather."

"I didn't say anything," Eric says.

Uncanny. He can read my mind.

*   *   *

Cassie visits for two weeks.

She falls in love with L.A., the apartment, the neighborhood, and Eric.

"What's the catch?" she says, staring at him in bed one morning. "You seem too good. Are you an ax murderer or something?"

"I don't think so. Unless I'm sleepwalking."

"I'm going to move here," she says.

"Oh, you'll discover my flaws then," Eric says. "I promise."

Cassie finds an apartment four blocks away and a job at a call center. She slides into Eric's social circle, although she's not sure about Chris. He's begun his second reincarnation as a rocker, talks about putting together a band. One evening, walking with Cassie to a café to meet Eric, Chris describes his current job.

"The greatest job in the world," he says.

"Yeah? Why's that?" Cassie says.

"I don't do anything all day. I sit in my cube and watch movies. The boss is never around. It's awesome."

"So, basically, you're getting paid for doing nothing."

"Yep. How great is that?"

Not great in Cassie's mind. Not great at all.

*   *   *

A year later, laid off from his job, deep into rock star mode—long hair, fingernails painted black, biker boots, leather pants squeaking as he walks—Chris heads back to Long Island for his ten-year high school reunion. Before he returns to L.A., he hits a strip joint. One of the dancers, a bleached blonde named Desiree, slithers over to him. He stuffs a bill into her G-string and asks for a lap dance. In a back room behind a torn dirty green drape, heavy metal scraping the walls, the air stinking of liquor, sweat, and lemon disinfectant, Desiree grinds on his lap and spills the sordid details of her life. Chris listens intently with the ear of a poet and the heart of a social worker.

The next day, he rents a U-Haul and moves Desiree and her pet bird to California.

*   *   *

"It's a good deal for both of us."

They sit at a falafel place around the corner. Eric pokes his salad with his fork, toys with it, his appetite gone. Chris smears hummus onto a slice of pita. "Totally win-win."

"I'm a little dubious," Eric says.

"Desiree will clean, cook, and share the rent. Where's the downside?"

"Well, I mean, you haven't known her that long."

"Nope. It was sudden. But sometimes you just know."

Eric exhales deeply. "She's a stripper, you say?"

"Exotic dancer, yeah."

"And how did you meet her again?"

"At a get-together. At a club. At a party. It doesn't matter. She's had a hard life. She wants a new start."

Eric pushes his plate away. He grips the ends of the table. "As long as we're talking, I want to respond to something you said, that you regard me as some sort of corporate sellout."

"Fine. Hit me."

"I don't see myself that way. I've been given an opportunity and I've chosen to take advantage of it. I am still *me*. I have not changed."

Chris freezes in midchew. He considers Eric. Shakes his head. Swallows. "Okay, man, straight up. I do think you have sold out. Maybe that's too harsh. Whatever. I'll put it like this. I don't agree with the choices you've made. I feel that you've gone the safe route and I have hung on to my artistic ideals. I'll put it like that."

"I guess we'll agree to disagree."

Chris grabs another slice of pita, dumps on the remaining hummus, folds the pita into a triangle. Eric, wavering, closes his eyes for a second. He knows what he should say, that he should reject this awful idea of Chris's stripper girlfriend moving into his apartment. Talk about a no-brainer.

"So, okay," Eric says. "I guess there will be three of us."

"Yeah, basically."

"Basically?"

Chris stuffs half the pita triangle into his mouth and chews ferociously. "She's got a stupid fucking bird."

That night, Eric tells Cass that Chris's new girlfriend, Desiree the stripper, and her pet bird, have moved into his apartment.

"I'm only going to say this once," Cassie says. "You will regret this."

*   *   *

Typically now, Chris lounges in bed until noon with Desiree and they get high or drunk or both in the afternoons and evenings, often ending up taking long, steamy bubble baths together. As Desiree lies around with Chris, she allows her bird the run of the apartment. Eric often comes home to bird shit dotted all over the living room floor, the stink magnified by bowls of exotic-smelling potpourri Desiree places everywhere—on the dining room table, on the coffee table, on the kitchen counter. Eric sees no sign of Desiree looking for work, no evidence that she has cleaned, and receives no contribution to the rent. He does see that Chris appears to be caught up in some new, crazy, decadent lifestyle. He's put everything on hold except her—his music, making a living, connecting with friends. Feeling uncomfortable in his own apartment, Eric spends more and more time at Cassie's place. When he does go home, he walks on eggshells around Chris and finds the apartment, the bird, and Desiree herself disgusting. For Eric, the "win-win" Chris described has turned into a big stinking loss.

Finally, he asks Chris if Desiree even wants a job.

"She hits the pavement every day," Chris says. "Nothing, man. Not even a nibble. Rough out there."

Eventually, Cass calls in a favor and gets Desiree a job at the call center. She shows up late the first day, later the second day, and on the third day doesn't show up at all.

Gradually, Chris begins to run out of money. Anxious to find a job and to start working on his music again, he feels his relationship with Desiree starting to unravel. He begins to see another side of her.

One morning after a long night, Chris and Desiree walk into a Starbucks. Chris steps up to the counter and orders his drink, smiling at the attractive barista. "Good morning. How you doing? Two grande no-foam lattes, please. Thanks. Have a good one."

They move to the pickup area. Desiree rages through her purse, finds a tube of lipstick and rolls a new coat over her lips. She flings the lipstick into her purse. "What the fuck was that all about?"

"What?"

"The way you said good morning to that girl. What the fuck was that?"

Chris truly has no idea what she means. "What are you talking about?"

Their drinks arrive. Desiree snatches hers, grabs his and throws it against the back wall.

"Fuck you and your new girlfriend," Desiree says and storms out.

Soon after the Starbucks incident, Chris finds a temporary job that brings in some cash and removes him from the apartment for hours at a time. When he comes back from work, he often finds Desiree in some state of distress, screaming jealous fury at him, accusing him of flirting with a co-worker, incensed that he brought leftover pizza to his job instead of leaving it for her. One night, he walks in on her in the bathroom and catches her cutting herself with a razor. He freezes in the doorway.

"What are you doing?"

"What does it look like?" she says, blotting the blood that bubbles and trickles down her forearm.

"I didn't know—"

"Well, now you do. Shut the fucking door and leave me alone."

He eases out of the bathroom, closes the door behind him. He walks into the living room, his legs feeling heavy. He leans against a wall for support, slides down onto the floor, and buries his head in his hands. He breathes deeply and feels his eyes filling up.

"Where am I?" he whispers.

*   *   *

Over Christmas 1999, in Ocean Springs, Eric asks Cassie to marry him.

A traditionalist, he first asks her father, a physician, for permission.

When he gives Eric his blessing, Eric gets down on one knee and asks Cassie for her hand.

"What are you doing? Is this for real?"

"I think so," Eric says, and hands her a box.

"Oh my God, *yes*," Cassie says, laughing, and opens the box, finding Eric's glittering fifteen-thousand-dollar engagement ring. "This is gorgeous. When did you—how did this happen?"

"The video game business has been very good to me," Eric says.

They return to Los Angeles, engaged. They set a date in April for the wedding. With the go-ahead from Cassie, Eric takes over planning and preparing every aspect of the event from designing the invitations to arranging the honeymoon. The wedding becomes his project, his production. He thrives on every detail.

First detail: where they will live.

"I think we should live in my apartment," Eric says.

"With Chris, Desiree, and the bird?"

"I'm going to ask him to move."

*   *   *

"You're kicking us out?"

"We're getting married."

"I'm fucking with you. Congratulations." They hug briefly, stiffly. "So, when do you need the apartment? Are you like in some rush?"

Eric wags his head, trying not to gag from the stench wafting up from the tureen of fresh potpourri in the center of the kitchen table. "Well, we're going to redecorate and repaint the whole place. Cass wants to make the apartment hers as well, you know? So, ideally, as soon as possible—"

"Uh-huh."

Within seconds, the temperature between them drops from unseasonably mild to blizzard frigid.

"Yeah, I mean, we need to get started," Eric says.

"Fine. We'll start looking."

"Good. Thanks. I'm actually going to start moving my things over to Cassie's place to get a jump."

"Got it," Chris says. "Great idea."

"Thanks for understanding."

Eric starts loading some of his books into a box.

*   *   *

I always rely on my instinct.

And now his instinct hums.

Desiree.

Something about her. Something . . . unnerving. He pictures the hard look she always gives him, the way she constantly seems to judge him, and his inner warning light flashes. He knows he has to remove everything he owns from the apartment as soon as possible.

"What do you think she'll do?" Cassie asks Eric as he shoves his box of books into her closet and starts folding together another box from the dozen unmade boxes that lie flat against the wall.

"I don't know. I just have a bad feeling. Like she'll fuck with my stuff."

"Then go with your gut," Cassie says.

Eric does. He moves everything out—clothes, books, lamps, silverware, dishes, videotapes—lugging it all in boxes the four blocks from his apartment to Cassie's. Overnight, he turns her already small one-bedroom apartment into a cramped one-bedroom storage locker piled floor to ceiling with boxes. Feeling claustrophobic, fenced in by the wall of boxes in her bedroom, he says, "This isn't forever, Cass. Just until Chris finds his own place."

"I'm desperately trying to be patient," Cassie says.

"Wish I could say the same," Eric says.

In early February, Eric mails the wedding invitations.

Chris receives his and promptly returns the enclosed engraved RSVP card.

He will not be able to attend.

*   *   *

Late one night, Chris, wearing only his boxers and flip-flops, and Desiree, in tight jeans, T-shirt, and tons of jewelry, pack up the apartment. They take their time, stopping often to argue. Desiree packs her stuff listlessly, moving in virtual slow motion. Jobless, she's afraid of becoming homeless. She blames Chris.

"We'll find something," he assures her.

"Really? You don't know shit. Like this was such a great fucking idea."

Oh, love that sarcasm. So sexy.

In fact, he did once find her edginess hot. No longer. Now he finds her overall personality just plain nasty. If he could, he would eject her from his life. But he feels stuck, caught, and responsible for her. Maybe that's why he allows her to scream at him, to swear at him, to belittle him, and even sometimes to hit him.

"I'm not doing this," she says, tossing an armload of her clothes onto the floor. She slams herself onto the couch, sits cross-legged, and glares at him.

"Fine," Chris says. "It's like two in the morning. We'll pick it up to-morrow."

"I mean *ever*, asshole. I'm not fucking moving."

Chris bites his lip. "We kind of don't have a choice. This is not our place. We have to move out."

"Yeah? Make me."

Great. A 2:00 A.M. throwdown. Like I need this. I have to stop dating strippers.

"Desiree," Chris says. "It's real late. Let's start fresh in the morning."

He reaches for her hand. She pulls it away.

"Don't fucking touch me."

"Seriously. Let's go to bed."

He rests his hand on her shoulder.

She grabs his hand, holds it for a moment, then bends back one of his fingers.

"Ow! Son of a *bitch!*"

"Did you call me a bitch?"

She slaps Chris across the face.

He staggers back, rubs his cheek. "Fuck."

"Did you call me a *fuck?*"

She leaps off the couch, charges him. He backs away, holds up his hands to fend her off. She howls, trips over the base of a lamp. The lamp pitches forward, hits the floor and shatters. Chris circles to the back of the couch.

This is insane. She is insane. This is like a scene in a bad movie.

"Okay, I give. You win. Whatever. I'm going to bed."

He retreats into the bedroom, slams the door. He hears the couch cushions sag and creak as she jumps on it.

"You're killing me!" she screams. *"You're fucking killing me!* HE'S KILLING ME! HE'S KILLING ME!! HELP!!!"

Chris races back into the living room. Desiree stands on the couch, her face deep red. "HE'S. KILLING. ME!"

"Shhh. Jesus." He grabs her around the waist, pulls her down onto the couch. He climbs astride her, pins her with his chest and slams his hand over her mouth. His hand rises and falls as she breathes, his palm wet from her saliva. "Bring it down. People are gonna hear. Come on. Shh."

She moans, thrashes beneath him. He loosens his grip. She drives her knees into his back, slams his tailbone. She thrusts with her pelvis and he falls off the couch. She hurdles him, rolls over, gets to her feet.

"He's killing me!" she howls. "HE'S KILLING ME!"

She darts through the living room, zigzagging, smashing vases, lamps, throwing books on the floor, ripping down a curtain, knocking over a chair, the bird suddenly appearing, nosediving in panic, squawking, feathers flying.

Desiree braces herself in the far corner of the room. Her breathing comes fast—she's panting now—her face a fiendish shade of purple. She grits her teeth, closes her eyes. A moment later, she opens them wide and growls.

Then she punches herself full in the face.

She hits herself again.

And again.

Then she slashes her cheek with her rings until blood spills down her face.

She claws her earlobes, grinds her rings into her neck. Chris, his eyes tearing, his sight blurred, presses himself into a wall, gaping, helpless, staring at Desiree, her lips puffed and sliced, her face blue with bruising, her cheeks gouged and running with blood.

Four shapes fill his vision. They rush toward him, a voice booming in his ear, "LAPD." Rough hands yank his arms behind his back, and he feels cold metal clasp onto his wrists. His mouth caked, he mumbles, "Psychotic break" and "I never touched her," and Desiree screams, "HE'S KILLING ME!"

Spitting blood.

*   *   *

He calls Elaine.

Divorced from Jimmy Love III, she now lives in San Diego, struggling to get a new business venture off the ground. She and Chris check in with each other regularly. She answers the phone on the second ring, sounding surprisingly awake and alert.

"Mom," Chris says. "I'm in bad shape. I'm in jail."

"You killed her, didn't you?"

"No, I didn't kill her. But some bad stuff has gone down. I need you to bail me out."

"I'm on my way."

Chris hangs up.

Then he calls Eric.

*   *   *

3:23 A.M.

The phone, on low volume, jangles softly. Half asleep, disoriented, one arm entangled in the sheets, Eric reaches his hand toward the phone, misses, manages to grab the receiver before it hurtles to the floor.

"Hello?"

"Eric. It's Chris."

"Wow. Okay. What time is it?" He squints at the alarm clock, makes out some fuzzy numbers. "It's like three thirty in the morning, Chris."

"I'm in jail, man."

Eric sits up. "Do you need me to do anything? Come over there or—"

"My mom's on her way."

"That's good. What happened?"

"That crazy bitch. We got into this blowout fight. She lost her mind, man. She went fucking crazy. She started tearing up the apartment. Throwing shit all over. I tried to calm her down but she's screaming at me, *screaming*, and then she starts punching herself in the face like Edward Norton in *Fight Club* and she's hitting herself, cutting herself, blood is gushing, and then the cops show up and it's a domestic disturbance and here I am. I can't believe it. It's fucked."

As Chris talks, Eric pictures Desiree screaming and trashing the apartment, Chris trying to calm her, Desiree punching herself, the cops arresting them both, and a litany of questions bang through his brain, the most nagging and confounding—*Do I believe this story?*

I do.

He questions the choices Chris has made but never his heart. He would never hit anyone.

Eric focuses on Chris's voice on the phone, rambling, desperate, and he believes that Chris is grasping for the connection they had in their past. For a moment, Eric wants to return to that time again, to be that guy, that *Raiders* guy, but he can't find that place, can't locate that switch. He's moved on. He feels too far away, too hurt, too angry. He listens to Chris moan, "That crazy bitch," and feels like he's talking to a stranger.

He knows that they have reached not a crossroads but a dead end. Chris has criticized him, removed himself from his life, found other friends, chosen to become a *struggling artist*, borrowed money and not paid it back, decided against coming to his wedding. Now Chris is in trouble and Chris needs him.

I want to be a friend to him, Eric thinks, staring into the wall. *But I don't know who he is.*

*   *   *

Elaine bails him out. Chris goes back to the apartment, boxes up all of Desiree's possessions, stuffs them into a storage locker, leaves the key with the lawyer Elaine hires. He cages the bird and pays a pet store owner to keep her until somebody bails out Desiree. Chris packs up everything he owns, delivers a check to Eric for the expenses he owes—Eric has sent him an itemized bill—and prepares to go into hiding with his mom, in San Diego.

On his final sweep of the apartment, Chris finds something in the back of the closet that he determines belongs to Eric.

The first article ever published about *Raiders*.

He and Eric had the article blown up, laminated, and made into a poster.

Chris carries the poster outside and leaves it leaning against the front door of the apartment.

Then he escapes.

Butt-Numb-A-Thon

Orlando, Florida.
October 2000.

In a conference room, over coffee and bagels, the head of the lowest-rated department at video game giant Electronic Arts introduces their new manager of quality assurance. To polite applause, Eric Zala stands, wags his head, and, in a well-crafted few sentences that he practiced the night before, vows to do everything in his power to raise the rating of his department. He can't promise instant results, but he guarantees hard work. He will mobilize his department that afternoon, starting with the launch of the company's new game, *NASCAR Thunder.* Eric sits down to a smattering of applause and a beaming smile from his new boss.

A month earlier, Eric announced to Cassie, his wife of five months, that he'd reached the end of the line at Activision.

"I'm ready to spread my wings," he said, and told her of an opening he'd learned about in Florida at EA, *the* video game company. The job offered rapid opportunity for advancement with the potential to earn a hundred thousand dollars a year plus bonuses and stock options. Enticing. Especially for someone young and ambitious like Eric, who had just turned thirty.

"It would give us enough financial security to start a family," Eric said.

"I think we should go for it," Cassie said.

Eric does go for it, all the way, Eric's only way, attacking his new position, impressing his boss. In his first employee review of Eric, his boss writes, "Amazing. You managed to keep your job." High praise since he'd canned Eric's predecessor and thought of Eric's department as the company's black hole. Over the next few months, Eric turns his department around and receives the company's Exceptional Employee Award.

Looking into the future with Cassie, he envisions a quiet life living in Orlando, designing their own house, and raising a family, as the company where he works and thrives closes a pair of golden handcuffs around his wrists.

*   *   *

One Saturday afternoon, home from running errands, Eric thinks about *Raiders*. He rummages in a closet and finds a box filled with videotapes, his personal copy as well as dozens of others containing outtakes. *A seven-year home movie of my childhood*, he thinks. *I don't want to lose it.*

To preserve the footage, he has to transfer everything to DVD, which will cost five thousand dollars. *Worth it. And I can afford it.* He also digs up his CD of the original *Raiders* soundtrack. He'll bring that along to the digital transfer lab and have them play the audio over the menu on the DVD to give the final copies a classy touch. He'll mail a copy to Jayson. He's been in touch via e-mail. He'll see if he can track down Angela. His mom may be able to help him there. And, of course, he'll send a copy to Chris, if he can find him.

He shoves the box of videotapes into the trunk of his car and heads off. He stops at a red light and pops the *Raiders* soundtrack into his CD player.

The "Raiders March" comes on.

He hears the opening notes and lets out a tiny gasp.

He hasn't listened to that song in years. He can't remember when he last thought of *Raiders* or Chris. That familiar *dun-dun-dun-dun-dun-dun-dun* opening instantly transports him to his backyard and his basement. For a moment, he is twelve years old again.

He pulls over and turns up the volume. Staring ahead, cars whizzing by, he listens to the entire *Raiders* theme, all six minutes and four seconds. The music penetrates him. He sees Chris running out of the woods by the swamp, chased by the eleven-year-old Hovito Indians. He sees Chris running in his garage, the boulder rolling behind him, threatening to crush him. He flashes on Chris being dragged on his stomach behind the truck.

"I can't believe it ended the way it did," he says aloud. "I can't believe it."

When they left Los Angeles, he said to Cass, "I'm so done with him, so done. I don't even know if he's alive or dead and I don't care."

He plays the "Raiders March" again, leans back, and closes his eyes.

I do care. I do.

* * *

Koreatown.
October 2000.

The meth winding down, Chris Strompolos, twenty-nine, assesses his life and decides to kill himself.

When the high first hit an hour ago, he felt the charge tingle through him like an electrical shock. He thought about being broke, owing sixty grand on his credit card, and living here, in squalor, sleeping on the floor of this rat hole of an apartment, busting his ass to bring in enough money to spend on dope—fuck the bills—and the insane escapade with that skanky stripper and her fucking bird. All that made him laugh. Broke him up.

Now, coming down, unbearable sadness grips him around his throat, chokes him, and he feels lost.

Lost *Angeles.*

That's where I live.

Some fucked-up empty city of my mind.

And when he thinks about giving up drugs, breaking out, turning things around, the sadness comes.

My best friend's wedding.

Eric's wedding.

I'm sorry. I won't be able to attend.

Not his scene. Not his type of people.

That's the message he sent.

A lie.

The truth . . . the *truth* . . . a tear coming as he thinks about it, relives it . . .

The truth is . . . I was embarrassed.

He didn't want to deal with anyone.

Didn't want anyone to compare.

Eric, corporate executive, married man, life ascending.

Chris, meth head, hourly wage slave, stripper lover, life . . . fucked.

I'm done. I can't do this anymore.

His apartment wall shakes. A desperate *bam-bam-bam* like someone banging out a code. The phone rings. Ray. Drug friend. Drug fiend. Meth head.

"Chris!"

He can't speak. His lips feel glued together.

"*Chris!* Are you there? There's a snake under my bed! It's huge! It's gonna eat me. Shit, man, it's eating me. SHIT! CHRIS!!!"

I have to fucking end this.

*   *   *

Cold turkey.

He unearths his buried work ethic, dusts it off, turns it on.

The harder you work, the luckier you get.

Once his motto. Now his mantra.

So—

He flushes his drugs down the toilet.

He starts exercising, eating right, cooking again.

He hires a lawyer, declares bankruptcy.

He starts paying off his debts.

He hooks up with a hard rock band in Long Beach, takes over as lead singer, main writer, booker, and manager.

He moves out of the dump in Koreatown and into a decent one-bedroom in Long Beach.

He commits himself to his job—DVD testing—at Intellikey Labs in Burbank. He doesn't mind the two-hour-plus commute. He listens to music, meditates, plans his future. The drive becomes his therapy.

He tosses around new names for the band. Rejects *Cold Turkey for Chris.* Too on the nose. Dave, the lead singer he replaced, fell into the deep end and checked himself into rehab or an institution or . . .

Daycare for Dave.

Mint.

He books the band around Long Beach, gigs in bars and clubs, and somehow interests a well-known record producer who's worked with big names, bands you've heard of.

He kicks ass at his job, earns a raise, a promotion, keeps clean, stays straight.

And one night, he gets lucky.

*   *   *

Onstage, fronting the band, cranking his voice, he notices her immediately. The short brunette. Bright brown eyes shaped like almonds. Dazzling smile that appears in shy spurts and causes her to lower her head. Swaying to the music, she seeks out his eyes. Finds them. His eyes bore into hers. *She's Mexican*, Chris guesses. *Or European.*

Exotic.

After the gig, they move in a group to the record producer's house. He loses her then. Beer in hand, he drifts from room to room, his mind still on her. *Maybe I dreamed her.*

And then he sees her in a small pack, laughing. Closer up, he's drawn in by her aura, her look, her flair. He moves through the people around her, faces her, and blurts the three words that change his life:

"Dig your jacket."

"Thank you," she says. "It's what I do. Clothes designer."

"I really like it. I'm Chris."

"Monica."

*   *   *

They marry on March 22, 2003, in an art gallery downtown. Monica designs and makes her own wedding dress, a striking combination of an early-century classic and art deco. Chris wears black leather. The guests, an assortment of artists, musicians, fashion designers, and Chris's coworkers, decorate the gallery, hang their artwork on the walls. Monica and Chris announce the attire as *Come as you are.*

Surrounded by his friends, Chris stands in the center of the gallery with its soaring fifty-foot ceiling and Gothic interior, and as he whispers his wedding vows to Monica and kisses her to seal the deal, he feels a tremor go through him. His body vibrates. *I've come a long way in three years, a helluva long way,* he thinks, basking in the light of this cathedral of art. He's not a religious man, but at this moment, he feels as if he's been lifted from the gutter to God.

The reception under way, he moves from guest to guest, accepting congratulations and champagne, his wide smile a cover-up for how shaky he feels.

Unbelievable. Fantastic. *Strange.*

"You okay?" Monica whispers, slipping her arm through his.

"I'm fine. My pants are just a little tight."

I'm fucking married.

Man.

This rocks.

*   *   *

Austin, Texas.
December 2002.

Eli Roth feels the heat. *Cabin Fever,* a horror film he's directed and co-written about five college kids stranded in a cabin with a mysterious flesh-eating virus, has just premiered at the Toronto Film Festival. Even though the film won't be released for almost a year, the buzz has started. People leave the theater unnerved and grossed out. Audience members and eventually reviewers call the film "gory," "gruesome," "funny," "nail-biting," and "particularly disgusting." Nobody knows yet that the word "blockbuster" will fit best, since *Cabin Fever* cost only 1.5 million and will bring in more than $33 million at the box office. After years of struggle and obscurity, Eli finds himself in demand. His phone rings off the hook. Producers and film executives want to pitch him their ideas and hear his.

Eli decides to take some time to himself and head to Austin to attend the "film geeks' Christmas," the Butt-Numb-A-Thon (BNAT) film marathon, which Internet movie giant Harry Knowles hosts every year in celebration of movies and his birthday. This year, over the course of twenty-four consecutive sleepless hours, BNAT will show a dozen or so movies, among them vintage films *The Mask of Fu Manchu* and *Machine Gun Kelly*, the new Rob Zombie film *House of 1000 Corpses*, and the world premiere of the most anticipated film of the year, which Harry calls *Salome II* but everyone knows to be *The Lord of the Rings: The Two Towers*.

The previous year, Eli met Harry Knowles when the two traveled to Spain for a film festival, then met Tim League, owner of the Alamo Drafthouse Cinema, when Harry screened *Cabin Fever* at his horror movie marathon. Eli, a lifelong movie geek, fell in love with the Drafthouse and, as Harry wrote, with Harry's and Tim's "insanity." The day the horror movie marathon ended, Eli announced, "I'll be back for Butt-Numb-A-Thon."

Since Butt-Numb-A-Thon honors Harry's birthday, Eli wants to bring him a present, something unique that has a meaningful connection to movies. Harry's entire life is movies, watching them and writing about them in his *Ain't It Cool News*, the ultimate Web site for film fans. Eli remembers a funny poster he saw in the lobby of the Drafthouse, a replica of the original *Indiana Jones and the Temple of Doom* poster with Harry dressed as Indiana Jones, and it hits him. The perfect gift.

The tape.

*   *   *

Flashback: 1996 or 1997. Eli's good friend Gabe Friedman, the editor at Troma Studios in New York, gives Eli a copy of a videotape, which Frank Reynolds, the editor before him, had passed on to Gabe.

"What is this?" Eli asks.

"*Raiders of the Lost Ark* remade shot for shot by kids," Gabe says.

Eli watches the tape, amazed, and takes it with him when he moves to Los Angeles. Occasionally, Eli brings it out and shows it to friends. The film always receives the same reaction: People are blown away.

The tape now sits on a shelf.

Waiting for Harry.

*   *   *

Eli hands the tape to the man mountain of movies. "Happy birthday, Harry."

"Thank you, man."

Eli gushes. "You've never seen anything like this."

Harry looks at the label, squints at the familiar logo. "It's *Raiders of the Lost Ark*. I've seen something *exactly* like this."

"No, no, no. You've never seen *this*. It's a remake of *Raiders*, shot for shot, made by a bunch of kids somewhere in this world. They spent like ten years working on this thing. You watch them age before your eyes."

"What is this, like a tall tale?"

"No, man, these guys are legends."

"Well, is it cool?" Harry says.

"I'm telling you. You've never seen anything like this. You should show it during Butt-Numb-A-Thon."

"If you say so." Harry plunges his hand into the bushy red beard flaming down over his massive round chin. Harry's no-mustache beard and bulk make him look like an Amish bouncer. "Give it to Tim. Maybe we'll run it during the breakfast break. The audience won't mind. They'll probably all be asleep."

*   *   *

9:00 A.M.

The breakfast break.

The Butt-Numb-A-Thon audience has sat through twenty-one straight hours of movies, all day, all night. Before the marathon closes with *Salome II*, Tim allows everyone an hour to stretch, sleep, or snack. In the projection booth, he considers a couple of alternatives for something to show during the break, then decides to pop in the videotape Eli gave Harry for his birthday. He sends word down to Harry and Eli.

A second before the movie begins, Eli rushes to the front of the screen and sticks up a hand to get the crowd's attention, many of whom are eating, rustling fast food wrappers, talking, dozing. Eli says, simply, "I'm Eli Roth. What you're about to see is my birthday gift to Harry." He nods at the screen. "I don't know these guys, never met them, but I feel like this has to be seen and you are the perfect audience. Harry hasn't seen it either. So, happy birthday."

Eli takes his seat and just like that—no introduction, no explanation—*Raiders of the Lost Ark: The Adaptation* begins.

The audience stops eating. They wake up. They hush others for quiet. They focus completely on the kids on the screen. They cheer Chris as he runs from the giant boulder. They laugh and applaud as he escapes from the Hovitos. They howl at Angela. They roar at Snickers the dog playing the Nazi monkey. They watch, at first enchanted, then mesmerized, and then transported into the familiar yet unique world of this *Raiders*. They experience magic.

An hour in, Tim pulls the tape so he can start *The Lord of the Rings* on time.

The audience boos, hoots, stomps, in Harry's words, "goes riot."

Harry lumbers to the front of the screen. "I want to see the rest of this *Raiders of the Lost Ark* thing, too. And we will schedule a screening. But right now, we've got to show *Salome II*."

The audience jeers, then cheers again, not for *Salome II* but for the miracle they've just witnessed, and for the promise of seeing it all the way through.

As Harry Knowles will say, *Raiders of the Lost Ark: The Adaptation*— "this little bitty film that nobody ever heard of . . . not even a rumor on the Internet that this thing exists"—stole Butt-Numb-A-Thon.

*   *   *

A few weeks later, Eli takes a meeting with Paul Lister, an executive at DreamWorks, Steven Spielberg's production company. As the meeting winds down, Eli brings out the videotape of *Raiders: The Adaptation*.

"I want to show you something," Eli says. "I gave a copy of this to Harry Knowles, and he showed it last month at Butt-Numb-A-Thon. The crowd went insane."

"What is it?"

"*Raiders of the Lost Ark* remade by kids. You have to see it to believe it. I had nothing to do with it. I just know I have to show it to you."

Paul Lister takes the tape from Eli. "I'll take a look."

A week later, Paul calls Eli.

"That tape? Unbelievable. Steven watched it. He loved it. He wants to write them a letter."

"Are you kidding me? They'll go nuts."

Eli feels a rush of collegial pride. He doesn't know these guys but *he knows these guys.* When they were twelve remaking *Raiders* in their backyard, pretending to be Indiana Jones, he was acting out scenes from *Texas Chainsaw Massacre* in his backyard, pretending he was Leatherface.

"Eli, I just need their addresses."

"I'll get them to you. All I have to do is find them."

Not easy. In February 2003, MySpace was still a few months away, Facebook had not launched, Twitter did not exist.

Eli begins by scouring the credits. He identifies the three main forces behind the making of the film: Eric Zala, Chris Strompolos, and Jayson Lamb. He types their names into the Yahoo and Google search engines and finds dozens of matches and phone numbers. He calls all the numbers, leaves messages. He knows he must sound like a rambling lunatic, but he doesn't care. He's on a mission. Finally he locates a Jayson Lamb in Vacaville, California. He calls him, leaves a message on his answering machine.

"Jayson, you don't know me. My name is Eli Roth. I'm a filmmaker. I just got a copy of your *Raiders* movie to Steven Spielberg. He loved it and he wants to write you guys a letter. I'm serious. I'm trying to find Eric and Chris, too. Please call me back."

A few hours later, the red light on Eli's answering machine flashes.

Eli hits PLAY. Jayson's voice comes on, slowly, thoughtfully, taking his time.

*   *   *

Sitting at his desk at Electronic Arts, Eric receives an e-mail from Eli Roth. Two dense paragraphs, beginning with *Hi, Eric, you don't know me, but my name is Eli Roth and I'm a filmmaker. This might sound crazy but Steven Spielberg has seen your* Raiders *movie and he loves it and—*

"What the hell is this?" Eric says aloud. "Okay, who's pulling my leg?"

He reads Eli's e-mail twice, hits REPLY, sends him back a cautious response.

Eli hits him back with more details. He tells Eric about *Cabin Fever* and Harry Knowles, Butt-Numb-A-Thon, and his meeting at Dream-Works. He feels that Eric is a kindred spirit. He asks Eric to call him and e-mails him his phone number. Less cautious but more confused, Eric e-mails Eli that he'll call him when he gets home from work so they can talk without interruption.

After dinner, Eric starts to dial Eli's number, stops, takes a deep breath. He picks up the phone again and finds that his hand is shaking. Eli answers on the second ring. He tells Eric how much he loved his movie.

"And that Andy Kaufman joke you put in the credits? Brilliant."

Eric frowns. "The um—not sure which Andy Kaufman joke you mean—"

"That you spelled Spielberg's name *Spielburg*."

A long pause.

Finally, Eric whimpers, "We did?"

"Yes. You didn't know?"

"No. It was unintentional. You're the first one who's pointed that out. Wow. We threw on the credits in the middle of the night. We hadn't slept in days—"

"You got all the shots in Spielberg's movie right but you spelled his name wrong? That's hilarious!"

"I guess so. It's kind of embarrassing."

Eli roars. Giddy from this surrealistic conversation, Eric lets loose and laughs with him.

"Man, there's so much I want to ask you," Eli says. "The boulder, man, how did you do that?"

"Well, as you might imagine, there were several failed attempts—"

They talk for two and a half hours.

The next day, Eli e-mails Chris in Los Angeles.

Chris doesn't reply.

*   *   *

The letter arrives a week later.

Sitting at the kitchen table, Eric stares at the envelope, *SS* written above the return address.

"Let me get the camera," Cass says, and hustles into another room.

Eric folds his hands next to the envelope.

Unbelievable. All those years ago, when we were making the movie, we actually talked about this moment. We actually said, "What if Steven Spielberg ever saw this?"

Cass returns, aims the camera. Eric picks up a letter opener, tilts his head at her. "This is unreal."

He holds the envelope up to the light, turns it over, turns it over again.

"Open it," Cass says. She hops impatiently, squints through the camera.

"I will. I am." Eric exhales. "I'm unbelievably nervous."

He slices open the top of the envelope with extreme care, as if filleting a fish. He eases out the letter and spreads it open on the table. He reads:

"February 6, 2003. Dear Eric, Wanted to write and let you know how impressed I was with your very loving and detailed tribute to our *Raiders of the Lost Ark . . .*"

He finishes reading, ends with, "All my best, Steven Spielberg."

"Did he spell it right?" Cass says.

"Yeah. He got it right," Eric says, then blows out, "Wow."

He reads the letter again and again, thinking, *It can't get any better than this.*

*   *   *

Chris receives the letter the same day. He riffles through the mail, sees the envelope with *SS* embossed over the return address, and tosses it onto the pile of mail on his desk.

"DreamWorks," he groans. "More DVD documentation stuff."

I've got to get a new job. Something that pays more money and involves less bullshit.

He feels a headache coming on. So much going on. The wedding. The band. Money worries. Keeping himself clean.

Life, man. A constant fucking clamoring in my brain.

And if he'd allow it in, *Raiders.*

He's tried to bury it, keep it locked away as part of his past. But two days ago, somebody sent him an e-mail with *Raiders* in the subject line. Some guy named Eli Roth. Chris still hasn't opened it. *It was a home movie. I'm a different person now.*

He looks at the envelope with *SS* in the corner. He picks it up, flaps it into his palm, lays it back down. He hears Monica's car roll up and walks out of the room, the letter teetering on the pile.

Later, Chris returns to his desk. He stares at the letter, rips it open. He begins to read.

"Holy shit."

"What?" Monica says, appearing in the doorway.

Chris scans the page, goes back to the beginning, gasps, and reads, "Dear Chris, Wanted to write and let you know how impressed I was with your very loving and detailed tribute to our *Raiders of the Lost Ark . . .*"

"All my best, *Steven Spielberg?*" Monica, in chorus with Chris, reads the signature over his shoulder. "What is this?"

Chris tries a smile, but he's literally having trouble breathing.

"This is unbelievable," he says. "It happened. We used to pretend Spielberg would see it, but it really happened."

"*What* happened? I don't get it. What is this *Raiders* thing?"

Chris tugs at the ends of his hair brushing his neck. "I did this movie when I was a kid. Me and some friends. It doesn't mean anything to me anymore." He pauses. "It didn't."

Monica gently touches Chris's forearm. "Let's watch it."

*   *   *

Chris ransacks his desk drawer and digs up the DVD Eric sent him. He slides it into Monica's computer. They pull up chairs and the film starts. Chris, twelve years old, dressed as Indiana Jones, walks through the jungle. Monica bursts out laughing. She watches the rest of the movie riveted and applauds at the end.

"This is amazing. Why didn't you tell me about it?"

"I didn't think you'd be interested."

Monica waits. She knows Chris is struggling to say more.

"I didn't want to think about it, so I buried it," he says. "It was my childhood and things were . . . hard . . . and now Eric and I—" Chris feels a catch in his throat. "I was ashamed of it."

"You shouldn't be," Monica says. "It's *amazing.*" She taps the letter. "Ask Steven."

The next night, Eli Roth calls Chris.

"I got your phone number and address from Jayson Lamb," Eli explains. "Did you get Steven's letter?"

"I did, yeah. Incredible. He mentioned my performance. So weird."

Eli laughs. "I'm totally starstruck. I'm talking to Indiana Jones."

Chris roars.

They speak for over two hours.

In the nearly five hours that Eli speaks to Chris and Eric, neither mentions that Chris and Eric no longer speak to each other.

*　　　*　　　*

The moment he hangs up with Eli Roth, Eric goes online to Harry Knowles's Web site, *Ain't It Cool News,* and trolls through the archives in search of Harry's write-up about *Raiders.* He finds it, stares at it, stunned. He reads *Ain't It Cool* every day, has for five years, yet he somehow missed the review of his own movie. He prints out the write-up, puts it next to his letter from Steven Spielberg, keepsakes he will cherish for life. Later, in bed, still wired, he says to Cassie, "Chris and I used to joke when we were painting the hieroglyphics in my mom's basement . . . *wouldn't it be cool if Spielberg saw our movie?* It was a pipe dream. This stuff doesn't happen in real life."

"I guess it does," Cassie says.

The next night after dinner, Eric answers the phone.

"Is this Eric Zala?"

"Yes."

"Hey, Eric. This is Tim League. I run the Alamo Drafthouse Cinema. I'd like to fly you, Chris, and Jayson down to Austin. I want to do the world premiere of *Raiders.*"

Magic

May 2003.

Eric straddles a chair in the kitchen and stares at the phone.

Should I call him? He twists the phone cord. *No. E-mail.*

He drags his chair to the computer, finds Chris's e-mail address, and types: *Wow. So we're going to Austin. This is pretty cool, huh?*

He hits SEND and waits.

Nothing.

He paces, forages in the fridge, pulls out an energy drink—his new addiction—roams in the cabinet among neat rows of crackers and cookies, looks for he has no idea what, then sits back down in front of the computer, trying to will Chris to respond. He swigs half his energy drink. *I'm making myself nuts.* He's reaching over to close the computer when his e-mail pings.

Chris.

Way cool. Off the hook, man.

Eric blasts out his reply: *Looking forward to seeing you.*

Within seconds, Chris replies: *Me, too.*

*   *   *

May 30, 2003.

Over the crackly intercom, the flight attendant announces in her husky Texas twang that they've begun their final descent. She asks that all passengers return to their seats.

I would love to, Chris says to himself in the bathroom, his face hovering over the toilet. *If I could stop the dry heaves.*

He groans, stands, weaves, yanks his shirt out of his pants, pats his face with a wet paper towel, and glares with horror at his reflection in the mirror. His hair, short, styled, sticks straight up as if he's been electrified. He shoves his shoulder into the door and staggers down the aisle. He feels green. He arrives at his seat, seriously considers crawling back up the aisle to the lavatory.

"You okay?" Monica stands, helps him into his seat.

Chris's stomach rumbles. "No."

He fastens his seat belt with a *click*. The noise makes him grimace. Monica folds his hand into both of hers.

"I'm so fucking nervous." Chris speaks through quivering purple lips stitched tight. "My stomach's in knots."

"What can I do for you?"

"Seriously? Shoot me."

* * *

Tim League, at the wheel, looks into his rearview mirror and catches Eric and Jayson sitting in the backseat. Cassie, pregnant with Quinn, rides shotgun. Tim speaks into the mirror. "How long has it been since you've seen each other?"

"Let's see," Eric says, doing the math. "Fourteen years?"

"That sounds right," Jayson says.

"Long time," Tim says.

"Indeed." Eric nods and smiles at Jayson, who grins back. For the occasion of the *Raiders* world premiere, Jayson wears an army jacket and backpack. *He's gone totally hippie*, Eric thinks. *So typically Jayson.* Eric smiles again and shakes his head, feeling a rush of affection.

"What about Chris?" Tim says, eyes on the road. "How long has it been since you've seen him?"

"Same," Jayson says, wiping a speck of dirt off his boots.

"Feels longer," Eric says, low, his voice cracking.

* * *

They pull into Tim's driveway an hour before the premiere. Tim and his wife, Karrie, have opened their home for a pre-premiere celebration. Eric and Cassie follow Tim into their living room, Jayson scrunched between them. *I'd forgotten how short Jayson is*, Eric thinks.

"And here's the other two." Harry Knowles, the myth, filling up the room, offers his hand. Eric takes it and thanks Harry.

"I should be thanking you," Harry says.

Then Eric hears someone call his name. Or thinks he does. He whips around toward the sound and sees Chris, trim, hair styled, black shirt, standing in the archway of the next room. He shoots Eric a nervous half-smile and a halfhearted wave. Eric holds for a fraction of a second, bobs his head, and walks toward him. Chris moves through the room. They meet in the far end of the League living room.

"Hey," Chris says.

"Hey," says Eric.

They throw their arms around each other and hang on, the years of silence, disconnection, and anger melting away.

The idea, the dream—the crackpot notion—of remaking *Raiders of the Lost Ark* brought them together. The realization of that dream twenty-one years later has brought them together again.

Later, Eric says, "It was like all that bad shit never happened."

*   *   *

The line for the Alamo Drafthouse Cinema curls around the block. Tim drops Eric, Chris, their wives, and Jayson at the front of the theater and drives to the back entrance with Harry.

"What is this?" Eric asks Chris, genuinely confused, gesturing toward the crowd.

"It can't be for us," Chris says.

Jayson walks up to the first person in line, a guy their age. "Hey, what are you here to see?"

"The remake of *Raiders of the Lost Ark* with kids."

"Shit," Chris says.

A half hour later, three hundred people pack the theater. Harry, beard freshly trimmed, adjusts his thin granny glasses, leans on his cane, and limps to the front of the crowd. Arms flailing, beyond excited, he dives into his introduction. He explains how Eli Roth gave him the videotape for his birthday and how the movie stole Butt-Numb-A-Thon. "All of a sudden, the opening sequence happens. And they're seeing it and they're noticing, that's a *kid* as Indiana Jones. And you're sitting there and it's a much better shot-for-shot remake of *Raiders of the Lost Ark* than, say, Gus Van Sant's *Psycho*, right? Because this thing's done with *love*. Every frame you see, you know that there were some mad, insane children somewhere in the world, right, that were just insanely faithfully doing this. Why? None of us knew."

The audience erupts with laughter.

Harry continues the story of how the audience booed and nearly rioted when he pulled the tape at BNAT so the audience could watch *Salome II*. "Well, what happens in this thing is that you have to realize that this isn't today. This isn't, you know, kids with DV cams, or insane money from somewhere. If you were a child of the eighties, you know how fucking hard it was to do anything with those oversized shitty cameras. You couldn't get anything to work. And here, against all odds, is a giant boulder gonna smoosh this little Indy kid! I swear to God, it's a fucking boulder the size of this room. And I'm thinking, *They're gonna kill the kid.* I mean, how is he gonna live? There's somebody behind this boulder pushing it to try to kill him because, yeah, wouldn't it be funny if he died by a giant boulder shooting a remake of *Raiders of the Lost Ark*, okay?"

The audience loses it, Eric and Chris roaring with them, and then Harry continues talking about how the audience at BNAT got caught up watching the movie, asking themselves, as he himself did, "How are they gonna set the bar on fire? These are kids. They can't do that. They do! You think of them saying, okay, I'm a stupid kid, I've got some crazy friends. We're making *Raiders of the Lost Ark*. Now, how do we get a submarine?"

Harry has the crowd on the edge of their seats and he hasn't even started the movie.

*   *   *

When the lights go down and the movie begins, Chris and Eric hold their breath, almost as if they are one person. The same thoughts shoot through their minds: *What if nobody laughs? What if they hate it? What if this is a total embarrassment? What if I sit here in agony and humiliation for the entire 100-minute running time?*

They needn't have worried.

Within the first thirty seconds, they own the crowd. The audience laughs, cheers, screams, and stomps. When the lights come up after the film, all three hundred people leap to their feet and give the film and filmmakers a raucous ear-bending four-minute standing ovation.

But at some point before, as the movie plays, although they will not admit it to each other, Eric and Chris feel overwhelmed by what they see before them, by what they have accomplished, by the love they felt toward each other, by the loss of their friendship, and by the loss of that time in their lives, their youth. They summon up all those summer days when Chris Strompolos gave every ounce of his body and heart to playing his hero—to *becoming* his hero—and Eric Zala devoted every waking moment of every day to committing him faithfully to film. And in the dark, apart and together, as they watch their younger, long-lost selves, they silently weep.

* * *

Soon after the world premiere of *Raiders of the Lost Ark: The Adaptation*, Harry Knowles posts a long review on *Ain't It Cool News*. He writes, "This is the best damn fan film I've ever seen," and closes the review in caps and in bold, "Be prepared to be blown away by **PURE MAGIC.**" Readers flood his comments section, many of them gushing over the experience of having seen the film. Hours later, Harry's review catches fire over the Internet, goes viral. Magazines call Chris, Eric, and Jayson. They want to write about them, as Jayson says succinctly, to tell the story of their impossible dream that came true. With several major magazines requesting exclusives, Eric and Chris convince Jayson that they should go with the prestigious and popular *Vanity Fair.*

"Isn't that a ladies' fashion magazine?" he says. "Why do we want to be in a magazine about women's underwear?"

Eric and Chris prevail. At Dave and Mary's suggestion, the boys invite the *Vanity Fair* writer and photographer to conduct the interviews and hold a photo shoot at Manyoaks.

*   *   *

December 14, 2003.

Back in Los Angeles, Chris takes point on the costumes. He ships a box from Paramount's costume shop containing Indy's costume, the bullwhip, Belloq's safari outfit, pith helmet, and Panama hat. He and Monica arrive at Manyoaks for what will be a total of four days of interviews and photographs. As Eric and Chris prepare to dress for the photo shoot, Eric says, "It feels as if we're making the movie again, only this time with a budget."

A few minutes later, Eric, dressed as Belloq, comes out of the bathroom to find Chris, outfitted as Indiana Jones, checking himself out in the bedroom mirror.

"What do you think?" Chris says, posing in Indy's leather jacket, tipping Indy's fedora.

"This is so weird," Eric says. "You look . . . perfect. This is what I always wanted."

"A long way from my spray-painted Members Only jacket, huh?" Chris pauses. "I've been thinking. I want to talk to you about something. Now's probably not the time—"

"What?"

Chris grins.

"What?"

"I'm thinking this ended up all right, you know? We really do work well together—"

"The last time you said something like that we spent seven years making a movie and another fourteen before anybody saw it."

"And three years pissed off at each other."

"You're right," Eric says, laughing. "Let's talk about this later."

The perfect host and hostess, Dave and Mary set tables with tablecloths on the lawn and cater a buffet with endless platters of food and unlimited bottles of wine and soft drinks. The photo shoot includes a shot of the three boys posing by the boulder (fiberglass maven Mic Sajway decides Manyoaks is the rock's rightful home), which Eric and Chris place in a prominent spot on the lawn. After the interviews and photo shoot, the party roars late into the night, the highlight—or lowlight—involving Jayson skinny-dipping in the swamp in front of the female photographer's assistant.

"Some things never change," Chris says.

He and Eric clink wineglasses.

*   *   *

May 2004.

"Raiders of the Lost Backyard," Jim Windolf's article in *Vanity Fair*, hits newsstands and the Internet. The New York media take notice and Hollywood calls. Eric, Chris, and Jayson fly to the Coast for meetings with talent agents, late-night talk show appearances, and to tape a segment for the *Today* show. Riding around L.A. in a rented convertible, adrenaline pumping, drunk with disbelief, Jayson says, "We will meet Spielberg."

"And you know this how?" Chris says.

"I get premonitions."

Chris's cell phone rings. He picks it up, listens, says little, his face turning an ashy gray. He clicks off, stares at Jayson. "Tomorrow. Noon. Spielberg."

For the rest of the trip, Eric and Chris call Jayson "Jaystrodamus."

*   *   *

He strides into the conference room, grayer than they expect, and shorter, his hand gripping each of theirs firmly, his smile broad, as if they are favorite cousins he hasn't seen in a while. "Hey, guys, how's it going?"

They find seats at the table and spend the next forty-five minutes speaking as old friends and movie buffs. Steven and Chris talk about *Casablanca,* a film they both love. Eric shifts to the process of moviemaking, asks Steven if he enjoyed shooting *Raiders.*

"I did," he says. "Actually, when I started *Raiders,* I was depressed. *1941* had just come out and it had bombed. I wanted to prove to the world that I could make a really good yarn, you know? *Raiders* felt like my comeback."

Steven talks about the physical challenges involved in making the film, location issues, special effects mishaps and backfires, stunt redos, and then he offers to show them a blooper reel. They follow Mr. Spielberg into his office and huddle on his couch, watching a DVD of *Raiders* outtakes. *I feel like I'm watching a home movie from Steven Spielberg's private collection,* Eric thinks.

The meeting wraps up, and Chris asks if they can take their picture with him. Steven calls in his assistant, who snaps several shots with Chris's camera. They thank Steven for taking the time, shake his hand. They start to leave. Jayson, who until now has been subdued and mostly silent, says emphatically, "I don't care what anybody says, I liked *The Color Purple.*"

A long uncomfortable beat.

"Oh, okay, thank you."

Eric and Chris hustle Jayson out of there.

* * *

A few days later, Jayson returns to his life in Oakland. Chris and Eric begin a flurry of appearances at nonprofit film festivals, introducing *Raiders of the Lost Ark: The Adaptation* to audiences all over the world. They meet Quentin Tarantino and Kevin Smith and other notable filmmakers, people they idolize. They fly back out to L.A. and attend the Hollywood premiere of their movie at the famous Grauman's Chinese Theatre, where they at last meet Eli Roth in person. As they travel the world with their film, critics and fans continue to echo Harry Knowles's words, calling their *Raiders* "the greatest fan film of all time."

Then, one night, watching their movie on an outdoor drive-in movie screen at Spudfest in Driggs, Idaho, the sun setting behind the Tetons, Chris finally pops the question, the one he never asked Eric at the *Vanity Fair* photo shoot.

"So, here's what I want to talk to you about," Chris says. "You ready?"

"Hit me."

"I have this idea to make a movie."

"You're pulling my leg."

"I'm dead serious."

He pauses. And then he speaks the same words he spoke in their very first phone conversation back in Mississippi, when he was eleven years old and Eric was twelve.

"I was wondering if you wanted to help."

*   *   *

In June 2005, committed to making another movie with Chris, their friendship cemented, Eric resigns his job as director of quality assurance at Electronic Arts in Orlando. Encouraged and supported by Cass, pregnant now with their second child, he sells his house, cashes in his stock options, wriggles out of his golden handcuffs. They move back to Ocean Springs, buying a small house a short distance from Manyoaks. Eric takes a job as director of a cultural arts center at half the pay and twice the hours. On weekends, several times a year, he and Chris hit the road with *Raiders*, nearly always playing to sold-out audiences, ranging from rabid *Raiders: The Adaptation* fanatics to fellow filmmakers to the merely intrigued. In hotel rooms between screenings, on plane rides and car trips, Eric and Chris work on the screenplay for their second movie, a Southern Gothic thriller. They keep each other in check and sane, one lifting the other when spirits sag, when money issues press, when finding time to work gets tight, when life butts in.

"I'm not going to give up. You?"

"Hell, no."

They won't.

Miracle

Ocean Springs, Mississippi.
September 2005.
The aftermath.

Taking a break from shoveling mud, Chris emerges from the Zalas' basement and looks toward the Gulf. The glint of the sun bouncing off the water causes him to blink, and then something catches his eye.

Or rather, the lack of something.

"Hey, man, where's the boulder?"

Eric, bearded, filthy, Red Bull in hand, ducks his head out of the basement, moves next to Chris. He lays a hand on Chris's shoulder and tips the Red Bull toward the space where the boulder had stood since the *Vanity Fair* cast reunion and photo shoot two years ago. "Gone. Blown away, I assume. Taken by Katrina."

"This fucking storm, man."

They say nothing more, stand slumped in front of what was once the porte cochere and squint into the Gulf.

"Come on, man," Chris says. "We got a lot of work to do."

"I know," Eric mumbles. "Overwhelming."

"Hey, I'm not giving up. You?"

Eric forces a smile. "Hell, no."

For the next two weeks, the family works in the stifling heat, living without running water, electricity, or air-conditioning. Finally, they start to see signs of progress.

"The house doesn't look defeated anymore," Eric says. "It looks *defiant*."

One afternoon, the sun murderous, the mosquitoes swarming, the boys take a breather. Chris decides to go for a walk. Ten minutes later, he appears at the farthest corner of the property. He waves frantically at Eric.

"Eric! Yo! Come here! And bring waders!"

                              *   *   *

They stand together at the rim of the swamp.

"Unbelievable," Eric says.

"A fucking miracle," Chris says.

Eric shifts his weight, and the waders, snug, up to his thighs, crackle and sing. "Ready?"

"Let's do it."

They step into the swamp, tentatively at first, then plunge into the warm brackish water and thrust forward little by little.

Facing them, trapped in the center of the swamp, caught in a mesh of debris and sour smelling green vines, floats the boulder.

They wade deeper in, nearly up to their waists. They reach the boulder at the same time.

Eric holds the boulder in place while Chris disentangles the vines, freeing it. Then they push the boulder out of the swamp and onto the grass.

"It fucking stinks," Chris says.

"We'll clean it up, be good as new."

Standing behind it, shoulder to shoulder, they roll the boulder up a slight hill toward Manyoaks and the family working on the front porch.

Someone shouts and someone else claps.

The boys smile, wave.

Applause from their family showering down on them, Chris and Eric roll the boulder home.